HEAVEN
and Your
SPIRITUAL
EVOLUTION

—

A Mystic's Guide
to the Afterlife *&* Reaching
Your Highest Potential

Barbara Y. Martin *&* Dimitri Moraitis

SPIRITUAL
ARTS
INSTITUTE

ENCINITAS, CALIFORNIA

SPIRITUAL
ARTS
INSTITUTE

Spiritual Arts Institute
527 Encinitas Blvd, Suite 206
Encinitas, CA 92024

(760) 487-1224
Toll-free: (800) 650-AURA (2872)
https://spiritualarts.org

Publisher's Cataloging-in-Publication data

Martin, Barbara Y., author. | Moraitis, Dimitri, author.
Heaven and your spiritual evolution: a mystic's guide to the great beyond and reaching your highest potential / by Barbara Y. Martin and Dimitri Moraitis.
Includes bibliographical references. | Encinitas, CA: Spiritual Arts Institute, 2021.
LCCN: 2021906525 | ISBN 978-1-954944-02-2
LCSH Heaven. | Future life. | Eternity.| Reincarnation. | Karma. | BISAC BODY, MIND, & SPIRIT / Afterlife and Reincarnation
LCC BL535 .M37 2021 | DDC 202.3–dc23

Printed and bound in the USA by Bang Printing
First printing
Cover and interior design by Nita Ybarra

While the authors have made every effort to ensure that telephone numbers and internet addresses are accurate at the time of publication, neither the authors nor the publisher assume responsibility for errors or changes that occur after publication. The authors and the publisher have no control over and take no responsibility for third party websites or their content.

Dedicated to the Immortal Ones who reached

the summit of human achievement.

CONTENTS

Dedication v

Foreword
DIMITRI MORAITIS   1

Introduction
BARBARA Y. MARTIN   3

Part 1
YOUR SPIRITUAL ASCENT

Chapter 1
YOU DON'T GO TO HEAVEN, YOU GROW TO HEAVEN   13

Defining Heaven • A Celestial Experience • Heaven Is about Human
Potential • How These Things Are Known • A Quick Metaphysical Primer

Chapter 2

YOUR COSMIC STORY   27

The Pilgrimage Begins • A Cosmic Vision • Where Is Heaven?
• Spiritual Cosmology • Heaven Is Without, Heaven Is Within

Chapter 3

HOW THE HEREAFTER RELATES TO LIFE HERE AND NOW   43

General Conditions of the Spiritual Worlds • Activities and Lifestyle on the
Other Side • How Your Actions Here Relate to Life on the Other Side
• Bringing Inspiration from the Spirit Worlds to Earth

Chapter 4

A HISTORICAL UNDERSTANDING OF THE HEREAFTER   57

Ancient Heavenly Traditions • Abrahamic Traditions of Heaven
• Heaven in the Eastern Spiritual Traditions

Part 2

GROWING THROUGH THE
SPIRITUAL WORLDS

Chapter 5

BEGINNING YOUR SPIRITUAL ASCENT—
THE ROAD ALREADY TRAVELED   83

The Astral Worlds • Acclimation–The First Astral Plane • The Dream State—
The Second Astral Plane • Conscious Awareness—The Third Astral Plane

Chapter 6

AWAKENING TO THE SPIRITUAL LIFE—
THE FOURTH ASTRAL PLANE   95

Beginning Your Physical Incarnations • Visiting the Fourth Astral Plane
• The Spiritual Awakening

Chapter 7

UNFOLDING THE HIGHER SELF—
THE FIFTH AND SIXTH ASTRAL PLANES   107

Understanding the Higher Self • Building Character—The Fifth Astral Plane
• Reaching the Higher Self—The Sixth Astral Plane

Chapter 8

THE REALM OF ENLIGHTENMENT—
THE SEVENTH ASTRAL PLANE   125

Chapter 9

PREPARING FOR HEAVEN—
THE INTERPLANETARY WORLDS   135

Building Your Full Soul Power • The Mental World
• The Causal World • The Etheric World

Chapter 10

THE GLORY OF HEAVEN   149

The Seven Heavenly Perfections • The Heavenly Incarnations
• Spiritual Etheria—The First Heaven • The Kingdom of Light—
The Second Heaven • The Kingdom of Creation—The Third Heaven

Chapter 11

THE HIGHER HEAVENS AND THE CELESTIAL LABORATORIES   169

Focusing on God • The Kingdom of the Gods—The Fourth Heaven

• The Kingdom of the Inner Light—The Fifth Heaven

• The Kingdom of the Spirit Light—The Sixth Heaven

• The Kingdom of the Seven Spirits—The Seventh Heaven

Chapter 12

RETURNING HOME—FROM HEAVEN TO GOD   185

The Divine Reunion • Working with Souls from The Kingdom of God

• Assimilation and the Great Rebirth

Part 3

PITFALLS ON THE PATH

Chapter 13

YOUR ASCENT IS NOT A STRAIGHT LINE UPWARD   195

What Can Cause You to Fall Off the Spiritual Path?

• Reclaiming Your Spiritual Heritage • False Prophets

Chapter 14

THE NETHERWORLDS   213

The Animal, Beast, and Brute Netherworld Kingdoms

• The Demonic Realms and the Darkest Places in Creation

Part 4
EXERCISES TO ACCELERATE YOUR SPIRITUAL DEVELOPMENT

Chapter 15

YOUR PASSPORT TO ETERNITY IS THE LIGHT YOU EARN   225

Make Spiritual Growth Your Priority • Apply Truth in Everything You Do
Until It Becomes Wisdom • Pursue Quality Spiritual Education • Transform
Distresses into Blessings • Ten Keys to Success in Your Spiritual Growth

Chapter 16

MEDITATIONS TO CONNECT WITH THE SPIRITUAL WORLDS   237

The Higher Self Meditation • Receiving Spiritual Inspiration
• Accelerating Your Spiritual Growth • Overcoming Tests and Challenges
on the Spiritual Path

Chapter 17

SLEEP AND TRAVELING TO THE WORLD OF SPIRIT   253

Facilitating Nighttime Spiritual Blessings

Chapter 18

THE ROAD TO HEAVEN IS PAVED WITH LOVE   269

Acknowledgements   273
Index   275
Author Biographies   283
About Spiritual Arts Institute   284

ILLUSTRATIONS

2.1 *Ascending through the Spiritual Planes* 40

6.1 *Awakening to the Higher Life* 104

7.1 *The Temple of Healing* 118

7.2 *Dropping the Personality Ego* 123

8.1 *Enlightenment and the Temple of Love* 131

9.1 *Mind Over Matter* 140

9.2 *Reconciling Past Lives* 144

9.3 *The Mystic Marriage* 147

10.1 *Entering Spiritual Etheria* 160

16.1 *The Meditative Pose* 241

FOREWORD

ORKING WITH BARBARA on this book has been an immeasurable honor. The wisdom offered is based on a lifetime of experience, and the writing has been years in the making. In many ways, I think this book is her masterpiece, as it brings together many of her spiritual talents and experiences to reveal the inner life of a mystic and teacher. Having worked with Barbara for many years, I can say that of all her spiritual gifts, the gift of helping souls grow through the spiritual dimensions of life is the greatest of all. And of her many clairvoyant talents, the ability both to consciously travel to the spiritual worlds and to help others connect with those worlds is particularly extraordinary, and also one of the most difficult and demanding.

Exploring the process of soul evolution is a monumental task, as many aspects of metaphysics need to be woven together to tell the story. This book follows the grand mystical, cosmological traditions you can find in the works of theosophy, the Kabbalah, and the Rosicrucians, to name a few. In exploring the many facets of the spiritual worlds, it can feel dizzying to contemplate the grandness of the journey in the same way that mountain climbers, looking at Mount Everest for the first time, can feel initially daunted by the grandeur before them. Let your intuitive, divine nature be your guide. Think of these spiritual realms as already nestled within you, yearning to be discovered and expressed.

Each of us has a spiritual ladder to climb. Not only do you want to leave this Earth better than the way you found it; you want to leave this Earth at a higher level of consciousness than when you started. In pursuing the spiritual path, you are both a scientist in the detail and attention you need to succeed and an artist in your creative expression of unfolding your soul's potential. As you ascend the ladder, you become more expressive in every way. Life does not necessarily become easier, but it does become more exciting and more fulfilling, and you feel you are making a deeper impact on the greater good.

There is much to contemplate in these pages. Take the time to envision not only the beauty of the other side but the breadth of your own evolution. Truly, your spiritual ascent is the most exquisite adventure there is, because there is not one part of you that doesn't eventually get involved.

Having walked this mystical path for many years, I can share that it is worth every effort. You can reach your potential. Be courageous and follow your heart and highest inspiration. Take the long view of life. Your spiritual potential unfolds gradually, each step beautiful in its own way. In Aesop's fable of the tortoise and the hare, it was the slow but steady tortoise who won the race. And it is the steadfast path that leads to your spiritual victory.

May you find joy and fulfillment on your mystical journey.

In Light and Love,
Dimitri Moraitis

INTRODUCTION

I AM THRILLED TO present this book on the heaven worlds and your spiritual growth. As a metaphysical teacher, my most essential role is to help people reach their spiritual potential. My goal to give you a better understanding of the process of spiritual unfoldment that leads you to that grand place we call Heaven—the destiny of every human soul on Earth. There has never been a better time to grow spiritually than today. More and more people are waking up to their spiritual potential. Yet with all this enthusiasm, many people do not have a clear idea what the spiritual path actually looks like. If you want to become a doctor or a lawyer, there is a clear road to take. Yet when it comes to the most important goal—your soul's growth—that process is far less clear.

The road to Heaven is a grand study. Not only will we explore the metaphysical perspective of Heaven, we'll look at the many spiritual dimensions that lead there and how we experience these dimensions as part of an evolutionary path. We'll look at how your spiritual ascent does not begin when you cross over to "the great beyond" because you have already started the journey! We'll explore how everything in physical life is a manifestation of that which was first created in the spiritual worlds, and how all your actions are either drawing you closer to or further away from the divine objective.

The wisdom and knowledge I share of the spiritual worlds is based on my own training and clairvoyant experiences. From age three, I could see the auric field—the spiritual energy that every soul embodies and radiates. I spent decades honing these gifts to become a trained clairvoyant. My experiences in the world of spirit also began at a very young age. I know this can sound unbelievable. Aren't things like experiencing the hereafter or Heaven reserved for when we die? Can one visit and interact in the afterlife and return to tell the tale?

The truth is, we are all part of the spiritual world. We come from these realms before we are born. They sustain us here in physical life, and we will return to these inner worlds when our time here on Earth comes to its end. The challenge is that most of us do not retain conscious awareness of these inner dimensions. Those memories and experiences are submerged while we journey through physical life unless something rekindles that wisdom. Still, there have been countless cases of people reporting other worldly experiences.

I started having inner world experiences as early as eight years old. They would usually happen when I would take a nap during the day. These started as simple experiences of being taken to pastoral settings on the other side—not unlike a beautiful location you might visit on Earth. These experiences occurred quite often and didn't last long at first. I did not try to make them happen; they seemed to happen on their own. I knew that I wasn't dreaming, and I wasn't scared or apprehensive that I might be dying. Rather, they were uplifting experiences, as I was taken to happy places.

These inner world experiences supported me while growing up during the Great Depression. Some of those years were difficult for my family and myself, as they were for so many others. These spiritual experiences took me out of those challenges and made me realize there was a greater life. When I came back from these spirit visits, I felt renewed. However, I quickly learned not to share my experiences with others, as they did not understand what I was going through.

As a teenager, these travels to the spirit world increased. The visitations started happening at night while I was sleeping. These weren't dreams but vivid, real experiences. I learned that these travels were not happening by themselves; I was being escorted to the inner worlds by celestial beings. Throughout this book, I'll refer to these wonderful divine beings as angels and archangels or as "the Higher" or the Holy Ones. The Holy Ones were there all along but did not reveal that it was they who were taking me to these spiritual realms until I was old enough to understand and appreciate it. They took me to many places on the other side, where I slowly began to realize the vastness of the spiritual life.

Gradually, I started to be trained in the spirit worlds. I would be taken to special training centers or "temples," as they are called. There is a great variety of such temples, each with its own specialty. These are magnificent buildings, filled with Divine Light, where education takes place and blessings are given. The angels would usher me into these realms, support me the entire time, then bring me back. They would help me with things going on in my physical life and teach me about my spiritual gifts and how to use them.

This nighttime work continued until I was around nineteen, when I got involved in the world of entertainment. My family had moved to Los Angeles after having lived in many parts of the country. My father was a Greek Orthodox priest. He was also a builder of churches. The diocese would send him to a new town, gather the parishioners, build the church, and then assign him to another city to do the same thing. He was excellent at this but was paid a meager salary. I was one of six children, and it was difficult on my mother moving so much and raising a big family on a priest's income.

When my father was assigned to build a church in Pasadena, we all moved there. My mother fell in love with California. She told my father he could go wherever the church needed to send him next, but the family was staying in Los Angeles. I fell in love with California as well. We moved at the time of the Golden Age of Hollywood in the 1940s. I had a brother who was an excellent actor. Through him, I was introduced to the world of show business and, still only nineteen, I started my own variety show. I was the producer and also wrote some of the comedy sketches and music. We toured locally, especially at army bases, and became popular. Eventually, I had 300 people working under me.

During this time, I was trying to live a "normal" life and not be so involved in my clairvoyance activities and metaphysics. I enjoyed being part of the world of entertainment and thought this might be my life's work. After a couple of years running the show, I received an offer to take our act to Las Vegas. Entertainment was just beginning to get big there, and they needed talent. I was presented with a lucrative contract. It was the most money I had ever been offered. I was ready to accept when the Holy Ones came to me and revealed that it was not my destiny to be in entertainment. Rather, my destiny was to become a metaphysical teacher. They granted me a glimpse of my life as a spiritual teacher. Naturally, I saw the wisdom in what they were showing, but it meant I had to let go of my showbiz career. This was not an easy decision, but I turned down the offer, much to the dismay of the rest of the troupe who did not understand the reason for my declining the opportunity.

With a commitment to follow my spiritual path, a wonderful new phase of metaphysical training began. I was shown the breadth of the inner life and taken to dimensions beyond my wildest imagination. The Holy Ones gave me strong direction and instruction, which I followed to the best of my ability. It was truly a fantastic time. This inner training went on for many years, although you wouldn't know it based on what my outer life looked like at the time. I was not yet teaching metaphysics. No one knew what I was going through as I kept it to myself. During this time, I got married, had two wonderful children, went through a divorce and the death of a loved one, and had workaday jobs while raising my two children on my own. It was a beautiful yet challenging time.

Then my father unexpectedly died. I loved him very much, but because of his work and travels, I didn't get to spend as much time with him as I had wished. In my grief, I wondered how I was going to move my life forward. I didn't feel lost, but I did feel a great sadness. By divine grace, it wasn't long after my father died when I met one of the most important people in my life: my mentor and spiritual teacher, Inez Hurd. It was she who would prepare me for life as a metaphysical teacher.

Inez was a remarkable woman. She was born of Austrian aristocracy but had to flee the country and came to the United States. She, too, was born clairvoyant and at first lived a "normal" life. She married and had children. When she was in her late twenties, she got food poisoning from eating tainted lettuce and almost died. She prayed that if she lived, she would dedicate her life to God and spiritual work. She lived, of course, and became a remarkable teacher. She trained for many years, receiving some of her instructions in India while studying with a mystic who was part of the Theosophical Society. Inez had many spiritual gifts. She could see the aura with uncanny accuracy. She was strongly in touch with the spiritual hierarchy and had developed a profound understanding of the inner worlds. She only taught privately in small groups. Speaking to large groups of people was not her mission. Yet it was Inez who told me that not only would I become a metaphysical teacher, I would share my spiritual work with many people and become a public figure.

She helped me to sharpen my spiritual gifts and prepared me for the rigors of metaphysical teaching. An important part of her training was to deepen my work in the inner planes. We would go to the spiritual worlds together under the guidance of the Holy Ones, and she taught me many things. This training went on for almost ten years in various phases, some more intense than others. By the time this training was complete, I was ready to be a metaphysical teacher. And shortly after that, I began my career in earnest.

Through all my years of teaching and the many people I have been privileged to help, my relationship with the Divine has only deepened. Now that I am in the maturity of my life, my inner world travels continue to be a blessed experience. I am profoundly grateful to my co-author, Dimitri Moraitis, for his remarkable work in the writing of this book. We have been writing together for many years, and I have been grooming him to continue this work when my tenure as a teacher comes to its completion. He has been going through much of the training I describe in this book. In addition, I'm grateful to my students—my fellow spiritual travelers—who have been so supportive during the writing to make sure the book got done. I'm delighted with the illustrations Jonathan Wiltshire has created. He has done a wonderful job bringing to life the feeling and majesty of the spiritual worlds.

You do not need conscious memory to be part of the spiritual worlds. At the right time, your own direct experiences of the inner life will open up to you. The most important thing is to pursue your spiritual growth with all the joy, motivation, and enthusiasm you can muster. Be the best person you know how to be, and you will deepen your connection to Heaven and the inner life. Live by your highest ideals and aspirations and refuse to let anyone or anything discourage you. There is a marvelous spiritual support system that is inspiring you to reach your highest self and the celestial realms of glory.

May God bless you abundantly on your spiritual journey.

In Divine Light and Love,
Barbara Y. Martin

PART

I

—

Your Spiritual Ascent

Chapter 1

YOU DON'T GO TO HEAVEN, YOU GROW TO HEAVEN

The life so short, the craft so long to learn.
—Chaucer

HERE IS A home, an everlasting house, where the tributaries of life gather together. It is a place where life flows in its fullness; where love, peace, and joy reign supreme and justice prevails; where you are creative, strong, healthy, vibrant, and alive as can be. No matter where you are or how far you travel, this home is there for you. When you feel lost, sad, desperate, or forgotten, the everlasting house is there to warm the heart and stir the soul. Shadows of the past fade in this eternal place. You are where and who you are meant to be.

We call this blessed place Heaven. Many of us build our lives on the principle of a great beyond and that our actions on Earth determine the kind of life we will have in the hereafter. Heaven gives us purpose. It reaffirms that our actions have meaning and that life isn't random or happenstance. Of course, there are those who say that heaven is a human fallacy—a superstition we sustain to deal with the difficulties and ambiguities of this world. At best, we make our own heaven or hell by the way we live our lives. And then there are others who feel heaven is a question that can only be answered when we die.

No book can prove (or disprove!) that Heaven exists. That is something every person must decide in his or her own way. What I *can* share with you is what metaphysics teaches on this timeless topic and what my own clairvoyant experiences over the course of a lifetime have taught. As these pages will illustrate, Heaven is not only real, but it is also the key to attaining all the potential that is in you as a human soul. It is not just a place; it is a state of consciousness. To be part of Heaven and the consciousness it embodies, you must unfold your spiritual potential.

Metaphysics teaches that you don't go to Heaven just because you have been a good person; you *grow* to Heaven through the gradual, majestic process of spiritual evolution. To become a citizen of Heaven, you must first unfold all that you are capable of becoming, which means learning to express every goodness, every talent, every character strength, and all of your spiritual power. As you unfold, step-by-step, into who and what you really are as a soul, you grow spiritually. As you experience life in its great variety, the soul gathers up wisdom, which helps to unfold its power and potential. Mystics call this spiritual growth an ascent—your spiritual ascent.

If you are reading this book, it likely means you have had a spiritual awakening or that something has stirred your interest in understanding the greater life. The goal of this book is to motivate you to make your spiritual path a stronger priority and to give a clear picture of what spiritual growth is about and what the road to Heaven looks like. To do this, we will take an extraordinary journey through many spiritual dimensions that exist in the hereafter. I will share with you some of my own clairvoyant experiences in the spirit worlds to inspire you to live a fuller, more rewarding life. Meditative exercises will be offered to help increase your awareness of the spiritual realms and your potential as a human soul.

DEFINING HEAVEN

Understanding Heaven means many things. It means accepting the idea that there is life beyond the physical world and that there is a grander organization in the universe than only the physical planets, stars, and galaxies. It means there is a greater intelligence that inspires, supports, and interacts with us on a daily basis and that life does have purpose, even when we feel lost or helpless.

Each culture and spiritual tradition describes Heaven in its own specific way. Dictionary definitions generally refer it as a place ruled by God and populated by angels and the righteous after they have died. Its original meaning is simply "sky, or firmament." Metaphysics defines Heaven as *the realms of God's domain*. To understand this definition, we must realize that the other side is not one place; it is many places. The creative process of life has many dimensions in ascending order. All aspects of creation are in the loving embrace of the Divine, yet not all dimensions have the same awareness of the Divine. Some spiritual realms are more elevated and enlightened than others. Spiritual realms that are particularly close to the divine source we call Heaven. In the heaven worlds, the power and glory of the Divine is in full expression. The citizens of these celestial realms are in a joyful oneness and creative expression with the divine source.

The heaven worlds are the celestial laboratories—the prototypal realms where things are first created before being objectified on Earth. In the heaven worlds, we directly participate in the inner workings of nature, learning to be co-creative beings with the Divine. Some may think such lofty aspirations are unattainable. Yet the truth is, we are all mystics in the making. It is our destiny to become part of the heavenly realms and all they embody. All souls are precious, even when they make terrible mistakes. No soul is past redemption. It is not a matter of *if* you will reach heaven; it's a matter of *when*.

Many see Heaven as something to experience when you die, something in the distant future when you are done with this life. Yet, you are partaking and receiving from the heaven worlds every day. They sustain and inspire you now. They are the source of all inspiration, spiritual light, and guidance. No matter your belief system, heaven is for everyone.

In making a more conscious effort to connect with the spiritual worlds, you unlock more of your creative potential and accelerate your spiritual growth. Each spiritual realm plays a part in the unfolding divine experience and reflects a different aspect of your spiritual self. In walking the path to Heaven, think of it in three ways:

1. An actual place you will one day be part of.
2. An enlightened consciousness to experience, embody, and express in physical life.
3. The evolutionary process it takes to attain this glorious goal.

A CELESTIAL EXPERIENCE

One of the great blessings of my life was working with my spiritual mentor and teacher, Inez Hurd. When I met her, I'd already had a lifetime of clairvoyant experiences. Yet, Inez took my talents to a new level and opened spiritual doors I didn't imagine possible. Inez possessed extraordinary spiritual talents. She taught me to become a *trained* clairvoyant and prepared me to become a spiritual teacher. With her help, I reached a pinnacle in my own spiritual quest. As part of her profound spiritual gifts, she possessed great knowledge of the inner worlds from

her own experiences, and taught me how to be a more conscious participant in this intricate work.

During the most crucial years of working with her, I lived in her
home. We would meditate often and would have many spiritual experiences together. One time while we were in meditation, the energy was
particularly high. Suddenly, two celestial beings appeared in the room.
They were radiant with Divine Light that took your breath away. Inez
was thrilled but not surprised. We were taken out of our bodies and
found ourselves in a realm of extraordinary beauty. As I oriented myself, I realized we were in the heaven worlds—a place known as Spiritual Etheria. I looked at Inez and saw that she was in her heavenly form.
We had traveled to many places together on the other side, but this was
the first time we traveled together to the heaven worlds. She looked
radiant. In her earthly body, she had put on weight, but her heavenly
form was slender and graceful. Her aura was expansive and magnificent
and emanating pink light. She was wearing a gold robe and smiling at
me. It was fascinating to see this side of Inez, and I understood more fully
the exquisite soul I was privileged to work with. I looked at my own celestial body and felt its power. I found myself wearing a robe of aqua blue.

The celestial beings who brought us here helped us to acclimate to
these heavenly vibrations. They remained quiet but I could see them in
their full, grand form. They were incredibly tall and remarkable. We
were standing on the grounds of a magnificent temple building. There
were flowers and trees of a variety I had never seen. A gorgeous vista
overlooked a landscape of exquisite beauty. The temple was huge and
elaborately designed. Inez told me that it was a temple of divine peace
and that we were going inside.

As we walked down a beautiful path toward the temple, I could
see a pale blue light permeating the atmosphere. This ethereal light is
a feature of Spiritual Etheria. The holy presence was everywhere and

in everything. As we neared the temple, colorful light rays emanated outward. It was filled with divine power. There were other people here, but I could not see them, so it felt like we were having an intimate experience in this grand, expansive place. As the angels ushered us into the temple, Inez took me to a large, ornately designed room. She showed me an altar lit with candles. She knelt down and motioned for me to do the same and said we should pray together.

I knelt down and found myself praying for devotion to the Divine. In my earthly life, I was going through inner turmoil. Living with Inez and pursuing the spiritual path was putting a strain on my family. It was unclear how I would make my metaphysical pursuits work practically. I knew there would be difficulties ahead when I started my teaching work. As we were praying, the celestial beings were blessing us, and I felt my heart opening up. Then I had a revelation: I had to give my life more completely to God. It wasn't enough having spiritual talents; I had to surrender myself even more than I already had. I knew well the power and value of the spiritual life, but we are still human, and there was a level of commitment I had yet to make.

The divine beings who brought us here started singing about love, which had a deep effect on me. I felt I could let go my concerns. I looked at Inez, and she was praying for me. She had already made the level of commitment I had yet to make. Her presence was reassuring. Then the singing stopped. One of the celestial beings asked me to pledge myself to the Divine. And in that moment, I made a pledge that I have kept to this day and will continue to honor until I pass from this world. The challenges that lay ahead would not just disappear, but I felt an inner contentment that came with my commitment. Inez and I soon found ourselves back in our bodies in the meditation room where this all started. It felt strange coming back into the physical body. There was a touch of sadness after leaving that glorious place. The Holy Ones were still with us, though, sending Divine Light. We stayed in silence for a while; no words were needed. We both knew what happened.

This experience unified many of my previous spiritual experiences and put them into perspective as part of a grand plan. I understood my life in a new way and gained greater insight into the people I loved. I was newly motivated in my spiritual journey and strengthened by the knowledge that preparations were being made for my becoming a teacher and helping others in their spiritual quest.

HEAVEN IS ABOUT HUMAN POTENTIAL

Locked inside each of us are great powers that are meant to be accessed and developed. These spiritual powers are the key to success in every field of human endeavor. In ancient Greece, foreigners who first saw the Acropolis with its majestic Parthenon were in awe. They thought gods built such structures and lived there. People who were close to the genius of Mozart were amazed. They could not understand how a human could have so much musical talent. We look at the wonders of today—unlocking the mysteries of the atom, sending people to space, building computers, unraveling the human genome—and are dazzled that humans could conceive of such things. Great accomplishments that benefit humanity are inspired acts of spirit, even if we don't think of them that way. Yet nowhere is human potential more profound than in the arena of spirituality.

Every person on Earth has a spiritual potential. It drives everything you do. To unfold your spiritual potential, you need to awaken divine powers and consciousness that are latent within you into active expression. And to develop those latent powers, the soul must embark on a pilgrimage through creation where it unfolds its power, eventually making its way back, fully realized, to its divine source. In this cosmic picture, life on Earth is a schoolhouse and all your experiences are part of your spiritual growth. Lifetime after lifetime, the soul comes to experience existence in all of its wonders, mystery, and contrasts. Yet, behind all of your experiences lies your greater spiritual purpose. Whether pleasant or painful, the things you go through in life are learning experiences.

From the metaphysical perspective, each soul is precious and essential. We are all ultimately destined for greatness, but we are not all at the same place in our evolution. We're growing at our own pace. Regardless of where you are in the journey, it is beautiful. What is asked is for you to unfold the spiritual powers and talents you are meant to. This will help you reach that place in the evolutionary process you are meant to reach. It is the greatest thing you can achieve. There is no delight so sweet as reaching your potential and fulfilling your part in the divine plan.

HOW THESE THINGS ARE KNOWN

How can you know about the other side without dying? There have been countless cases of people reporting experiences in the spiritual worlds. These out-of-body experiences fall under categories such as near-death experiences and astral travel. Near-death experiences happen when someone is going through life-threatening trauma. During these times, the person can be temporarily dead, yet the soul can be quite active. These experiences can be life-changing events where people are given a glimpse of the greater spiritual life. Other out-of-body experiences can be more simple and earthly such as witnessing your own surgery. They can also be terrifying for those who have had menacing encounters with lower elements on the other side.

There is a type of out-of-body experience called astral travel. Astral travel can be voluntary or involuntary. It happens when, under certain conditions and not due to trauma, people find themselves out of their physical body with awareness. With astral travel, they are not really going to the other side. They are still on Earth but in their non-physical, astral form. They can move around in their astral body, visiting places and people. Some have a talent for astral travel in the same way some people are psychic, but I do not recommend this type of travel, as it can be dangerous. Like near-death experiences, astral travel demonstrates there is life beyond the physical dimension.

There is another type of out-of-body experience that metaphysics refers to as the ability to consciously go to the spiritual worlds. This type of experience is a hallmark of the mystic life. Consciously going to the inner worlds is a cooperative effort between the Divine and the human to experience the world of spirit as part of the soul's spiritual education and unfoldment. These experiences can happen during waking hours or at night while asleep. Building a conscious connection to the inner worlds is a process every soul goes through to become a fully enlightened being. The spiritual experiences I describe fall under this category of consciously going to the inner worlds.

A QUICK METAPHYSICAL PRIMER

Throughout this book, the term metaphysics means "that which comes after the physical." It is the study of the spiritual root of physical life. In this way, metaphysics shares similar goals with other noble studies such as theology, philosophy, mysticism, theosophy, and ontology. This sacred undertaking follows a global tradition from time immemorial and is making a strong resurgence today.

Throughout the ages, there have been various schools of metaphysics. While they shared common themes, each has an emphasis to accommodate the audience the teachings were directed to. The school of metaphysics presented in this book is a mysticism known as *The Kingdom of Light Teachings*. This grand system of spiritual study can be traced back four thousand years to the ancient Hebrew and later Christian mystics. It is part of a nondenominational, universal teaching being given to humanity at this time. Inez called these teaching Christos Wisdom. In this book, the terms "metaphysics" and "The Kingdom of Light Teachings" are used interchangeably.

To better understand how metaphysics sees the process of spiritual evolution, here are three basic metaphysical principles:

Reincarnation—You Can't Do It All in a Single Lifetime

Many people see life as a journey from womb to tomb. You are born, you live, you die. This philosophy takes the position, do the best you can, because you have only one shot at life. Others see this life as a kind of purgatory: How you conduct yourself determines how you will spend all eternity in the hereafter. That's a lot of pressure! Metaphysics teaches that you can't learn every life lesson and unfold all of your spiritual powers and talents in a single life no matter how good that life is. There are simply too many stages of growth to metamorphose from an aspiring soul to a spiritually matured, enlightened being.

This is where reincarnation comes into the picture. Reincarnation is the principle that the human soul goes through *many* incarnations in physical life to gradually perfect itself. By incarnating on Earth time and time again, you accumulate experience and wisdom and earn the right to become part of the heavenly realms. Some reach this goal of spiritual maturity sooner than others. Regardless of where you are in the journey, every soul will eventually reach perfection.

You have already had many lives, accomplished many things, and had countless adventures. In your many incarnations, you've succeeded and failed. You've been rich and poor, brilliant and dimwitted, the saint and the sinner, male and female. You've lived in just about all corners of the world, experiencing the variety of races and cultures. Through each life, you gradually mastered skills, talents, and character traits that become part of your immortal self. Reincarnation teaches that you always have a second chance. If you make mistakes, which we are all bound to do, you are given the chance to return in another lifetime to correct those mistakes so you can succeed in your goal of spiritual mastery.

Reincarnation is also about the time the soul spends "between lives" in the spiritual worlds. When you are on the other side, you are not just waiting to reincarnate back into physical life. In the worlds of spirit, you have a rich, full life. You have activities, friends, experiences, adventures, and things to accomplish. You review and assimilate the things you've experienced on Earth and prepare for the things you are meant to accomplish in your next incarnation.

The Spiritual Hierarchy—You Are Never Alone

One of the most beautiful aspects of Heaven and the spiritual worlds is the support you receive from celestial beings. We call the organization of these divine ones *the spiritual hierarchy*. The spiritual hierarchy is the administrator of God's divine plan. This holy order includes angels, archangels, and other exalted beings. They work on different levels of unfoldment, which is why it's called a hierarchy. Together, they form the evolutionary chain that links all life together. We need these great beings as they connect us to the Divine.

You receive loving support of the angels and archangels every day, regardless of your awareness or belief. The reason you may not be aware of these beings is that there is a veil between the physical and spiritual worlds. These divine ones work "behind the scenes" to guide and steer life on Earth. In the spiritual worlds, there is no veil between humans and the divine ones; there is a regular, natural interaction with the spiritual hierarchy. Your life in the hereafter is strongly directed by the angels. They teach, heal, and guide you. As you climb up the spiritual ladder, interactions with the Holy Ones greatly deepen. You discover new facets of this marvelous spiritual order—its stunning breadth and depth.

The Aura and the Divine Light—Fuel for Your Spiritual Growth

Everyone has an aura. It is the energetic blueprint of the soul. The aura is the individual expression of the universal life force. Everything going on in your life is reflected in your auric field. Your thoughts, feelings, talents, health, and well-being all have an energetic foundation in your aura. Where you are as an evolving soul is clearly delineated in the aura. No two people have the same aura because no two people will express the universal life force in exactly the same way.

The aura reflects how the soul is embodying and utilizing Divine Light. What is Divine Light? It is the lifeforce that emanates from God. It is the "conduit of consciousness." Through the Divine Light in all of its spectral colors, creation is inspired and uplifted. There are many attributes of the divine life to embody, so there are many aspects of the Divine Light to integrate in your aura. As you develop the spiritual attributes of love, wisdom, compassion, intelligence, peace and so on, you build up more spiritual energy in your aura[1].

---

[1] We will use the terms "spiritual energy" and "Divine Light" interchangeably in this book.

Your aura is the key to your spiritual ascent. It is where you forge your spiritual mettle. As you change your aura, you change your life. To evolve your soul, you need spiritual power. This power cannot just be given; it must be earned. The more Divine Light you earn, the higher in consciousness you climb. Light and consciousness walk hand in hand. You don't take your fame and fortune to the other side when you pass on, but you *do* take the Divine Light you have accumulated. Divine Light is the most precious thing you possess. It determines your state of consciousness. It determines where you are in your spiritual evolution. While there are no shortcuts to spiritual growth, meditating with Divine Light and applying that power in your life can help set a conducive environment to accelerate your spiritual growth and better connect you with the celestial power that flows from the spiritual worlds.

Chapter 2

YOUR COSMIC STORY

*Spiritual evolution...is the inner fact which alone
illuminates the problem of earth existence...apart from it,
our life here has no intelligible significance.*
—Sri Aurobindo

Y OUR SPIRITUAL ASCENT is truly a miracle of life. The ability
to grow through the various dimensions of creation is the most
exciting adventure imaginable. To understand the scope of your evolution, let us start by telling a story—your cosmic story of where you
came from and where you are headed.

Most children ask the question, "Where did I come from?" As soon
as we have gathered enough awareness of our life and surroundings, it's
a basic human need to want to know our origins. And yet it is common
to think of your life as starting with your physical birth. While this
was the beginning of your life on Earth, it is not the beginning of you!
Metaphysics teaches that you are not your body. You are a soul, and
your soul existed long before your physical birth and will go on long
after you pass through the portal we call death. Your soul is an individualized spark of immortal life, which means that your soul, in some
form, has always existed and always will.

Your soul is not alone. The life that is you is part of the same life that is me. We are all part of an infinite *sea* of life. This infinite sea has gone by various names (although ultimately it is said to have no name). In this book, we call it "The Unknown Root of All Existence." We are all part of the Unknown Root. It is at the heart of everything. Everything in the universe springs from the Unknown Root. In the Hindu philosophy of the Upanishads, it is the principle of Brahman, "the ultimate reality." It is the essence of the Chinese philosophy of the Tao.

There are times when the soul is meant to rest in the sea of the Unknown Root, and times when it needs to leave the Unknown Root and move into states of creative expression to evolve and mature into higher levels of consciousness. And this is where our cosmic story really begins: It begins with God.

God is the supreme, definable expression of the Unknown Root of All Existence. As metaphysics sees it, God is the Creator of all that has been, is, and shall ever be. God is omnipotent, omnipresent, and omniscient. He[1] is boundless, eternal, unlimited, and infinite. He is eternal mind and everlasting love, the fountainhead of all creative power, the designer of the Divine Plan. God gives order and expression to life. As we are always part of the sea of life, we are always a part of God. Since God is eternal, He is creating new experiences and new dimensions of life through eternal cycles of activity and rest, motion and repose, experience and assimilation. Life is eternally unfolding, eternally evolving. When God decided to create our universe, He out-breathed His creative Holy Breath and began a new cycle of creative life.

Through the unfolding of this creative cycle, our immortal souls were born. United in love, the dynamic and magnetic aspects of the Divine, the Father/Mother God, gave birth to the human expression of our immortal soul. We were born in the highest spiritual realm—

---

[1] The masculine is used in its neutral, non-gender sense.

The Kingdom of God. All that is part of creation ultimately draws its nourishment and power from this divine source. This stupendous realm encompasses within it all creation at every level, including the heavens and the earth. As the Divine teaches us, it is a place of indescribable splendor, love, and beauty, not just for humans but for all the hierarchies of life including the angels and archangels. Every human soul started its journey in this divine realm, as we are all children of the same God.

We were born without form—spiritual infants in the embrace of the Divine. Being spiritual infants, we were unable to communicate with God but were aware and responded to the divine impulse. We rejoiced in the celestial splendor nursed by our Divine parents. Yet from the beginning, the plan was for us to leave this divine place to experience creation. God prepared us for the extraordinary journey of discovery and evolution we were to embark upon. We were sent to distant lands to experience and grow so we could return to The Kingdom of God as fully matured human souls and become co-creators with the Divine. By our birthright, we were given spiritual freedom to be creative, to express ourselves, and to make our unique contribution to life.

We were born as part of a life wave of untold numbers of other human souls—our brothers and sisters in light—with whom we would walk on this divine pilgrimage. We were not the first life wave of human souls and would not be the last; God gives birth many times. This means we will encounter souls who are "older" than we are, more experienced and further along the spiritual path. We will look up to these souls for guidance and direction. And we will encounter souls who are not as far along the path as we are. These souls are "younger" and less experienced in their human journey. It is our job to support these younger souls. Regardless of where we are in the journey, we are all equally loved by the Divine, and we are all equally essential.

Once we absorbed the beauty and power of our divine infancy, it was time to start the spiritual pilgrimage. To initiate this great journey, the Divine empowered us with many essential tools. We were given a celestial body that would remain in The Kingdom of God. This body would be made "in the Image and Likeness of God." It would be the body we would one day inhabit when our pilgrimage was complete and we returned Home. This celestial body would act as a guiding light for the countless other bodies we would inhabit in the various dimensions of our spiritual journey. It would be the ultimate ambassador for the Divine Light and inspiration that would flow to us.

We were also given a spark of the God Spirit to keep us close to God during the journey. This is the "God within" that we would gradually awaken throughout the many spiritual realms we would inhabit. This God spark is kept close to our heart, closer than our hands and feet, so the creative fire of the Creator would burn bright in each of us. This God spark would become our spiritual compass, so that wherever the spiritual path took us, whatever we experienced, wherever we directed our free will, we would never completely lose our way Home. We were then given a Higher nature with its own divine individuality, so that no matter the persona we would wear in the realms we would inhabit and the incarnations we would experience, we would always retain the mark of our true identity. In this way, we could not fully forget who and what we are. We were blessed with a Divine Spirit that would become the parent to our soul, working with the spiritual hierarchy and teaching the soul countless lessons that creation would offer.

To crown our preparation before leaving The Kingdom of God for the great pilgrimage, God paired us up with another new-born soul who vibrated perfectly with us. A complete soul in its own right, this is our "soul mate" or "spiritual mate." It would be our confidant and loving companion on this long journey through creation. Our soul mate would be going through its own spiritual journey as well, learning and growing. Together, we would share in the joys and sorrows, the tests, challenges, successes, and triumphs of the pilgrimage. There would be times in the journey when we would share in adventures together and other times when we would be apart. Ultimately, our soul mate is destined to return with us to The Kingdom of God.

The spiritual hierarchy would always be with us through every aspect of the pilgrimage, guiding and inspiring us. Yet once we were no longer in The Kingdom of God, the awareness of God would be concealed in the many spiritual realms and domains of life we would experience. It would be our job to rediscover God and the eternal experience of life in every facet of creation through the many spiritual enlightenments. Each discovery, each illumination, would bring us into greater conscious awareness of God and greater maturity in our relationship with the divine nature of life.

THE PILGRIMAGE BEGINS

As the pilgrimage began, the Divine gently ushered us down through every spiritual realm we would one day evolve through in our journey back Home. Mystics call this descent into matter *involution*. Involution is the process of immersing the soul into creation. This is not the same thing as *de*volution—the loss of spiritual ground due to serious missteps and misuse of talents and abilities. Involution wasn't due to any missteps, sin, or punishment. Just the opposite. It was how our Creator gave us the opportunity to become greater spiritual beings than we otherwise could have.

During our descent through the heaven worlds, we were given celestial bodies associated with each heaven to establish a connection and give us the means to experience these realms when we began our evolution back up through them. With each level we descended through, we were invested with spiritual power. The Divine started building our auric field as well as the mental and emotional tools we would need. As the soul was going through this descent, it was partially aware of its surroundings and amazed at the vastness of the heavens and how much there was to experience. Each heaven we descended through became more dense; and while we were becoming more aware of the realms we were in, we were becoming less aware of where we came from.

From the heaven worlds, we descended down through the other realms of life. These include the interplanetary worlds, the astral worlds—the realms where many of us are ascending through right now—and down through primitive realms we evolved through long ago. As we passed through each realm, we continued to be blessed with spiritual power and tools, though we would not use them right way. When we reached the farthest place in our descent from The Kingdom of God, the seed was planted, and our soul was now a part of creation. Along our descent, the Divine had built the entire auric framework for our spiritual return. We now possessed all the tools we would need to start experiencing life and begin the slow, steady process of evolution. The pathway Home was laid out, even though it would take eons of time to complete.

During this descent, however, we lost awareness of God and our divine origins. We forgot who and what we really were. Once again, this wasn't due to any missteps on our part. Rather, this forgetfulness was an inevitable outcome of immersion into creation and part of our learning experience. Our soul started to identify with its immediate surroundings and forgot the glorious realm it came from. It would now need to exert itself through striving and aspiring in order to learn and grow. This would become the evolutionary drama: the tension between the sense of separation from the root of life and the eventual rediscovery of this unity and oneness through each spiritual dimension it would experience.

While immersed in creation, the soul did not completely forget who it was. The seeds of knowing were always there—the echoes of the celestial chord reverberating in our consciousness and intuitively reminding us of the truth of our origins. The joys, loves, and triumphs of the pilgrimage would encourage us to go further and remind us of the beauty of life. The pain, suffering, and sorrow would remind us that regardless of the realm and condition we found ourselves in, this was not the ultimate destination. Something greater awaited.

We began our spiritual evolution upward through primitive yet beautiful realms—realms we passed through long ago. When it came time to experience physical life as part of our spiritual ascent, the process of reincarnation began. We would incarnate on Earth many times, in all the varieties of human experiences, learning and growing along the way. Between each incarnation, we would go back to the spiritual realms to assimilate what we learned, continue our experiences and evolution in those inner worlds, then return to Earth to further develop our skills and attain insights. Earth became the great spiritual schoolhouse—an essential but temporary residence to re-vitalize the needed momentum in our spiritual journey.

Since our immersion into creation, humanity has been going through an extraordinary journey of spiritual exploration and development. To get to the evolutionary place we stand today, both individually and collectively, we have already passed through many realms of life. Yet compared to the spiritual glories that await, we are still children. The journey until now has been grand, yet the return journey ahead of us is even grander!

A COSMIC VISION

———

Early in my teaching career, I went into meditation, as I normally did, to prepare for a class I was teaching. In the meditative state, I unexpectedly found my consciousness being raised to an extraordinary place. I was still very much in my body, but I was being granted a spiritual vision. In this visionary state, I was shown the planets and stars. I could see them clearly in my mind's eye. I was moving through the cosmos at tremendous speed. I saw myself outside the solar system, traveling through other solar systems and star clusters. It was incredible to witness the beauty of the galaxy, how vast and intricate and active it was.

As the vision continued, I saw myself being lifted beyond the stars, up and up beyond our Milky Way galaxy and seeing it from the outside. It was a stunning experience. The galaxy looked like an exquisite jewel of infinite facets. As I gazed in wonder, I became aware of where I was as a human soul in the cosmic order of things. Rather than feeling insignificant amidst the unimaginable grandeur of the cosmos, this vision made me feel an intimate part of it. It stirred something inside me that I can't put into words but made me realize even more how sacred it is to be born of the Divine.

I then started to feel the God presence and an awe and reverence for the holy vibrations I was experiencing. As the presence got stronger, the galaxy started to "open up" like the petals of a rose, each petal a spiritual dimension of life. It took my breath away as the image revealed the many dimensions of life—dimensions that interpenetrated each other yet were unique in their own right. This vision of the galaxy unfolded in a dazzling array of light and color.

As I was witnessing these multi-dimensions in my mind's eye, I felt whole and complete. All of these spiritual dimensions were part of the great whole; every individual soul was part of the great whole. Despite such grandeur, the Divine was showing me that even the glory of the galaxy in all its dimensions and staggering creativity is an expression of something greater. I fell into a state of spiritual ecstasy. The bliss, the joy, was indescribable. And as glorious as this was, I was still aware that it was "only" a vision, granted by the Divine. I was not actually in these cosmic dimensions. Yet I couldn't help but think, *If this is a vision, what is it like to actually be in these spiritual dimensions?*

During my experience, nothing was spoken, yet so much was understood. Then I saw myself accelerating back "into" the galaxy through the stars and finally to Earth. However, I didn't just travel through the physical planets and stars but also through a panorama of spiritual dimensions. How glorious it was! As the vision ended and I found myself back in my physical consciousness, I could still feel the stars, the planets, and the moons stirring within. I knew that all these spiritual dimensions were a part of me, as they are part of every soul. It truly made me feel the glory of life.

I have kept this vision private, never before sharing this experience. I consider it one of the sacred moments of my life. I share it now to inspire and help you feel the glorious, spiritual heritage you are a part of.

WHERE IS HEAVEN?

When we look up at the sky, we marvel at the breadth and grandeur of the universe. It staggers the imagination. As students of spiritual evolution, the more we learn about the physical structure of the galaxies and stars, the more we wonder where God is in all this grandeur and how we fit in as human souls. The more we know, the more we yearn to know. A deeper understanding of physical life calls for a deeper understanding of spiritual life.

Heaven and the hereafter is not a fantasy or dreamland. The other side is real. In many ways, it is more real than physical life. It is also not a nebulous, non-distinct, primordial energy. The spiritual worlds are well-organized and structured. Everything we see in physical life—and much more—exists in the spiritual realms. As grand and expansive as the physical universe is, the spiritual universe is even grander and more encompassing. As Paramahansa Yogananda relates in his book, *Autobiography of a Yogi*, "The entire physical creation hangs like a little solid basket under the huge luminous balloon of the astral sphere.[2]"

To orient ourselves to the spiritual worlds, we have to change the way we see the universe. If you were able to look at our solar system with a spiritual telescope—a telescope that could see *all* the dimensions of life and not just the physical—you would be shocked. You would see much more that you possibly could with even the best of physical telescopes. The planets would look much more encompassing: larger and more active as you could see their spiritual dimensions. You would see many planets that do not exist in the physical realm, all of them teeming with life and activity. Even our sun would look more beautiful, grand, and dynamic. You would truly appreciate the mystic phrase, *spaceless space*: that which appears as empty space is, in essence, full of life and activity.

It is these spiritual dimensions that comprise what we call "the other side" or the "hereafter." They cohabit in the grand space of the universe. When we experience the other side, either as an out-of-body experience or through the portal we call death, we cross over into the spiritual planets and worlds from where we came. We have done this countless times, through every incarnation. We have made dying something to dread, but in truth, it is not. It is one of the most natural things there is. It may be the end of our experiences in the present physical body, but our soul goes on. Death is merely a passing from one dimension of life to another.

---

[2] Yogananda was quoting his teacher's (Sri Yukteswar) description of the astral worlds.

Why are we not consciously aware of these spiritual realms? Our immersion in physical life cloaks our awareness of nonphysical realms. To pierce the veil of matter, you have to seek out the spiritual. This is part of the pilgrimage: to find the divine in everything you do by living a spiritual life. As you live a holy life, love and care for each other, and pursue your purpose and potential, you gradually awaken to the reality of the spiritual realms and build a conscious bridge to the inner worlds.

SPIRITUAL COSMOLOGY

In our pilgrimage through creation, there are many planes of consciousness through which to evolve. The study of these many realms and our place in the divine scheme of evolution is known as *spiritual cosmology*. Spiritual cosmology is one of the most ancient of all metaphysical sciences. It is considered a master key to the divine mysteries. The ancients saw the study of the planets and stars as a spiritual experience. It is ironic that today, many see the study of the cosmos as something completely unrelated to their personal lives. Yet our life experiences here on Earth are intimately tied to the cosmos. As the poet Francis Thompson wrote,

> *All things by immortal power*
> *Near or far*
> *Hiddenly*
> *To each other linked are,*
> *That thou canst not stir a flower*
> *Without troubling of a star.*

We too often miss the personal significance of the cosmos because our personality is so engrossed in its own affairs. Yet we live on a planet utterly dependent on its resources to survive. We are utterly dependent on the sun for our life; even small changes in its behavior can have dramatic effects here on Earth. We are greatly influenced by the moon. The rhythms of the day and night, the calendar of days, weeks, months, and years, as well as the seasons are all contingent on planetary influences. And the influences don't stop here. On a spiritual level, we are utterly dependent on the cosmos for our spiritual sustenance and support.

When you look at the universe, you are looking at your celestial home. The ancient mystics saw the universe as one great house—a palace—in which you and I reside. The old depiction of the Earth at the center of the universe, surrounded by planets and stars, was much more than a primitive, geocentric model. It was a concealed system of spiritual ascent from earth consciousness to the consciousness of the heavens. For countless centuries, this technique has successfully ushered souls back to their immortal Home.

It is ironic that this ancient wisdom, understood and appreciated in its day, has been buried in modern times, seen as an old superstition or folk tale that we have outgrown. We pride ourselves in material science that has created the wonders of the modern age. But this is not the full story. Regardless of the age we live in or our beliefs, we are still the same spiritual souls we have always been. True, we outgrow old superstitions about the physical and spiritual worlds. This is normal and natural. Yet more than ever, it is time for science and spirituality to walk together hand-in-hand as greater truths emerge.

No one knows the full scale of creation, the dimensions upon dimensions of life. We can only see the realms we can relate to as evolutionary human souls. And while the terminology of these spiritual dimensions has varied from mystical tradition to mystical tradition, don't be confused. They are generally talking about the same things. Here, we will use The Kingdom of Light Teachings, but we will refer to other traditions in the hope of discovering the underlying unity of spiritual truth.

Throughout this book, we will be exploring four broad areas of the spiritual worlds separate from the physical world and their connection to our spiritual growth:

The Astral Worlds

While evolving through these spiritual realms, the soul begins incarnating in physical form, builds its intellectual powers, and awakens the awareness to divine life that eventually leads to spiritual enlightenment.

The Interplanetary Worlds

These realms are where the enlightened soul brings together all of its accumulated talents and experiences in preparation for the ascent to Heaven.

The Heaven Worlds

In the heaven worlds, the soul reaches a state of perfection, earns its way "off the wheel" of the cycle of reincarnation, and learns to become a co-creative being with the Divine.

The Kingdom of God

Here, the soul reaches the summit of human achievement and becomes a fully matured, co-creative being with God. The soul has returned Home.

The Kingdom of God

The Seven Heavens

Kingdom of the Seven Spirits
Kingdom of the Spirit Light
Kingdom of the Inner Light
Kingdom of the Gods

Kingdom of Creation
Kingdom of Light
Spiritual Etheria

The Interplanetary Realms

Etheric Worlds

Causal Worlds

Mental Worlds

Astral Worlds

Ascending through the Spiritual Planes : ILLUSTRATION 2-1

HEAVEN IS WITHOUT, HEAVEN IS WITHIN

The miracle of the spiritual realms is they are not only worlds to experience as actual locations but internal states of consciousness as well. By studying, developing, and awakening the divine within, you unfold the heavenly part of you. The spiritual realms are interpenetrating you now. You are not aware of them until you awaken the spiritual faculties that allow for that perception. In this way, the Divine is not "out there somewhere" but is an innate part of you.

As the mystic and theologian Emanuel Swedenborg described his experiences in the afterlife:

> *...for heaven is within us, and people who have heaven within them come into heaven. The heaven within us is our acknowledgment of the Divine and our being led by the Divine.*[3]

---

[3] *Heaven and Hell,* Emanuel Swedenborg

Chapter 3

HOW THE HEREAFTER RELATES
TO LIFE HERE AND NOW

There is more to heaven and earth, Horacio,
than is dreamt of in your philosophy.
—Shakespeare

WHEN I WAS nineteen, my family, after years of constantly moving, settled down in a modest but lovely home in
Los Angeles. Up to this time, a good deal of my inner world experience was related to spiritual development. Then I had an experience
that would change my perspective on how the divine life relates to life
here on Earth. On a journey to the other side, the angels took me not
to a temple or training center but to a beautiful home in a scenic setting by an ocean. The home looked strong and sturdy and seemed to be
made of stone. It was a modern design but had a Mediterranean feel. I
had been taught that people did have homes on the other side, though I
wondered why I was taken to this particular home and who lived here.

The angels led me inside. The rooms were spacious and bright with
many views of the ocean. Although it wasn't a mansion, it was palatial
in roominess and decorum. No one seemed to be there, but candles
were lit in one of the rooms, so someone was clearly living here. The

angels led me to a veranda overlooking the ocean with another stunning view. I thought that whoever lives here is fortunate indeed. As I acclimated to my surroundings, I felt a sense of familiarity. When we went back inside, I was greeted by a German Shepherd dog. He was handsome and friendly and seemed to know me. I petted him and felt I knew him, too. Then I realized where I was: This was *my* home!

The angels smiled and confirmed what I thought. This is where I lived before incarnating on Earth! During my incarnation, the home was being maintained. This made me realize even more how familiar life is on the other side and the many similarities to life in the physical world. I started tuning into the vibration of the person living here and almost went into shock. I didn't have to tell the angels what I was thinking; they knew my thoughts and nodded in the affirmative. The person living in the home was my soul mate! I didn't see him, but my heart filled with joy that I was so close to my beloved. Soon after this, I found myself back in my physical body in my home in Los Angeles. This experience stayed in my heart for a long time. It made me realize how supported we are.

In this chapter, we will explore how the spiritual worlds are very much a part of your life while here in physical world. Earth life and spiritual life are both part of the *one* life. You cannot separate the two. The things you do here affect your life on the other side, and your life on the other side affects your life here. The goal of understanding the workings of the spiritual worlds is not to remove you from physical experience but to better appreciate how precious your time on Earth really is.

Physical life is a spiritual necessity. You cannot mature as a human soul just by living in the spiritual worlds. Physical experience is an essential ingredient to your spiritual growth. In fact, you can grow faster in physical life than you can anywhere else. Why? Because in physical life, there is resistance. Things aren't easy. But because you have to exert more effort to achieve, you become stronger and build more spiritual light.

You are meant to bring heaven to earth. You are meant to bring more of the operating qualities of the inner worlds here into physical expression. This is meant to happen individually and collectively as a society. The inner governing powers are meant to be reflected in the governing forces on Earth. The more you understand life in the beyond, the better you organize life here. It inspires you to live to a higher standard and encourages you to take bolder steps in your spiritual unfoldment. The more your physical life mirrors your inner life, the better life will flow for you.

GENERAL CONDITIONS OF THE SPIRITUAL WORLDS

To understand the relationship of the physical and spiritual worlds, let's start with an overview of the spiritual realms. A general understanding will orient you to the incredible sweep of what the spiritual worlds are about. In later chapters, we'll look at these spiritual planes in more detail. There are challenges, however, to offering a general description of the hereafter, as there is so much variety. There are many spiritual planes, each with their own unique experiences. This is what makes the inner life such an exciting adventure!

The basic forces of nature are the same on the other side as they are here. Heaven and the many spiritual realms leading to Heaven are composed of spiritual suns and planets yet on a grander scale than in the physical. All spiritual realms have an atomic structure. In addition, a type of spiritual electromagnetic energy exists. Gravity also exists on all spiritual planes, but with variations in expression, especially in the higher realms where it's possible to harness the mystery of gravity in ways not possible in physical life.

In addition to the forces of nature we recognize, there are spiritual forces at work. While they operate here in physical life, we are not aware of them unless one has developed the faculties to perceive them. Still, we benefit from their influence. In the spiritual worlds, we gradually become more aware of these spiritual forces. We start to understand the extraordinary influences of the Divine Light in its many spectral colors. We become aware of other spiritual powers that pervade creation. As you learn to incorporate these powers, you can produce results that are truly breathtaking.

In the spiritual realms, you find a wider variety of landscapes and expressions of nature. Some are simple settings; others are far more magnificent than on Earth. In the spiritual realms, there are vistas, lakes, trees, oceans, mountains, and more. There are animals, variations in weather as well as seasons, night and day. These nature settings can be extraordinarily beautiful and offer deep insights into the mystery of life.

A key feature of life in the spiritual worlds is the interaction with the spiritual hierarchy. Angels, archangels, and other spiritual beings work with us here in physical life. But because there is a veil between the spiritual and physical worlds, we cannot perceive the Holy Ones unless we have developed spiritual senses. In the spiritual worlds, this veil isn't there. Their loving and commanding presence brings an enormous sense of trust and stability. Their presence is very reassuring. We know we are in greater hands, even if there is much to life we don't understand.

What body are you in if it isn't physical? A body appropriate to the realm you are in. If you are in the astral world, for example, you inhabit an astral body. If you are in the etheric world, you inhabit an etheric body, and so on. But no matter the realm, these spiritual bodies have similar qualities and characteristics as your physical body. Otherwise, you would feel disjointed inhabiting non-physical forms. Spiritual bodies look like you and can change appearance from one incarnation to the next. When you transition to the other side, you do tend to revert back to a younger, more youthful state of appearance, but that is not always the case.

Spiritual bodies don't die the way a physical body dies. In fact, we do not die on the other side. For example, the astral body—the form we inhabit when it's time to cross over to the other side—can be seriously injured but not to the point of death. In this way, the astral body is indestructible. If the astral body becomes hurt, the Divine can heal it. If it becomes severely injured, the person goes into a type of dormancy or hibernation until the Holy Ones revive them. This means that we do tend to be more adventurous in the spiritual worlds because we have stronger, more resilient forms. This is not to say that the countless pains of physical life do not exist in the spiritual worlds. There is suffering on the other side, but it's expressed differently.

Is there violence on the other side? In the less developed realms, yes. But not to the same degree and level of cruelty that unfortunately exists in physical, earthly life. In the higher realms, there is no violent behavior as we think of it. There are dramas and challenges but not the behavior of hurting someone to gain benefit. This nonviolent behavior also extends to the animal kingdom. In the spirit worlds, animals don't kill each other as there are other ways to gain nutrition. We do not eat animal meat; all are essentially vegetarians on the other side. We take nourishment in other ways.

In the spiritual worlds, there is no procreation. As there is no death on the other side, there is no birth. While there are babies and children, these souls made their transition to the other side in those forms.

When children die in the physical world, they retain their child body and childlike state of consciousness. They continue to "grow up" on the other side. There are also no marriages or families as we think of them. Yet there are family-type groups to raise spiritual children.

If there is no procreation, is there sex and romance? Yes, there are intimate relations. You experience profound and loving exchanges, but without the same emphasis on sex as experienced here. The expression of love in its infinite variety is an operating principle of the spiritual worlds. Especially in the higher realms, love is at the root of all activity. We experience loving exchanges in more beautiful, exquisite, and direct ways than we generally do in physical life. One of the most rewarding and profound experiences we have on the other side is the experience of love.

In the spiritual worlds, there are natural talents and abilities that all humans share, such as telepathy. Telepathy, in its simplest form, is the conscious ability to pick up thoughts from and transmit thoughts to others. This happens here, but we often aren't aware of it. You may be in the grocery store, and your spouse is sending you the thought to buy tomatoes. Although it wasn't on the grocery list, you end up buying tomatoes as you unconsciously picked up that thought. In the spirit worlds, this is done on a much more conscious level. Because telepathy is natural, it is more difficult to conceal secrets or hide your feelings from others. It makes for more open and honest relationships. As you evolve to the higher planes, the talent of telepathy greatly deepens. You telepathically communicate with the angels and other holy beings. Their minds are operating at such exalted frequencies that these mental exchanges are life-changing moments.

ACTIVITIES AND LIFESTYLE
ON THE OTHER SIDE

There is a traditional image of people in Heaven suspended on clouds, wearing white robes, and playing harps. In truth, a wide variety of activities exist in the spiritual realms. You learn, play, work and explore. You have a home, wonderful relationships, and pursue work and activities that you enjoy.

You are not that different in character on the other side from who you are here. When you cross over, you do not suddenly become a saint if you have been living a life of lying and cheating. There is a continuity. If things were very different, living on the other side would be too disjointed. You would not be able to relate to yourself and your environment. At the same time, the spiritual worlds do bring out qualities and characteristics that are sometimes subdued in the physical world. So, you aren't completely the same person on the other side as you are here.

In the hereafter, activities break down into the three broad areas. In the first, there is a period of acclimation once you've crossed over. During this time, you rest as you disengage from earthly life. You are healed of any illnesses as well as mental and emotional distresses. Your life on Earth is reviewed to see where you succeeded and where you could have done better. If you have done misdeeds, you'll spend time understanding why what you did was wrong. Behavioral issues can take a long time to be resolved. Weaknesses in soul qualities take even longer to work through and often require future incarnations to strengthen. If you did a lot of good while on Earth, you'll enjoy the fruits of those labors and often continue in the good work you were doing. My father, for example, was a Greek Orthodox priest and excellent at what he did. I was honored to see him on the other side after he died, and he showed me that he was continuing his priestly work to great effect.

The second area involves activities you participate in that have nothing to do with earth life. They are part of what it means to live in the world of spirit. These activities can be very exciting. Some are connected to your evolution, while others are part of the spiritual dynamics of the realm you live in. The third area of activity is related to upcoming incarnations. This is when you prepare for things you will be doing when you reincarnate again into physical life. In many ways, you plan and build your earthly destiny before you incarnate, using that incarnation to achieve the goals of the divine plans you've prepared.

What about loved ones who have died? Do you see them? The answer is a resounding *yes!* Death does not sever the bonds of love. If you truly loved someone and they loved you, you will have reunions and they are joyous occasions. On the other hand, if there was no bond of love on Earth, such as in a loveless marriage, there may not be the same reunions. Loving reunions also extend to our pets! Animals we've deeply loved will wait for us on the other side and welcome us into our new life in the world of spirit.

As wonderful as it is to see loved ones, our relationship with them will be different. For example, a loving parent/child relationship on Earth is not the same on the other side because we no longer play the same roles. Also, our loved ones are often involved in activities unrelated to what we shared with them on Earth, so we may not spend the same kind of time together again. Plus, once we become a citizen of the world of spirit, we rediscover wonderful friendships with other souls we have known in earlier incarnations. It's a remarkable time to rekindle those relationships.

Is there civilization on the other side? Most definitely, and in ways more splendid than here. There are no countries but there are regions that are like provinces. There are cities but not the congested concentration of life you would find in Manhattan, London, or Tokyo. In general, life is more provincial. There are trains and boats that can take you from one place to another. There are some cars and a few airplanes, but they aren't quite the same as we have them here. There are governing bodies overseen by the spiritual hierarchy, so there is no corruption or self-serving interests. There are human ministers of politics who participate in governing and work closely with the Holy Ones. These relationships and interactions demonstrate how effective and satisfying politics can be when attention is focused on the betterment of the people.

Interactions with the Holy Ones influence all areas of human activity. Doctors learn more about healing from the angels of healing. Artists learn about their art from angels of music, art, and literature. Those of legal mind may work with great celestial beings such as the Lords of Karma—the very embodiment of divine law—to understand how the eternal laws of life work. Angels who are adept in the sciences inspire the mathematical and scientific minds. There is even business and industry, as every invention that has benefitted humanity was conceived and created on the other side. Every field of human endeavor is lovingly inspired and guided by the spiritual hierarchy.

Fortunately, there are no wars because there is no death and no quest for land and goods. However, because there *are* evil spirits, there is a type of psychic warfare that happens in some spiritual dimensions. This can be as devastating as any warlike situation but is part of life experience. Is there pain and suffering in the spiritual worlds? Yes, we still have the same human frailties. Anger, rage, fear, worry, jealousy, resentment, depression, mental and emotional disturbances, intolerance do exist on the other side.

Cultures and customs also continue. If you enjoyed the culture you were immersed in while on Earth, you can continue in that experience. At the same time, there are customs unique to the other side. You can also keep your religious faith. On the other side, you are taught the beautiful original meanings and intentions of all religions and how they draw their inspiration from the same divine source.

You live in communities, although as mentioned, there are no families other than those who take care of children who have crossed over. You tend to live with other people, although many live in their own home. The pace of life varies and dramas do unfold, but in general, there is a more gradual flow of life that is quite different from the kind of stressful living that exists on Earth. People are more considerate and compassionate.

Among the many inventions we don't have here is a type of holographic TV, but not with the volume of programming you see on Earth as people are engaged in many other activities. People engage in artistic activities such as going to or participating in plays and musical concerts. In the more enlightened realms, musical concerts are particularly exciting as you can see the energetic thought patterns created by the music, which are spectacular to witness!

We have jobs on the other side! They aren't the nine-to-five jobs that exist here, but everyone is expected to serve the greater good. Some are more cooperative and industrious than others at this. There are lazy and undisciplined people as well as dedicated, hardworking souls. As you progress to the heaven worlds, everyone is productive. People are very motivated in what they do and are given inspiring assignments that do much good for many people. At the same time, there is fun and play time, laughter and joy. You can participate in sporting events but on the more causal side; there are no professional competitive sports as we have here.

It might be surprising to know that there is a form of money in the hereafter. There is no paper or coin money, but there is a type of credit system. And while there are no banks as we think of them, there are financial centers where these credits are kept and administered. You earn credits through work and application which allow you to do more things. Prosperity is a divine attribute, so the building up of prosperity is a spiritual quality. It is also a talent that some are better at than others. Here you learn the value and importance of abundance as a means of mastering the powers of the realms you are in. Once you reach the heaven worlds, the expression of abundance dramatically increases as you tap the divine flows of prosperity directly.

It's comforting to know that extreme poverty does not exist on the other side because there is no inequity of resources. This doesn't mean that everyone lives the same. There are those who live a modest life as they have not yet learned to harness the powers of prosperity or aren't making the needed effort. In the same way, there are those who are very industrious and live a more abundant life.

What language is spoken? Language is sacred in the spirit worlds. It is recognized that there is spiritual power in words, and they carry vibrations that reach out into the creative fabric of life. On the other side, you can speak any of the languages on Earth, yet each spiritual realm also has its own sacred language. The languages on Earth are in fact a reflection of these spiritual languages.

Finally, while the hereafter is not exclusively focused on spiritual evolution, a great deal of activity is. There is an understanding that the spiritual planes are places to evolve, and most people interact with divine ones from higher dimensions. There is regular spiritual training that goes on like any educational pursuit, much of which takes place in specially constructed training centers. It's exciting to be taught spiritual topics by celestial beings. You know they speak from experience, and you are captivated by their instructions, blessings, and wisdom.

HOW YOUR ACTIONS HERE RELATE TO
LIFE ON THE OTHER SIDE

———

Most spiritual traditions teach that your actions here determine your life in the hereafter. Dante, in *The Divine Comedy,* spent a great deal of time detailing where people on Earth (at the time of Dante) found themselves in the hereafter based on their character and behavior. Without question, your actions have meaning both in the physical and spiritual worlds. If you lived the saintly life of a Mother Teresa, for example, not only were you a blessing to many, your wonderful work continues on the other side. If you did destructive things on Earth, hurting yourself and others, you are shown the repercussions of such actions. The soul will then have to go through a period of remorse and begin a process of redemption. Some souls accept seeing their missteps; others resist. When actions are particularly destructive, such souls have lost so much power, they can find themselves in the netherworlds. These are not eternal hells but dark places where souls need to come to terms with their misdeeds.

What happens to your talents and accomplishments when you cross over? They continue. A Mozart or a Beethoven may continue writing music. That talent does not just disappear. My older brother, Phillip, was a world-class operatic tenor. After he passed, I saw him on the other side continuing to sing and perform. As for wealth, you cannot take your money and possessions to the other side. But if you used your wealth wisely—if you were generous, kind, and giving and you accrued good money karma—this will come back to bless you. If, on the other hand, you were wealthy but greedy, hoarding your wealth, you will find yourself in a challenging situation on the other side.

BRINGING INSPIRATION FROM THE
SPIRIT WORLDS TO EARTH

One of the most intriguing aspects of the spiritual worlds is how many things accomplished on Earth are first generated there. You spend time in the spirit worlds preparing for your upcoming incarnation. If you are a talented artist and it is part of your life purpose to create wonderful works of art in your upcoming incarnation, you start to develop these artistic creations in the spiritual worlds. When you incarnate on Earth, you build your talents and attune yourself to that inspirational mind so the creativity that was already manifest in those worlds can flow down into physical life. You may have no conscious memory of this, but you may be amazed, not only of an inspiration, but at how complete and natural it feels. This is because you are, in essence, bringing inspiration from one realm of life to another. Not only does this bring creativity to Earth, it helps to align you to the inner worlds from where the inspiration came.

The key is to be open to inspiration. This can be difficult when we get distracted. Why is it that sometimes we get our most original ideas when young? Because young minds are often more open and flexible. And yet masters in the arts and sciences have the ability to create throughout their lives. The ancient playwright Sophocles was writing masterpieces at ninety-four! If you design your life effectively, inspiration will grow and mature as you do. The saddest thing is for your creative potential to be thwarted because you become rigid. When this happens, the things you generated in the spiritual realms will not have the chance to objectify themselves. It's a loss for the soul and a loss for humanity. It is thus essential to be creative, open-minded, flexible, and ready to learn new things.

Not everything is set in advance. Life is fluid in all realms, and there are many opportunities for new inspirations while in the midst of your incarnated life. When I was producing my variety show years ago, we had to come up with a song to introduce the show. I was working with some fine musicians, but we were having trouble coming up with the right song, something that would set the tone and draw people in. I am not a musician, but one day the entire song came to me in a flash, both the melody and lyrics. I raced to the musical team and sang what I was "hearing." They notated and orchestrated it, and it became the theme song of the show! This didn't come from me. I knew it was a gift from the other side.

Ultimately, your spiritual lessons are fully internalized in the physical world. You build up power in the spiritual realms, yet the final "test" to see if something is truly learned and accomplished happens in physical life. Once learned there, it becomes part of your eternal expression.

Chapter 4

A HISTORICAL UNDERSTANDING
OF THE HEREAFTER

There is no religion higher than truth.
—H.P. Blavatsky, based on an ancient Hindu saying

T HE DESIRE TO soar to the skies has been around as long as humanity has been able to think and dream. From the most ancient of days, humanity has wanted to touch the heavens—the celestial spheres of the Moon, stars, planets, and the Sun. It was believed by many ancient societies that the sky above was Heaven itself. When we died, our soul soared to the heavens to join our ancestors and the gods. Some ancients even thought that we became a star when we died. There was also a belief that our soul would descend to a region deep inside the earth where we would travel to the underworld. Today, humanity is exploring the cosmos while the wonder of Heaven is stronger than ever.

Heaven is the backdrop of almost every spiritual tradition. In this chapter, we will look at the theme of Heaven and your spiritual ascent in the context of various spiritual traditions. There are unique concepts found in each tradition, yet there are common threads of ideas and teachings. Every genuine religious and metaphysical teaching is essentially looking at different facets of the same universal truth. All spiritual studies are ultimately drawing their inspiration from the same source, regardless of the differing cultural presentations and the way institutions and people may interpret those truths.

There are challenges in facing a historical perspective on Heaven. The first is that many mystical teachings have been kept secret. To gain such wisdom, one had to join an ashram or mystery school where such things were taught. This was deliberate to preserve the integrity of the teachings for those who were ready to understand and receive them. In addition, there were periods of suppression and persecution, which forced metaphysical teachings to go underground.

Another challenge in understanding the history of Heaven is separating mystical insights based on direct spiritual experience from popular yet naive beliefs of the day. How cultures viewed Heaven was connected to how they viewed life. If the physical universe was not well understood, how could there be a clear understanding of the spiritual universe? For example, the ancient Akkadian word *etemmu* means "the animated existence beyond death in the form of a spirit". Yet the distinction between etemmu and the physical body was sometimes blurred, with some texts speaking of etemmu as if it were equivalent to the physical body. This is one reason the ancients put such strong emphasis on the burial process; they believed that the way a person was buried had a bearing on their afterlife experience. Even today in many religious practices, there are rules and restrictions regarding burial of the dead that go back to these ancient beliefs.

Yet, enlightened souls of ancient days *did* understand the underlying structure of life and the physical universe through their inner visions and spiritual training. But they could not talk about these principles openly as they could not prove their understanding. Those who tried were usually rejected.[1] This meant that mystics would teach one way privately and another way publicly. For those in the "inner circles" of spiritual learning, the instruction would be clear and direct. In presenting metaphysical concepts to a general audience, however, they couched their teachings in the customs and modes of the day. This makes reading ancient spiritual texts difficult. The historian and philosopher Gershom Scholem expressed this challenge when speaking of the Kabbalistic masterpiece, *The Zohar*:

> *Again and again, one is struck by the simultaneous presence of crudely primitive modes of thought and feelings, and of ideas whose profound contemplative mysticism is transparent.*[2]

I have experienced this dual way of teaching, the exoteric and esoteric, in my own spiritual education. When I was eleven years old, I was fortunate to study with a hermetic scientist. To the world at large, she ran a well-known theater stock company of which I was a part. Privately, she was a mystic clairvoyant and a third-generation hermetic scientist—one of the most ancient metaphysical traditions. She never let on about her spiritual gifts and talents unless she sensed that talent in others. She could clairvoyantly see that I had the mystic sight but that I didn't know how to use that talent.

At that time, I was having many spiritual experiences, and Dorothy helped me to put these experiences into perspective. She was my first spiritual teacher giving lessons in metaphysics. It was an inspiring time

---

[1] The ancient Greek astronomer and mathematician Aristarchus of Samos correctly theorized the heliocentric notion of the Sun at the center of the solar system and placed the planets in their correct order from the Sun. He further surmised that the stars were suns like our own only much further away. His thinking was not generally accepted in his time. Ironically, centuries later, Copernicus gave credit to Aristarchus for his heliocentric theory.

[2] *Major Trends in Jewish Mysticism* by Gershom Scholem

to finally understand what I was experiencing. As part of her teaching, she showed me old, hand-written books on Hermetic science that came from Europe. They were hundreds of years old and were based on even older manuscripts. In these books were explanations of many spiritual principles including color interpretations of the aura with accompanying illustrations. It was incredibly illuminating.

These unpublished books were different in style and content from the historical Hermetic fragments available to the public today. As inspiring as it is to study the published Hermetic texts, these unpublished manuscripts were written for a different audience and purpose. Designed for those undergoing mystic training, they were clearly written, and there was no question what they were trying to communicate. Even an eleven-year-old child could comprehend much of their content.

ANCIENT HEAVENLY TRADITIONS

The oldest surviving historical records of Heaven can be found in the Mesopotamian cuneiform tablets. There is the Sumerian epic of King Etana, "a shepherd who ascended to Heaven, who organized the lands (countries)." Toward the end of this story, of which we have only fragments, Etana soars to the heaven of Anu on an eagle, where he watches the Earth below slowly fading from view before visiting various aspects of heaven—part of a quest to find the "planet of birth" so Etana may have a son.

In Sumerian incantations of purification, we find the theme of the seven heavens within calling upon the powers of Heaven in healing:

Seven heavens and seven earths, seven firmaments...
Be exorcised by Heaven, be exorcised by Earth.

Clearly, when these tablets were written over 5,000 years ago, concepts of Heaven were already well-established.

Astro-Theology

The ancient understanding of Heaven, especially the seven heavens, is tied to astronomy and astrology. Mystics saw these sciences as master keys to the spiritual mysteries. The Sun, stars, and planets were far more than lifeless objects moving in space. They were living presences that reflected the relationship of humanity to Heaven itself. From the metaphysical perspective, the cosmos revealed the fundamental reason for living on Earth—the human ascent to the heavens. Spiritual practice was part of the great journey of spiritual growth. Manly P. Hall aptly phrased the ancient view on astronomy and astrology as "astro-theology."

The ancients devised a celestial system of the universe (with variations) that was remarkably resilient up to the time of Copernicus. It combined the theological and scientific understanding of its day. Today, we call this system the "geocentric model" of the universe. While we now know that this model is not how the universe really works, ancient mystics used this accepted picture of the cosmos as a symbol of humanity's personal ascent from Earth-centered consciousness to the celestial consciousness of the Divine.

In the mystical interpretation of the geocentric model, Earth is at the nucleus. This represents material, human consciousness before spiritual illumination. Circling the Earth are the Moon, Sun, and the five planets visible to the naked eye. These seven celestial objects represented the seven heavens. They reflected the spiritual processes the ascending soul goes through to reach the summit of spiritual enlightenment. Above the seven heavens, there were three more realms. First was the realm of the "fixed stars." Above that was the realm of the Primum Mobile—prime mover of all celestial objects. Above that, highest and grandest of all, was the Empyrean. Here is where God and the angels lived—the source of creation. Mystically, these upper three realms represented the ultimate destination of the human ascent back to our divine origins.

Ancient Egyptian Tradition

In the glory days of Egypt, there existed some of the greatest metaphysical training centers the world has ever known. *The Kybalion*, a 1908 Hermetic text, teaches that Egypt was once the center of the Hermetic tradition and that mystics of all lands drank from the spiritual waters of the Egyptian mystery schools.

The Egyptians called Heaven "The Field of Reeds." This belief presented the afterlife as a type of ideal earthly life where there was no pain and where things lost at death were returned. Perhaps the best source we have from this period on how a soul can attain Heaven in the afterlife is found in the ancient papyrus scroll called *The Egyptian Book of the Dead*, also known as *The Book of Coming Forth by Day*.

To earn your way to The Field of Reeds, you first had to go through the underworld, which the Egyptians called the Duat. Here, you had to pass several tests and trials. There were caverns and passages that were protected by monsters and gods of the dark. You needed special spells and incantations to successfully navigate the obstacles put in your way. If you cleared the chambers of darkness, you were confronted by Ma'at, the goddess of truth and justice. Here you would be tested with the "forty-two negative confessions" where you declared that you were not guilty of committing certain sins to prove how pure and righteous a life you lived.

If you could answer these questions satisfactorily, you then met the god Anubis, where your heart was "weighed" on the scales of justice against a feather. If your heart was heavier than a feather, you could not be admitted to Heaven. If you were a pure soul and your heart was "light as a feather," you were granted an audience with the god of the underworld, Osiris, one of the most important gods in Egyptian religion. He would grant you the final right to be admitted to The Field of Reeds to live in joy and in the eternal presence of the gods. In this story of the afterlife, we find a veiled allegory of the initiation ceremonies in the Egyptian mystery schools. The "coming forth by day" was the resurrection of the initiate into the revelations of the spiritual life.

The Ancient Greek Mystery School Tradition

Religion was central to the ancient Greeks. They had a fascinating combination of the rational and the mystical. They believed in the spiritual powers of the universe but also wanted to understand the physical universe through the power of reason and intellect. This thinking gave rise to the glory days of Greece as the cradle of Western Civilization.

The Greek word for Heaven is often translated as Ouranos, after the mythical god, Uranus. Uranus was considered "father sky"—the personification of the heavens. Yet the heaven that humans aspired to after death was called the Elysium or the Elysian Fields. This was an idyllic, blissful land. Homer described it as a place of perfection without work or strife. Hesiod wrote that the blessed were nourished by the sweet fruit that grew there. There was music and even sport. In the middle of this paradise was the most sacred part of the Elysian Fields: the Isles of the Blessed. The imagery of the Elysian Fields has inspired humanity for ages. The famous avenue in Paris, the Champs-Élysées, is named after the Elysian Fields. The German poet and playwright Friedrich Schiller described the fellowship and delights of the Elysian Fields in his poem, Ode to Joy. Beethoven immortalized the poem by setting it to music in his 9th symphony, creating one of the most iconic and recognizable melodies in history.

The Elysian Fields were part of a broader Greek conception of the afterlife called Hades ("the unseen"). The earliest depiction of Hades was of an ephemeral, misty, gloomy place. Departed souls went to Hades regardless of their actions on Earth and were shadows of their former selves. Over time, the concept of Hades evolved into different sections where departed souls found themselves based on their actions in life. If they did evil, they ended up in the dark pits of Tartarus, the Greek version of Hell. If they weren't bad people but hadn't distinguished themselves or made great accomplishments in life, they might find themselves in a place called the Asphodel Meadows ("remembered beyond the tomb"). If they lived a pious life and were remembered by the living, they could enjoy the fruits of Elysium.

Originally, the Elysium was only for demi-gods and heroes. Yet as the conception of the afterlife developed, anyone could enter if they earned their way. If a person lived a good and pious life, they could become immortal in the afterlife and, with their immortality, live in the Elysian Fields. There was a variation of this belief in that if a soul was able to attain Elysium by reincarnating back on Earth repeatedly, it could progress to the Isles of the Blessed and live there permanently in bliss. The ancient Greek mystery schools of the Orphic and Eleusinian traditions placed great emphasis on freeing the soul from the confines of physical life. Through the process of purifying and spiritualizing, the soul could attain enlightenment and earn its way to the immortal lands.

ABRAHAMIC TRADITIONS OF HEAVEN

It is remarkable that three of the great world religions—Judaism, Islam, and Christianity—and their metaphysical counterparts share the same spiritual father: Abraham. Many of our concepts of Heaven and the afterlife can be traced to these three spiritual traditions.

The Judaic Tradition

In the Jewish tradition, the afterlife is called Olam Ha-ba ("the world to come"). This can also be interpreted as "the age to come," meaning the time of the resurrection of the world that is to follow the coming of the Messiah. However one interprets Olam Ha-ba, modern Judaism downplays the role of Heaven and the afterlife, focusing instead on the spiritual life of the here and now. Because there is no standard belief regarding the afterlife in Jewish tradition, there is a wide variety of accepted beliefs regarding what happens when you die. Yet if you look at the ancient roots of Judaism's 4,000-year history, especially the Jewish mystical tradition, there is a rich heritage of Heaven and the afterlife. Heaven inaugurates the opening lines of the Hebrew Bible: "In the beginning, God created the heavens and the earth," setting the tone that Heaven is a fundamental tenet of Jewish belief.

In early Hebrew cosmology, the universe was divided into three parts: the Shamayim ("the heavens"), the Eretz ("the earth"), and the Sheol ("the underworld"). Shamayim also breaks down into two parts: *sham*, which means "sky," and *mayim*, which means "water." This reflects an ancient belief that the earth was separated from the heavens by water. Hence the Biblical quote:

And God said, "Let there be a vault between the waters to separate water from water." So God made the vault and separated the water under the vault from the water above it.[3]

God and the angels lived in Shamayim, the living were on earth (the Eretz), and the dead lived in the Sheol. In this conception, humans did not go to Heaven when they died. They went to the Sheol. Originally, this was thought of as a place of silence. It was neither bad nor evil but neutral. This understanding of the other side was tied to ancestral beliefs of being with loved ones and the ability to communicate with loved ones who had died. The idea was that those in the Sheol awaited the coming Messianic Age when they would be resurrected.

Over time, the concept of the Sheol changed. It, too, was divided into areas. One was an abode for the righteous dead, the other a fiery realm for the wicked. During the time of the Septuagint (the translation of the Hebrew Bible into Greek), the Sheol took on the Greek qualities of Hades. There were yet other Jewish writings where the Sheol was clearly a place closer to the modern concept of Hell.

Woven into this biblical tapestry were hints of a more sophisticated understanding of Heaven. There is the antediluvian patriarch Enoch who "walked with God, and then he wasn't there, because God took him."[4] This has been interpreted to mean that Enoch didn't die but was taken directly to heaven. Then there is the dream of Jacob's ladder, where the patriarch "dreamed, and behold a ladder set up on the earth, and the top of it reached to Heaven; and behold the angels of God ascending and descending on it."[5] There were inferences that one could choose where to go in the afterlife with biblical passages such as, "If

---

[3] *Genesis 6-7*
[4] *Genesis 5:24*
[5] *Genesis 28:10-17*

I ascend to Heaven, You are there; If I make my bed in Sheol, behold, You are there."[6] There is even the concept of a heaven of heavens (shamayi h'shamayim) as expressed by King Solomon: "Why, Heaven itself, even the heaven of heavens, cannot contain you; so how much less this house I have built?"[7]

Jewish Mysticism and the Merkabah Tradition

We know Jewish mysticism today as the Kabbalah, but the Kabbalah is the result of a long metaphysical tradition. These early Jewish traditions became known as The Ma'aseh Merkabah (Works of the Chariot) and The Ma'aseh Bereshit (Works of Creation). It was the Merkabah tradition that focused strongly on the heavenly ascent. Gershom Scholem, who is credited with reenergizing modern scholarly study into the Kabbalah, postulated that it was the ecstatic contemplations of this mysterious mysticism that was responsible for the flood of Jewish, as well as Christian, apocalyptic writings of the Second Temple Period (between 516 BCE and 70 CE) and centuries into the Common Era. In these writings, a robust vision of the seven heavens was explored with detailed accounts of mystics who were taken to these celestial realms. These accounts often ended with a vision of the future of the coming Messianic Age. The language was often ecstatic as well as symbolic. Many of these writings were a type of textbook for those who were undergoing mystical training. For example, the opening line of Hekhalot Rabbati is as follows:

---

[6] *Psalms 139:8*
[7] *1 Kings 8:27*

What are those songs (prayers, incantations) which he recites who would behold the vision of the Merkabah, who would descend in peace and would ascend in peace?

There are ancient Jewish legends of Moses having ascension experiences through the seven heavens. They happened at different times in his life: during his experience with the burning bush; on Mount Sinai when receiving the Torah; and shortly before his death. As he went through these celestial experiences, his body would gradually change form appropriate to the heaven he was in. He would visit heavenly temples and be granted visions and wisdom, all while beholding the glory of God. These remarkable stories, none of which are directly found in the Bible, seemed to be a way to bring elements of the Merkabah mystical ascension experience into the synagogue of the early Common Era.

The Kabbalah and The Tree of Life

Another running theme in Jewish mysticism related to ascension is the symbol of The Tree of Life—a universal theme found in many ancient cultures. Yet it is in the tradition of the Kabbalah that The Tree of Life, or The Tree of the Sephiroth, finds its most eloquent expression. In Kabbalah cosmology, there are four great worlds that were born of the Ein Soph—the Limitless and Boundless. These worlds are known as

1. *Atziluth*—the world of archetypes
2. *Ber'iah*—the world of creation
3. *Yetzirah*—the world of formation
4. *Assiah*—the physical world

From each of these great worlds radiates ten universal emanations or creative principles (the ten Sephiroth), each of which is organized into its own Tree of Life. The Sephiroth tree is the symbolic representation of how the universe is constructed and, at the same time, how each of us is constructed, spiritually and physically. It represents the way of holy living and the pathway back to the Divine Source, where we partake of the celestial Garden of Eden.

The Christian Tradition

Many of the concepts we have of Heaven are strongly influenced by the Christian tradition: Worship God, live a good life, help others, and you'll go to Heaven. This life is a preparation for the next life. The Christian understanding of Heaven is rooted in Judaism as well as influenced by the ancient Greeks, yet it was Jesus who gave humanity a new revelation about Heaven. He taught that there is a glorious spiritual kingdom we can attain if we live a godly life. From His teachings that "the Kingdom of Heaven is at hand" to the Lord's Prayer ("Our Father, who art in Heaven...") to His own ascension to Heaven, He showed a greater world that all humanity had access to. He lifted the veil a little between the spiritual and physical realms that we are all part of. He made Heaven a real, living spiritual experience in a way never done in public life. It was an inspiring message at a time when life for many was exceedingly difficult.

The teachings of Heaven were further expounded by the apostles and by St. Paul. In this famous passage, St. Paul says:

I know a man in Christ who fourteen years ago was caught up to the third heaven…was caught up to paradise and heard inexpressible things, things that no one is permitted to tell.[8]

Many scholars think Paul is speaking of his own experiences in Heaven. The canonical concept of Heaven was firmly established in The Book of Revelation and its eloquent, evocative, and dramatic presentation of the celestial realms:

At once I was in the Spirit, and there before me was a throne in Heaven with someone sitting on it. And the one who sat there had the appearance of jasper and ruby. Surrounding the throne were twenty-four other thrones, and seated on them were twenty-four elders. They were dressed in white and had crowns of gold on their heads…In front of the throne, seven lamps were blazing. These are the seven spirits of God.[9]

As the Christian movement evolved for over 400 years before becoming an established religion, so did the concept of Heaven. The early church fathers tried to answer basic questions: What is it like in Heaven? Do we have a body in Heaven? Do we see loved ones? Do we see God? The Greek bishop Irenaeus saw Heaven as a type of glorified physical world—a compensation for the difficulties and persecutions experienced in physical life. Saint Augustine first interpreted Heaven as a type of ascetic life, yet later started to incorporate ideas such as reunions with loved ones.

Through the centuries that followed, changes in how Christians defined Heaven often coincided with changes in society. In medieval Europe, art gave imagery and vision to Heaven and the spiritual life. As the Middle Ages progressed, cities and urban living developed. This

---

[8] *2 Corinthians 12:1-4*
[9] *Revelation 4*

gave rise to an image of Heaven not just as a paradise but as a God-centered, celestial city filled with Divine Light that emanated from the divine source. This b ecame a c entral f eature o f t he c elestial l ife. S t. Thomas Aquinas carried St. Paul's teaching of the "spiritual body" further by filling it with light, saying, "The body of the blessed will shines seven time brighter than the sun." The r obust m edieval c osmology of Heaven reached its zenith of expression in Dante's masterpiece, The Divine Comedy, bringing to life an understanding of Heaven with beautiful storytelling and poetry.

A major influence in the understanding of Heaven can be found in the writings of the Swedish theologian Emanuel Swedenborg. In his seminal work on the afterlife based on his own visions and experiences, *Heaven and Hell*, Swedenborg painted a detailed picture of life in heaven. His rich, vivid imagery captivated readers and influenced many. He said that souls in Heaven were productive and engaged in activities. They continued their spiritual development and loved each other. He taught that we do not suddenly change our character when we cross over; we have a similar personality to that in physical life. Souls no longer hid their inner nature, so both errors and strengths of character were more easily recognized. He emphasized that there were societies in Heaven and that people lived in communities.

He taught that in the spirit world, one did not gain immediate bliss or damnation. Rather, the soul was slowly educated in heavenly matters and then progressed into higher states of spiritual being as it perfected itself. There was a correspondence in Heaven with things of the earth. As he wrote, "Although the sun of the world is not seen in heaven, there is nevertheless a sun there, and light and heat, and all things that are in the world." This is a strikingly metaphysical interpretation of the other side. Swedenborg's visions helped establish modern Christian concepts of Heaven, which have endured to this day.

The Islamic Tradition

In Islam, the word for Heaven is Jannah, which translates as "paradise." Also known as The Garden of Righteousness, it is an afterlife of delights and pleasures for a life well-lived on Earth. The themes of Islamic heaven share similarities with the Jewish and Christian traditions yet have their own unique character.

Central to Islamic faith is Allah, the Muslim word for God. The ultimate goal of Heaven is to be in the presence of Allah. Islamic faith does not take the path that poverty is holy or that wealth is anathema to spiritual aspirations. Consequently, the Islamic depiction of the heavenly experience is divinely opulent and lavish. It is a place where all wishes are fulfilled. There are delights such as the famously beautiful maidens for men and young men for women. You are happy and free of sadness, hurt, or shame. Everyone is essentially the same youthful age and of equal standing. There are palaces made of bricks of gold, silver, and pearls with high thrones. You wear robes, bracelets, and perfumes and join in exquisite banquets served on priceless vessels as you recline on couches made of gold and precious stones. As the Qur'an states:

> *The description of the paradise promised to the righteous is that in it are rivers of fresh water, rivers of milk that never changes in taste, rivers of wine delicious to drink, and rivers of pure honey. There they will also have all kinds of fruit, and forgiveness from their Lord.*[10]

The theme of the seven heavens continues in the Islamic tradition. Each of the seven heavens is depicted as being composed of a different material and inhabited by Islamic prophets. The more good one has

---

[10] *Qur'an 47:15*

done, the higher the level of Jannah one can attain. The seventh and highest heaven is depicted as being composed of an incomprehensible Divine Light. The Tree of Life resides there and is the highest spiritual state humans can attain.

Perhaps the most famous account of visiting Heaven while still part of physical life is the account of Muhammed's night journey. Although it is only hinted at in the Qur'an, it is expounded upon in later Hadith literature. In the story, Muhammed is visited by Archangel Jibra'il (Gabriel) and taken on a journey first to Jerusalem. There he prays and passes a test. He is then ushered up through the seven heavens where he meets the prophets, among them Abraham, Moses, John the Baptist, and Jesus. He reaches the highest heaven and is taken on a tour full of miraculous sights. Ultimately, he arrives at the very throne of Allah. It is here that Allah tells Muhammed how Muslims should pray. Initially, the command is to pray fifty times a day, but that is eventually negotiated to five times a day. This has become the Muslim prayer practice ever since.

The narrative of Muhammed's night journey bears similarities to Jewish mystical literature and ascension stories and echoes the ascension of Jesus. Whether taken literally or interpretatively, it implies the mystic's deep connection with the heaven worlds. The idea that the journey happened at night reflects another spiritual mystery that all humanity has a connection to the world of spirit during sleep.

HEAVEN IN THE EASTERN
SPIRITUAL TRADITIONS

—

While the concept of Heaven is strong in Eastern spiritual practices, it is interpreted in a distinctly different way than in the West. There is a clear understanding that Heaven is not the ultimate objective. Heaven, like Earth, is seen as a beautiful yet temporary state. This is because in Eastern mystical traditions, the emphasis is on returning to the *ultimate reality* underlying Creation. It is described as a state of non-being—the ultimate state of consciousness, the ultimate bliss. In these philosophies, we reincarnate many times in different physical forms to eventually break the cycle of birth and rebirth and return to the ultimate existence.

In the Hindu faith, this ultimate existence is called Brahman. Brahman is the ocean of life, and we are drops in the great ocean. Through the process of gaining enlightenment or moksha, we can break the cycle of reincarnation and return to the state of ultimate bliss. In Buddhism, this ultimate reality is called Nirvana. In Chinese spiritual philosophy, the great aim is returning to the Tao, the natural order of life.

The Hindu Spiritual Tradition

There are many spiritual streams that co-exist in the Hindu faith which are reflected in the differing interpretations of the heavenly state. As the Hindus believe in reincarnation, souls transition to the spiritual realms after completing karmic actions on earth during their lifetime. They then reincarnate until they complete their reincarnation process.

In early expressions of the Vedic faith, the king god of Heaven is Indra, the god of thunder and lightning. In the Indian epic, *The Mahabharata*, the hero Arjuna seeks the help of Indra to secure weapons to protect Arjuna and his brothers in battle. He walks to the Himalayas and practices the ascetic life, which invokes a divine charioteer who takes Arjuna to Heaven. On their way, they see ascetics, heroes who had died in battle, and other virtuous people. After passing through the various regions of Heaven, Arjuna reaches the palace of Indra where Indra embraces and blesses him. Indra then gives Arjuna a thunderbolt to defeat the evil ones in battle.

In Sanskrit, *loka* means "plane of existence," both in consciousness and as an actual location. The sacred writings of the puranas speak of fourteen lokas, seven higher heaven worlds, and seven lower worlds. The highest heaven is Brahma-loka or Satya-loka. This is the realm where Lord Brahma resides. He is the creator god of the Hindu triune Brahma-Vishnu-Shiva (not to be confused with Brahman, the ultimate reality). Brahma-loka is beautiful and exotic with gardens and lotus flowers that radiate spiritual power. As the puranas state:

> *In that planet of Satya-loka, there is neither bereavement, nor old age nor death. There is no pain of any kind, and therefore there are no anxieties, save that sometimes, due to consciousness, there is a feeling of compassion for those unaware of the process of devotional service, who are subjected to unsurpassable miseries in the material world.*[11]

In the Hindu tradition of worshiping Lord Vishnu, the highest heaven is called Vaikuntha, a place without worry or distress. Vaikuntha is said to be beyond the sky and material world and given a location:

---

[11] *Bhagavata Purana, Canto 2: The Cosmic Manifestation*

"262,000,000 yojanas (209,600,000 miles) above Satya-loka."[12] Some of the most beautiful illustrations of the Hindu heaven are based on Vaikuntha. The Bhagavata Purana offers a reverent and colorful description of this glorious realm:

> *In the spiritual sky there are spiritual planets known as Vaikunhas,*
> *which are the residence of the Supreme Personality of Godhead and*
> *His pure devotees…all the residents are similar in form to the Supreme*
> *Personality of Godhead. They all engage in devotional service to the*
> *Lord without desires for sense gratification…the Supreme Personality*
> *of Godhead…is full of the uncontaminated mode of goodness, with no*
> *place for passion or ignorance…there are many forests which are very*
> *auspicious…they are filled with flowers and fruits because everything…*
> *is spiritual and personal…the inhabitants fly in their airplanes…*
> *eternally sing of the character and activities of the Lord.*[13]

The Buddhistic Spiritual Tradition

The story of Prince Siddhartha becoming the Buddha is one of the great world teachings of enlightenment. As the story goes, Siddhartha left the worldly pleasures of his palace seeking truth and the source of suffering. After going through the rigors of the ascetic life, he did not achieve the goal he was seeking. He then developed the idea of a "middle way" to enlightenment. One day, he found the truth he sought while meditating under a Bodhi Tree, and for the rest of his life, he taught others the way to liberation.

---

[12] *Bhagavata Purana, Canto 5*
[13] *Bhagavata Purana, Chapter 15, 13-17*

Like the Hindu tradition, the Buddhist spiritual system teaches that humanity is in a cycle of birth and rebirth. The kind of spiritual realms we experience on the other side will depend on the kind of karma we create while in physical life. The goal is to break the cycle of birth and rebirth and reach the ultimate state of Nirvana, when we no longer need to go through the dramas of pain and suffering, death and rebirth.

In the Buddhist cosmology, the spiritual realms aren't permanent. They are stages of development leading to the ultimate goal of Nirvana. Like the Hindus, the Buddhists have an elaborate cosmology of lokas or realms of life in addition to Earth. Twenty-six of these thirty realms represent various stages of heaven (sagga). These spiritual worlds are mental states of consciousness as well as realms to inhabit. Depending on the karma it creates, a soul is "reborn" into one of these heavens upon death. Once it spends the appointed time in the loka, it reincarnates back on earth for another opportunity to do better. The way to break this cycle of reincarnating is to release the attachments we have and the distress it creates. We accomplish this through meditation and right living.

These realms of heaven have varying degrees of refinement and beauty that break down into three broad areas with many divisions within each. These multiple layers of existence reflect the multi-layered nature of consciousness and our own spiritual make up. They are, from the least to the most refined:

KAMA-LOKA The worlds of sense desires and feelings. Here, dependency on the senses often binds us to our attachments and suffering. There is a lot of diversity in these realms. They include the four lowest planes of depravation, pain, greed, and conflict. Above these is the human realm, with a balance of pleasure and pain. This makes earth life an excellent place to learn how to break the cycle of rebirth. The six lower heavens are higher states of consciousness yet still bound by the senses and feelings. Those who do good deeds are often found in these heavens. Interestingly, all the realms of kama-loka, even the lower heavens, are still bound by the god Mara who is the tempter.

RUPA-LOKA The worlds of form or thought-form worlds. Those who have reached these realms have transcended sensuality and moved to thought-realms of the Brahma-lokas. These worlds are free from desire yet are still conditioned by forms and perceptions. People do not need to eat but feed on bliss. They are not yet perfected and are still subject to pride and wrong views. These heavens are attained by the realization of the Four Noble Truths taught by Buddha. Within this realms are the four jhanas or meditative states of mental absorption. Through concentration in meditation, through loving kindness, equanimity, and compassion, you climb up through the four jhanas, each ascending realm more beautiful than the other.

ARUPA-LOKA The formless worlds. These are the highest of the three spheres of existence in which rebirth takes place. As can be expected, these realms are difficult to describe and best understood when experienced. Here you find life in its infinite and unbounded nature. There are four realms in arupa-loka which correlate to four achievements in what is called "formless" meditation—meditative states where you are no longer associated with form. The four jhanas of this realm relate to the infinitude of space; the infinitude of consciousness; the awareness of no-thingness; and the awareness of perception/nonperception. It is taught that Siddhartha had reached this last state before becoming enlightened.

Reaching these higher worlds is difficult yet attainable through diligence and dedication. As the Buddha teaches:

> *In this dark world, few can see. Like birds that free themselves from the net, only a few find their way to Heaven. Swans fly on the path of the sun by their wonderful power. The wise rise above the world, after conquering Mara (the tempter) and his train.*[14]

---

[14] *The Dhammapada (13:174)*

PART

2

—

Growing through the
Spiritual Worlds

❧

Chapter 5

BEGINNING YOUR SPIRITUAL ASCENT—THE ROAD ALREADY TRAVELED

In my Father's house are many mansions.
—Jesus the Christ

I**N THIS SECTION**, we will explore the spiritual realms, both what they are like and the experiences that happen related to your evolution. We hope to give you an appreciation of the beauty of the spiritual path and how you can better connect with the inner worlds to strengthen your life. There are many planes of consciousness to experience. Life is rich and there's a lot to learn. Each spiritual realm is a unique, sacred adventure.

Where and when did our spiritual pilgrimage begin? It began eons ago in a primitive yet delightful state of consciousness. We have all had a rich evolutionary history that has brought us to the place we are now. The spiritual realms we went through when we took our first steps on the upward climb were wonderful in their own way. In these realms, human souls were in a state of consciousness the Divine affectionately calls "the little people." The fairies, gnomes, elves, and other creatures of folklore are often fictionalized accounts of these beings, but they are not fiction! They are as real as you and I. They *are* you and I in a much less developed state but still an important part of the evolutionary process.

The little people experience life, gain wisdom, and evolve. When we were little people, we were quite spiritual and delighted in harnessing the spiritual powers available to us. We had visionary experiences and lived close to the elements of life—water, air, earth, fire. By embodying the elements, we formed the foundation for our later, more highly developed evolution. Sometimes, little people take the wrong road. They can be mischievous, become influenced by evil, and incite unhealthy behavior. Fortunately, the Holy Ones help awaken the little people when this happens and steer them back into the Divine Light.

Little people inhabit various places on Earth. They live in nature as well as hidden corners in city environments. They can even live inside the Earth. They are quite social and live in groups. They are generally playful and love to explore. They rely on the spiritual hierarchy and understand the help the Higher gives them. They are often cautious about interacting with us directly, but if they sense a compassionate soul, they can make themselves known. When they do they come around, they often bring a lot of love, joy, and mirth.

While writing this book, we had a delightful visitation of five little people. They showed up in the living room where Dimitri and I were working. They were highly developed and formidable in their own right. They were about three feet tall with blue faces and bright auras! There was simple mental communication, but no language was spoken. They seemed happy and wanted us to know they lived in an area near where we lived.

THE ASTRAL WORLDS

———

When we completed our evolution as a little person, we began our journey through one of the most important realms in our spiritual development—the astral worlds. The word *astral* comes from the Latin for "starry." The astral worlds, or astral planes, are pivotal. This is where we began our incarnations in physical life and where we build up our intellect and learn to more fully express our free will. In the astral planes we choose to consciously walk the path of Light. With so much to do here, we spend a lot of time in the astral worlds.

The astral worlds are intimately intertwined with us here in earthly life. They are just as real and "solid" as the physical realm. The reason you cannot perceive the astral planes is that they operate in ranges beyond the physical senses. The astral world is made up of *astral atoms*. Astral atoms vibrate at a faster frequency than physical atoms, which is why we cannot see or touch the astral realms with physical eyes or hands.

The astral worlds have everything we have here and more. They are more encompassing and more populated than Earth. The astral worlds are not dream worlds as is sometimes depicted. They are real, actual locales yet have qualities that are definitely not earthlike. There are vistas, forests, lakes, oceans, magnificent flowers, and gardens but nature takes on fascinating expressions in the astral worlds. There are civilizations ranging from less developed to more developed than found on Earth. The astral worlds are very active with a wide variety of experiences, from primitive to highly advanced and everything in between. There are human dramas and struggles just as on Earth. Yet there are realms of extraordinary cooperation and productivity. Life is well-organized in the astral worlds.

Technology, science, art, philosophy, and religious and spiritual studies flourish in the astral worlds. There are wonderful concerts, theaters, and museums. As we have explored, if you have a gift or talent, you can continue developing that gift or talent in the astral worlds. As with all the spiritual realms, the Holy Ones do a magnificent job of guiding the evolutionary process going on in the various astral realms. While there are more evolved and less evolved levels in the astral, all are overseen by the Divine. One of our greatest privileges in the astral worlds is that we get to consciously interact with these great spiritual beings.

The astral worlds have levels or gradations. Each of the seven astral planes has seven sub-planes, comprising forty-nine gradations of astral matter through which we are evolving. Besides being beautiful, the astral planes have great learning and training centers. There are temples, chapels, halls of learning, sanctuaries, cathedrals, and other centers of creative activities. Each spiritual center is dedicated to some facet of the spiritual life. Because of the great knowledge available in the astral worlds, they are often called the *assimilating* planes. During our time on Earth, we are gathering up experiences, knowledge, and wisdom. When we return to the astral worlds, our soul reflects on and assimilates those experiences. Then at the appointed time, the soul reincarnates on Earth to gather more experiences.

Some metaphysical schools call the astral worlds the *desire* worlds. Desire is one of the defining features of the astral experience. In evolving through the astral worlds, you are learning many things, which include the maturation of your desire nature. Desire is the motor that compels life into expression. Part of your job while ascending through the astral worlds is transmuting your appetite for immediate self-gratification into a burning desire for the divine life.

Evolving through the astral planes takes time. Evolution is not an overnight process. This is why consciously walking the spiritual path is so wonderful; it quickens your ascent through the astral planes. Time spent consciously developing your spiritual nature, regardless of the form it takes, is time well spent.

ACCLIMATION—THE FIRST ASTRAL PLANE

When the soul completes its evolution as a little person, it graduates to the first of seven astral planes. The first astral realm is like an incubation period where the human soul becomes acclimated to astral life. At this point, it has not yet begun to incarnate on Earth. It is not even clothed in an astral body. Its job at this point is to become familiar with the astral environment.

This realm resembles the landscape of a barren planet, yet it doesn't feel desolate, as colorful light rays and sounds of light fill the landscape. Souls are clothed in an astral sphere-like form but not a body as we think of it. In starting the journey through the first astral plane, human souls are essentially "planted" in the astral earth. As the soul assimilates to these vibrations, it eventually evolves out of the astral earth and floats through the astral air. It mingles with the light rays radiating through the atmosphere. Here, souls interact with each other and learn to relate to one another in this new world. They make sounds like the "moos" of cattle. It's not pretty, but they are the beginnings of communication. Through the currents of spiritual light, these young souls acclimate to the astral world and build up their spiritual power.

THE DREAM STATE—
THE SECOND ASTRAL PLANE

When the soul has gathered up enough spiritual power through the process of acclimation and assimilation, it moves to the second astral plane. Here, our soul is given its astral body and a magical new life opens up. We now have a vehicle of expression in the astral world. We can perceive our surroundings and have freedom to move about and interact. Life on the second astral plane is primitive yet playful, innocent, and idyllic.

The astral body starts as oval-shaped and gradually gains human form and features. This reveals a defining quality of the astral body—its ability to change appearance. Through the countless incarnations we will go through, we will have the same astral body, but it will change appearance many times.

The astral body has a mind, but in the second astral plane, this mental expression is what we would call the dream state. This dream state allows the mental consciousness to freely explore and express itself without restriction. As our astral body develops, we learn to harness our mental faculties. Initially, the dream mind expresses its freedom as fantasy. It takes perceptions and experiences and creates mental scenarios based on its own wants and appetites. It is given the opportunity to do this without serious consequences. Our capacity to dream can be traced back to this magical time in our evolution.

As we interact with the astral world through trial and error, we learn to harness the dream mind. Fantasy starts to transform into creative expression. This mental part of us becomes stronger. What's more, souls on this plane can mentally connect together in a sort of collective consciousness through a telepathic trance state. It is a natural experience on this plane and creates a lively and exciting energy. At first, the collective experience is indulgent. As souls evolve, the collective consciousness becomes more creative and constructive. We learn important lessons in how to work together for a common good.

The soul delights in having an astral body to interact with and experience the astral world. Aspects of the second astral plane are like a playground, an astral nursery. There is no real sense of danger. Not only do we interact with each other, we interact with the spiritual hierarchy in a simple way and are responsive to their influence. We don't quite know who these beings are, but we know they are important, and we feel their power. Through the angels, we sense there is something greater in life urging us upward.

We consume food, as the astral body needs nourishment, but there is no eating of animal meat. There is a great variety of vegetation, and we get nourishment from eating delectable vegetables and fruits. The astral body does not die the way the physical body does. It can become sick, and if it gets hurt, diseased, or doesn't get enough nourishment, it can slow down like a car running out of gas, becoming inactive and, if unchecked, dormant. In those situations, the angels need to revive it.

There is weather with variations in humidity and temperature. There are even types of seasons. It rains and, in some areas, snows. There is companionship and social groups but no civilization. We experience love and feel happiness and sadness. There are affections between people and a primitive type of sexual attraction, yet this time is not for procreation; it's to experience intimacy. In addition to the collective mental experience, there is a primitive form of communication, but this is not yet language. Second astral plane souls make sounds and learn to intone—a type of singing. They communicate by the inflection of those tones.

As the soul evolves through this plane, the astral form becomes more defined. The mind is still in a dream state, but it has matured into more creative and productive mental activities. The group consciousness moves from simple cooperative experiences to more directed experiences. By the third sub-plane (remember that each astral plane has seven sub-planes within it), the astral body is fully molded into human shape. We learn skills like how to swim and develop simple building skills. As we grow from sub-plane to sub-plane on the second astral plane, we go through a type of astral metamorphosis. The astral body changes polarity from the male to female and vice versa, so we experience both sexes.

I was taken to a more developed level on the second astral plane as part of my spiritual education. It was startling to experience the enormity of it all. There were animals roaming around. I saw simple huts made of what looked like straw. I met a woman who communicated with me mentally, and I was surprised by the sophistication of her abilities. She looked like a teenager, wore plain, simple clothing, and had brown hair. There was a beauty in her appearance. I greeted her, and she greeted me back. I couldn't tell if she understood who I was, but she was eager to engage and wanted to know more about me.

CONSCIOUS AWARENESS— THE THIRD ASTRAL PLANE

As souls evolve to the third astral plane, dramatic changes start to take place. Our astral body becomes stronger and more resilient—a better tool of expression for our soul. Most importantly, it is on the third astral plane that a new expression of mind opens up—conscious awareness. We had awareness on the second astral plane, but it was through dream-mind consciousness. Now with conscious awareness, we are much more cognizant of our surroundings and each other. We are more aware of what we are doing and demonstrate greater flows of intelligence. It's a sobering experience to awaken out of the dream mind.

This attribute of conscious awareness is different from *self*-conscious awareness. Self-conscious awareness is the intellectual mind. It is the ability to mentally step outside yourself and "look back on yourself." Self-consciousness enables the attribute of abstract analytic thought. In reading these words, you are demonstrating self-conscious awareness. This trait differentiates us from the consciousness of animals. Animals are very much aware and intelligent, but they do not yet have *self*-conscious awareness except in a rudimentary form. They operate from instinct. Humans also develop an instinctual nature, which becomes a defining characteristic on the third astral plane. This is similar but not the same as the instincts of animals. Science defines instinct as an "innate, typically fixed pattern of behavior in response to certain stimuli." We tend to think of instinct as operating "without mind" and more like an impulse—a programmed behavior. We need these inborn tools to effectively react to and handle our surroundings. Without the instinctual nature, we would not be able to survive in a given environment.

With conscious awareness and the flowering of the instincts, there is a much stronger expression of the desire nature. This compels us to want things with greater intensity. We pursue our desires with zeal and determination. While there was affection and innocent sexual activity on the second astral plane, the sex drive opens up on the third astral plane. With the awakening of our instinctual nature, competitive elements come into play. Our interactions are more dramatic. We experience greater dynamics of life: courage, aggression, fear, triumph, tragedy, suffering, and joy. We are curious to know things; we explore and are inventive. Combined with conscious awareness, we develop basic skills such as problem solving, social development, leadership skills, and primitive arts and sciences. There are more challenges, but through these challenges, we learn greater resilience.

On the third astral plane, we have vivid dreams. When we were on the second astral plane, we *were* in the dream state and sleep was dreamless. Now that we are consciously aware, we go into deep dream states when we sleep. In our dream mind, we can play out scenarios that we will act out in waking life. We learn that mind has more than one dimension and that consciousness can shift between levels of mental activity. We learn crucial differences between fantasy and reality. The angels will often reach third plane souls during sleep in addition to working with them in waking life. They help us to understand that there is a higher life and something greater to aspire to.

There are greater varieties of vegetation and animal wildlife than on the second astral plane. Pristine landscapes look untamed and untouched as far as the eye can see. There is a variety of habitats, which includes valleys, mountains, deserts, forests, rivers, lakes, and oceans. A type of verbal language emerges on the third astral plane although there is no written language.

While not quite yet at the level of *civilized* living as we think of it, people live in larger, organized groups and share group traits and qualities. There are societies or tribes. Cultures and customs also come into the picture on the third astral plane. The astral body starts to reflect race types. From the metaphysical perspective, race is part of the spiritual experience. The race types we see here in physical life reflect the racial archetypes in the spiritual worlds. The dwellings that third plane souls live in take on more creativity and ingenuity than the simple huts of second plane souls.

Buildings constructed by angels can also be found on the third astral plane. Although not the sophisticated structures that exist in the higher astral worlds, they are beautiful. They are of moderate size, often made of wood or stone, found nestled within the nature that surrounds them, and filled with Divine Light. There are healing sanctuaries, chapels, and places of education. People are taken to these places and trained by angels and enlightened human souls in a variety of areas including healing, creative endeavors, and learning how to pray.

One of the most remarkable things that happen on the third astral plane is the beginning of earthly experience. These are not yet the physical incarnations that would begin on the fourth astral plane. Rather, they are extended astral visitations to Earth to acclimate to physical life. It's a type of incarnation even though it isn't physical. These third plane astral souls will experience differing sexes and differing races at various places in the world. When the time is right, souls return to the astral world and go through a type of review and assimilation. After that, they will "incarnate" again back to astral earth to continue the learning experience. This process helps prepare them for the back and forth that goes on with physical incarnations.

Having just described the process of acclimating to physical life, metaphysics teaches that it wasn't always this way. Ages ago, third-plane souls began their *physical* incarnations on Earth. These were the "caveman" days. Humans on the third astral plane inhabited physical forms such as the Neanderthal. As humanity passed through this evolutionary stage, third plane physical incarnations ended. Today, young souls start their physical incarnations on the fourth astral plane.

As we evolved through the third astral plane, we learned to mature our instinctual nature and became skilled in handling our environment. At the top of the third astral plane, there was a major leap in our evolution. We received the precious gift of *self-conscious awareness*. This aligned us with the qualities of the higher, inspirational mind and our Divine Spirit. Now we would unfold free will, because we had the mind to be self-aware to choose between right and wrong. This would initiate a new phase in our spiritual journey—the development of the intellect. With this new gift, however, there came a price. We became responsible for our actions. We would reap the benefits of our right actions and pay the price for our wrong actions. Thus, karma—the law of cause and effect—would come strongly into play. And life would start to take the civilized form that we recognize.

Chapter 6

AWAKENING TO THE SPIRITUAL LIFE—THE FOURTH ASTRAL PLANE

We are not human beings having a spiritual experience.
We are spiritual beings having a human experience.
—Pierre Teilhard de Chardin

As the soul evolves to the fourth astral plane, life starts to take on very familiar qualities. This realm is a pivot point in our astral journey. Of all the astral planes, we spend the most time on the fourth astral plane. It is the realm that is closest to the vibration of physical Earth. There are more souls on Earth at the vibratory level of the fourth astral plane than any other spiritual realm. There are aspects of this plane that are practically replicas of our physical earth. Some who die and cross over to the fourth astral plane find it so familiar that they don't think they have died.

Several key things happen on the fourth astral plane. Here, we cultivate our intellect, create societies, and learn to build civilization. With each sub-plane, civilization becomes more developed. On the higher aspects of the fourth astral plane, there are buildings and cities, but they are more provincial than bustling metropolises. As we have seen, everything in physical life was first generated in the spiritual realms, so civilization on Earth draws a lot of inspiration from the fourth astral plane.

Perhaps the biggest difference between astral and physical societies at this level is that the fourth astral plane operates in a spiritual rhythm. People are far from perfect at this stage, but astral souls are taught more directly how to cooperate with the Divine. Civilization on Earth is doing this only to a certain degree; the issue is how well—or not—humanity is responding and reflecting the divine plan. The fourth astral plane is cleaner, less congested, and doesn't have the dramatic discords experienced on Earth. There is no poverty or famine.

Nature is beautiful. As on Earth, humans have much influence on astral nature yet astral inhabitants are more respectful of nature. There are astral farms and gardens that are beautiful and well taken care of. There is a wonderful variety of vegetation that provides nourishment for the astral body's needs. Astral animals abound on the fourth plane. As astral people don't eat meat, animals in the wild are not so afraid. There is greater rapport with the animals. People keep some of them as pets.

Fourth astral plane souls behave very much like you and me. They have the same strengths and weakness. They are loving and kind but can be angry, vindictive, and fearful. They have excesses, but fortunately not to the same degree as experienced on Earth. Sometimes, people with bad habits in physical life will carry them into the astral worlds. For example, someone who is addicted to alcohol may carry that desire to the other side where it can take time to be released. There are no wars, but there is violent behavior. There are rehabilitation centers which effectively correct destructive behavior. There are astral hospitals, and doctors learn how to heal the astral body when it becomes ill or distressed.

There are trains, some cars, and even some airplanes that all run on a type of electrical power available to everyone. Mass transportation isn't found in the astral worlds as on Earth since people tend to do things locally. While civilization is built by human hands, other buildings and structures are clearly built by the angels. As on the third astral plane, these include sacred buildings of worship, prayer, and education. Culture comes into full bloom on the fourth astral plane—cultures on Earth reflect cultures in the spiritual worlds. Racial qualities are expressed in the astral worlds because race is more than just physical attributes; it is about energy patterns and soul experiences.

Some think of the other side as a place of rest, free from work and toil. While there is time for rest and regeneration, people are generally industrious and actively pursuing things they enjoy. They have homes constructed out of desires and dreams. Astral souls tend to live with other people, but this is not always the case. Sometimes people who knew each other on Earth live with each other in the astral worlds as love keeps them together. As we have seen, romance and sex exist but not for procreation. Sex is for sharing intimacy, though it's generally not as consuming an experience as it is on Earth and doesn't carry the same preoccupation.

There are no families as we think of them, yet infants and children who died on Earth continue their childhood in the astral worlds. There are foster parents who help raise the children with love. These astral parents are blessed by the Divine for the service they perform, and it can be a wonderful experience. Some of these parents weren't able to have children while incarnated and they now have the chance to experience such caring.

There are governing systems on the fourth astral plane with human leaders in every area of life. Each sub-plane has its own leadership structure. These leaders work hand-in-hand with angels and other advanced souls to guide human astral affairs and receive exceptional training.

A most wonderful quality of the fourth astral plane is the blossoming of the spiritual life, an experience first awakened through the religious spirit. Religions are beautifully expressed in the astral worlds and are a natural part of life there. As souls start to express their intellectual powers, they need to harness those powers to align with the Divine. Through the religious spirit, the soul learns morality and ethical living. It learns right from wrong by understanding how the divine laws work. Without a genuine, religious foundation, society could not flourish. Souls have been spiritual all along, but on the fourth astral plane, they learn to temper their intellectual power by living a spiritual life. Some resist this impulse for a time, but eventually the soul learns to embrace the religious spirit and the many life lessons it offers.

In the astral worlds, religious practices are in their original inspirational form. As all the great religions of the world are divinely inspired, you can practice them as they were intended without the institutional challenges they can have on Earth. Reflecting the various cultural influences, there are churches, temples, mosques, and synagogues in the astral worlds. If you loved the religion you practiced on Earth, you can continue that form of worship in the astral planes. Systematic prayer and meditation practices start on this plane. There are inspiring nondenominational training centers, called *The Halls of Learning,* where you learn the principles of the spiritual life.

As with all aspects of the astral world, there are some unique features that come into play on the fourth astral plane. For one, you can pick up other people's thoughts. It's a natural form of telepathy that exists on the lower planes but is now more pronounced. People practice a type of simple mental-to-mental communication. For example, one astral person can send a thought such as, "I want to meet you!" The other person can pick up the thought and mentally reply. This way of connecting becomes very important in the higher worlds, as a lot of communication is carried out this way.

BEGINNING YOUR PHYSICAL INCARNATIONS

As mentioned earlier, souls begin their physical incarnations on Earth while on the fourth astral plane. This opens up a vast new level of experience. The soul starts learning things it could only learn here. You enter physical form to experience and grow, and then die and return to the astral worlds to rest, assimilate, and integrate those new experiences. Then you incarnate in physical life again—hopefully more mature—to gather up new experiences and further develop skills and talents. The best spiritual training occurs on Earth.

Incarnating into the physical world is exciting and challenging from the start. The soul now has to learn how to manage a physical body and experience the vicissitudes of physical life. Yet in the midst of this struggle, the soul is forging its spiritual mettle. It is learning to harness the elements of life by its own efforts while experiencing pleasures it never had before. This is giving the soul a chance to grow in new ways that are not possible otherwise. As the soul meets the challenges of this difficult world, it feels a sense of accomplishment and gains an awareness of life it never dreamed of.

Our first steps into physical life provided a wonderful feeling of empowerment. Our life experiences became more vivid. With self-conscious awareness and free will, we started to go through a much wider range of emotions and experiences. Our desire nature took on new expression. We wanted to do, explore, and conquer. Initially, our physical experiences leaned to the selfish. But through trial and error, sadness and joy, we learned to consider and care for others and made new strides in our spiritual evolution. We also made big mistakes, creating unnecessary misery for ourselves and others.

Our first experiences of physical death were neither fearful nor full of grief. Once it became clear that we were crossing back over to the astral realms, another energy took over. There is an understanding of the dying process. Later, as we grew through the fourth astral plane and further developed our intellect, we put more weight on the death process, and it became a thing to dread.

VISITING THE FOURTH ASTRAL PLANE

I had a memorable experience on the fourth astral plane at an important turning point in my life. It was at a time when my metaphysical career was gaining momentum. People were hungry for spiritual instruction, and my classes quickly became popular. I had teamed up with a business partner to start a spiritual center. Unfortunately, that person had self-serving interests, and the project fell apart. The whole experience took a toll on me and my classes. I felt discouraged, as I had put much time into making this work. To compound things, I was also frustrated that many of my students were not following through on the spiritual opportunities being presented to them. I started to wonder if people were ready for serious metaphysical work. I decided to take a sabbatical from teaching to reflect, meditate, and write.

I was invited by a friend to stay in Santa Barbara, California. The beauty of Santa Barbara was the tonic I needed. I was writing, resting, and having wonderful spiritual visions and experiences. During one of my nighttime inner-plane travels, an angel took me through a panorama of life on the fourth astral plane. Our first stop was a small town. It felt like Earth with streets, buildings, and even trolley cars and was busy with people. The angel then took me to a hall in the center of town where a lot of people had gathered. It seemed they were all talking about something. The angel told me they were ready to have their spiritual awakening. They were good souls and happy but not yet awakened spiritually. The angel pointed out that they were going to need good teachers to help them. My heart warmed seeing these sincere souls. I wanted to help them.

The experience made me realize that even though I had setbacks and disappointments, my work was important. There were many people who could benefit. I realized anew my strong desire to help. Even though these astral beings were not yet incarnate on Earth, they reminded me of the people I was working with. I saw what an intricate process it was for the Divine to awaken souls and guide them into spiritual work. The angel helped me see things from a broader perspective and showed me how I was part of all this, telling me to live up to my best and to stay grounded. The experience reawakened my motivation to teach.

Then the angel took me to a vast staging area for inventions that were being prepared to be discovered and implemented on Earth. This is one of the most beautiful things that happens on the fourth astral plane. It was an amazing experience and felt like I was being given a glimpse of the inner workings of civilization—prototypes of new technologies that would benefit humanity. The angel showed me that many of these inventions and artistic creations were conceived and designed in the higher worlds, but when it came time to actually objectify them on Earth, they had to first be prepared in this staging area. I could not see anything specific but was told the area was related to technology. I interacted with one of the inventors, who explained how they work with people on Earth to inspire and guide them. It felt like I was in the very pulse beat of the innovative spirit.

I was then led to another scenic town. As we walked around this beautiful area, the divine being told me not to be discouraged. There was much more metaphysical work I needed to do. New things were coming up and other, more sincere souls would come along to help me move the spiritual work along. We came to a place where souls were interacting with angels. They had recently been awakened and were receiving blessings. They saw me and recognized I was of the earth. They had great interest in metaphysics and were eager to learn about the higher life. They started asking me questions and we engaged in a brief but wonderful talk. I saw, again, how sincere they were to learn.

The angelic being then led me to a beach where other people were swimming. The water looked so refreshing, and he told me to immerse myself in it, which I did. It was very stimulating. I felt a purification going on. Worry and frustration were being dissipated from my aura. When I came out, the angel gave me one more inspiration. He told me to be more careful choosing the people I work with, as I had not been wise in the business partner I picked. It was an important lesson as I entered a phase of my work where I needed others to help build the spiritual mission. I was deeply grateful to the angel for giving me such a powerful experience. Back in my body, I felt regenerated and grounded. I was more focused and motivated. I did restart my classes, and a new phase of my teaching and mission work began.

THE SPIRITUAL AWAKENING

As we cultivate our intellectual powers and temper those powers through ethical and moral living, we eventually reach a threshold. As we evolve to the higher realms of the fourth astral plane, we learn to be good people and develop a healthy intellectual life. For a time, we feel a sense of satisfaction but then feel something is missing. We begin to realize that even a healthy, developed intellect isn't enough. There is dissatisfaction, a searching that begins. The soul starts to more deeply contemplate the meaning of life. We have already formed a conception of the Creator—primitive at first—but which we slowly refine along with how we perceive the nature of our own being. But as we build momentum through the fourth plane, the soul yearns for greater understanding.

On the upper level of the fourth astral plane, a new door opens up on our spiritual journey: We have our spiritual awakening. This experience is different from the religious awakening we have already had but builds on that foundation. With this spiritual or mystical awakening, we receive a glimmer of our celestial nature and realize that there is a path of enlightenment. This awakening is the culmination of a long, gradual process of spiritual development. It's a time to rejoice as we earned this moment through long suffering and much travail.

When we have our awakening, it is a dramatic moment in our spiritual evolution—the pivot point leading to a greater life. With this awakening comes a decision: whether to follow through and walk the path to the higher worlds or stay where we are in our consciousness. The fourth plane is sometimes called the plane of division and decision because of this transformational time. Division means the ability to separate the life that brought us to where we are and the divine life that awaits. Once we understand the distinction between the two, then we decide which path to follow. It may seem like an easy decision, but following the path to the higher life means making changes. Some who recognize the value of divine life have weak willpower when it comes to actually following through. Our spiritual evolution is always in our own hands. The Divine inspires and guides, but it's up to us to choose the path of Light.

Eventually, every soul chooses the higher life. Once this decision is made, we prepare to evolve to the fifth astral plane. Whether souls actually make the jump depends on how well they heed the spiritual call and how dedicated they are in reaching the next spiritual plateau. The jump from the fourth to the fifth plane is the end point of one phase of life and the beginning of a new phase. Some souls are ready while others linger. Many good souls who have earned the right to the higher realms hesitate when it comes time to taking the actual steps leading to the greater life. They may feel comfortable where they are or resist exploring the unknown or something that may challenge current situations. There is nothing sadder than having a spiritual awakening and shelving it because you didn't want to change your life.

The interplay between the mental, the ethical, the religious, and the metaphysical occurs throughout our development through the higher spiritual worlds—not just on the fourth astral plane. While we initially harness our intellectual nature on the fourth plane, we continue to strengthen and develop it through our entire evolution. This reveals the importance of pursuing the spiritual path.

Awakening to the Higher Life : ILLUSTRATION 6.1

This illustration depicts a man having his spiritual awakening on the upper fourth astral plane. His soul is ready to pass through the door to the mystical life. With this awakening, a new chapter in the soul's evolution begins to unfold.

In his last incarnation, the man was of Hispanic heritage and became a Catholic priest. He was quiet by nature, accomplished, and intellectually strong. He was a good priest and helped many people. He had visions of angels and other spiritual phenomena. At the end of his incarnation, he had completed his life's purpose yet sensed there was something more. He didn't know he was getting ready for an entirely new phase in his spiritual journey. And even though it did not come to fruition in that earthly incarnation, he was preparing for things yet to unfold.

In this illustration, he finds himself in the auditorium of an elegant, non-denominational spiritual center. The room has white walls and tall, beautiful windows. It's bright inside, and there is a stage with an altar behind it. The man is sitting in a chair in prayer and meditation. Unbeknownst to him, an archangel appears behind him wearing magnificent gold robes. He has strong, heroic, yet compassionate features: handsome, blonde haired, and blue-eyed. The archangel blesses this man with a purple ray of light that stirs the man's soul. He cannot see the light but feels the upliftment. This is his spiritual awakening. The man does not fully recognize what is happening but is astonished and overjoyed as he comes to new realizations about life. This is the beginning of his metaphysical journey. There is a burst of energy about him; pink light surrounds his head expressing his excitement of the moment. With this new door that has opened, he will now start to pursue metaphysical studies. And in his next incarnation on Earth, he will rekindle his spiritual awakening and begin a new phase in his spiritual ascent.

Chapter 7

UNFOLDING THE HIGHER SELF—THE FIFTH AND SIXTH ASTRAL PLANES

Everyone of us is shadowed by an illusory person: a false self...
We are not very good at recognizing illusions, least of all
the ones we cherish about ourselves.
—Thomas Merton, New Seeds of Contemplation

AS YOU EVOLVE through each astral plane, your soul receives more tools of self-expression. In the first four planes, you were given your astral body, built your instinctual and intellectual natures, and began your incarnations through physical life. As you reached the culmination of the fourth astral plane, you had the spiritual awakening that opened the door to the divine life. From here, the ascent through the higher astral worlds begins. The fifth and sixth astral planes are about refining the skills you have earned and reaching your higher, divine self.

Life on the fifth and sixth astral planes brings a new understanding of service, love, integrity, ethics, philosophy, intuition, and inspiration. On these spiritual planes, the soul experiences a greater understanding of God. You build your spiritual sensing and feeling of things. Your instincts and intellect are now being honed to serve Spirit. You receive revelations about the spiritual path and gather experiences and understandings of the inner working of the universe. You are given the picture of the breadth of the cosmos and grandeur of the amazing journey you are on. As this happens, you start to move out of the material sensing of things and into spiritual realities.

A most beautiful aspect of life on the fifth and sixth astral planes is the relationship with our soulmate. When we began our spiritual pilgrimage, we were paired with another soul—complete in its own right—to be our companion through Creation. In the early experiences of the astral journey, you were close with your soul mate. Through the first three astral planes, you went through many life experiences together. But when you evolved to the fourth astral plane and began physical incarnations, the relationship with the soul mate changed. When one soul mate incarnated, the other would stay on the other side to provide spiritual support. When that person died and returned to the astral worlds, there was a reunion. The other soul mate would then take its turn to incarnate, and the other soulmate would remain and offer its support. This process continues while both soulmates evolve through the fourth astral plane, which is why you don't see as much of your soulmate during this period of spiritual evolution.

These soul mate dynamics exist throughout our incarnations in physical life, but as we evolve to the fifth and sixth astral planes, the relationship with our soulmate matures. We are still alternating incarnations, but we spend more time with them on the other side between incarnations and the bond of love deepens.

UNDERSTANDING THE HIGHER SELF

Before exploring these higher astral planes, let us look at that miraculous part of you known in metaphysics as "the higher self." When the human soul started its spiritual pilgrimage, it forgot where it came from and who it really was. Instead, the soul began to identify with whatever environment it was immersed in. This is an inevitable part of the evolutionary process. When a soul is immersed in material consciousness—physical, astral, or otherwise—metaphysics calls this consciousness "the lower nature" or "the lower self." Lower in this term does not mean less than. Rather, the term relates to its position in the divine order of things. Another name for the lower self could be the "immersed self."

As the soul is immersed in its lower nature, it starts to take on qualities and characteristics of that lower self, building its own persona. Metaphysics calls this the "Personality Ego." We all have one. Each personality is different because we each come from our own experiences and interact with life in our own way. The Personality Ego is like the mask an actor wears when he or she is performing a part in a play. Your name, your physical attributes, the environment and milieus you identify with, your habits, and so on are part of your personality, yet they are not the real you in the mystic sense.

The lower nature by itself could never climb the spiritual summit. It simply doesn't have the know-how to do so on its own. The only way the soul can aspire to greater things is if there is a part of the consciousness that is *not* immersed in material experience and is already spiritually aware. In this way, it can direct the lower nature. This greater part of you is the higher self. It is through this higher nature that you receive the Divine Light, wisdom, and inspiration. It is through your higher nature that the spiritual hierarchy connects with you. It is through your higher nature that you spiritually evolve.

The higher self has been with you all along. It was given to you before you started your pilgrimage. Because of your higher self, you could never become completely lost or completely forget who and what you are. There is always that reminder urging you upward. The higher self helps to steer your evolution. As you build powers and talents, the higher self becomes more pronounced. Metaphysics calls the individual stamp and character of your higher nature the "Individuality Ego." Your lower nature has its Personality Ego, and the higher nature has its Individuality Ego.

Most people spend their incarnated lives operating from their personality egos and never reach their true higher nature. They identify so strongly with their personality that they don't realize they have a greater self. Yet, this is the goal. Step by step, bit by bit, you learn to relinquish the hold that the personality ego has and claim your true higher nature as an Individuality Ego. This is not easy to do. The Personality Ego will resist your efforts to claim your individuality. Much of the inner turmoil you may feel in your life and spiritual work is the personality fighting your efforts to spiritualize yourself. Eventually, we all surrender the Personality Ego to fully claim the divine part of us. This is the noble job of our evolution through the fifth and sixth astral planes.

BUILDING CHARACTER—
THE FIFTH ASTRAL PLANE

While the fourth plane is very much like Earth, the fifth astral plane starts to take on the divine semblance. You can do things on the fifth plane you cannot do on the lower planes. It is a most intriguing and exciting place. All the astral planes have their glory and purpose, yet the fifth plane is an interesting combination of the spiritual and the earthly.

It is the most inhabited of the seven astral planes. Souls on this plane are coming out of the material sensing of life and building a spiritual foundation that will carry them all the way to the heaven worlds. You make incredible strides on this plane. Your soul starts to soar as you begin to experience the wonderment of the life of spirit.

This astral plane has been called Paradise. Everything looks brighter and more vivid as nature and the astral ambience take on a heavenly hue. The surroundings are still familiar, but it feels different from being on Earth as you start to experience the magic of the Divine. Your communion with nature is more profound. The vistas are more colorful and beautiful. You drink ambrosia made of delicious astral vegetation. It is common to find beautiful precious crystals and jewels in nature, and you commune with the mineral spirits. There are a greater variety of animals, and your interaction with them is delightful as they, too, are on a higher spiritual plane. You realize that all of nature is in a process of evolution.

You are motivated to do better because the environment around you encourages aspiration. Your interaction with other souls of this plane is more cooperative, satisfying, and productive than ever before. This is not to say there aren't challenges—there are. But they are of a different order than the interactions experienced on the fourth astral plane. Civilization is more advanced than you would find on Earth.

An exciting natural ability available on the higher spiritual planes is known as "float-walking"! This ability begins on the fifth astral plane and develops as you climb the spiritual ladder. Float-walking is not about flying like birds using force and pressure to move through the air. Rather, it reveals one of the profound secrets of the spiritual worlds— the expression of mind over matter. You learn to float-walk using the power of mind. You learn that mind is far greater and more encompassing than ever imagined. The entire universe, in all its dimensions, is a construct of mind, generated and sustained by Divine Mind.

The ability to move by using the mind is an exhilarating experience. There is a joy and excitement beyond description. And while this is natural, it does have to be learned, requiring effort and concentration. You begin by visualizing yourself somewhere, which starts the process of forward movement. At first you only go short distances to get the hang of it, and then you can travel further. The experience of float-walking dramatically increases when you are interacting with the Holy Ones. They can take you great distances at enormous speeds. It's truly a breathtaking experience to be with them in this way.

Extraordinary friendships are formed on the fifth astral plane. People you have known on Earth in various incarnations and others you may know on other astral planes become enduring friends that time cannot separate. You may not see each other for lifetimes, but when you do, you pick up the friendship right where you left off. Your loving nature blossoms on this plane and you start to see how deep spiritual love really is.

A most sublime experience on the fifth plane is when you interact with the angels. They have been there all along, but up to this point have made their appearance human-like to make it easier for you to be with them. Now you can start to behold them in their greater, celestial glory. It staggers the imagination to understand how holy and glorious the angels really are. This leads to interactions and communion with another class of spiritual beings—the archangels. They are of an evolutionary level even greater than the angels. Their presence is at first overwhelming as they are so grand. The term "spiritual hierarchy" takes on new meaning in the fifth astral plane as you become aware of just how many spiritual levels of consciousness there are.

As you tune into the power of your higher nature, you start to more clearly see your shortcomings, character flaws, and defects. You begin working through your personality blemishes, paying back old karma, and correcting your mistakes. Evolving through the fifth astral plane has a lot to do with mastering individual lessons and strengthening your character. This astral plane can be difficult to master because of these character lessons. Even though you are in paradise, there is a conflict between the human and the Divine. You still bring with you some of the consciousness of the earthly fourth plane and the karma created there.

As a result, you can procrastinate and resist looking at these parts of you. Regrets and remorse come into the picture as you start to see through the false self and your own past mistakes. It can feel like you are moving backward instead of forward because there will be times when you make great progress but then fall into old bad habits and behavior patterns. You then feel your mistakes more keenly yet still want to better yourself. This back and forth of progress and setbacks eventually smooths out as the momentum to evolve and ascend urges you onward and upward. Because each soul's lesson is different, each person's experience through the fifth plane will be unique. One person may have to learn more compassion while another more confidence and so on. The gift of working directly with the Holy Ones is that they support you in learning your lessons.

The Astral Temples

There is another miracle of the spiritual life that starts on the seventh degree of the fifth astral plane and continues through the higher worlds: the temples of Divine Light. The term temple refers to the many spiritual training centers in the spirit worlds. They are at the heart of what the other side is all about. In physical life, we have universities, research centers, hospitals, museums, and political, business, religious, and cultural centers. In the spirit realm, there are temples. They are constructed and maintained by the Holy Ones to help unfold our creative talents and potential and to aid in the spiritual evolution of our souls.

Here you receive knowledge, guidance, and inspiration, which you are then meant to put to practical use either in the astral worlds or on Earth. There are many temples, each one dedicated to a specific task. For example, there is the Temple of Love where you learn about the qualities of Divine Love. There is the Temple of Wisdom Light where you learn about the dynamic attributes of life and receive guidance on dilemmas that come up. There is a Temple of Purification where you can release old habit patterns and negative energy in your aura. You may be taken into specific temples relating to your own talents and abilities. If you are a musician, you may be taken to the Temple of Music where you are given inspiration to write a song. If you are a writer, you might be taken into the Temple of Literature or the Temple of Drama, and so on. Through your interaction with the temples, new worlds open up.

You don't visit these temples on your own; you are always taken to them by the angels. This is because the temples are operating at a very high frequency, and the Holy Ones don't want the energies to be mixed or somehow become unbalanced. This is not to say you cannot ask to be taken somewhere if you feel the need. You can, but the Divine will decide whether to grant your request.

The knowledge that comes from this inner-plane work is both powerful and wonderful. As you evolve to the top of the fifth plane, you will have mastered some key character weaknesses and imperfections. Your spiritual evolution has greatly stabilized, and your yearning for the divine life increases. You will be carefully watched to see how well you implement this knowledge before advancing to the next degree of learning. You are then given a fuller picture of the journey that lies ahead, preparing you for life on the sixth astral plane.

A Day in the Life on the Fifth Astral Plane

To give you a better picture of the astral world, I'd like to share a story of what life is like there. While this story is fictionalized, everything is based on my own experiences. We will follow a man, Richard, as he goes about his life in the astral realms. Richard was a professor of mathematics while he was on Earth. He was married and had three children. He was a good man and believed in God, but he wasn't very religious. He died in his early sixties in a car accident. According to his karmic chart, it was his time, and he is staying on the other side for a while before reincarnating back.

As we start our story, Richard has been on the other side for about twenty years by Earth time. He looks about thirty and is in full health and vigor. Because he lived a good life in his last incarnation, he earned the right to be on the second rung of the fifth astral plane. He lives in an English Tudor style home of moderate size that was built for him based on his own thoughts and desires. The house has nice grounds and a beautiful garden. His home is located in a valley with flowers, trees, and a small lake. It's an idyllic setting with other homes near him.

Richard lives alone. He begins his day energetically after waking up from a relaxation period. He walks into the kitchen and takes a drink of ambrosia which he made himself from the elements of the astral world. It's like a protein shake that energizes and nourishes his astral body. This is his breakfast. He then walks into the bedroom and picks out something to wear. He has a full array of light and easy-fitting clothing in various shades of colors. He takes a shower, dresses, then puts on some sweet-smelling cologne. There are no radios or TVs in his home, but he doesn't seem to need them. He is already aware of what is going on and what his day will be about.

He then walks outside. The air is fresh, the sun is shining, and beautifully shaped clouds are floating in the sky. The surroundings are vibrant with their own inner life. Richard walks through the neighborhood, where he passes by other people whom he greets. His walk accelerates, and he begins to float walk! He gains some height, maybe fifteen feet. This feels natural, and he is able to cover a great area quickly. He passes by others who are doing the same thing.

He soon finds himself in the center of a small town. It isn't crowded, and the buildings are not too close together, but you can tell it's a central gathering place. Richard walks to an impressive looking building, something you might find on a college campus. Others are walking in and out of this building. It is called The Halls of Music. He goes to a room that has pianos and instruments of various kinds, some recognizable and others not. A man who looks to be in his fifties greets him. It turns out that Richard is taking voice lessons and this man is his voice teacher. On Earth, Richard had a good baritone voice. He had a strong desire to sing but never an opportunity to pursue it. Here, he is encouraged to sing. The man teaching him has been on this side much longer than Richard, maybe sixty years. He has a sense of humor and enjoys what he does.

The teacher sits at a piano and the lesson begins. Richard is good and has been practicing for some time now. The teacher has an excellent tenor voice. It turns out Richard is preparing for a musical he is going to perform in. Today he is learning a new song he will sing at rehearsal that evening. When he finishes his lesson, he leaves the building and float-walks across town. He has prearranged to meet Paula by a lake they like to visit. Paula is Richard's girlfriend. She is a cute brunette with blue eyes and loves to laugh. On Earth, she was unmarried, a schoolteacher and an artist. She has been on this side for about six years and is continuing her studies in art.

Richard and Paula like each other a lot. They love to hike together and sit by the lake and talk. They met in The Halls of Learning and love to discuss the many interests they have in common, especially the arts. There are strong affections between the two. They embrace and kiss. They spend the afternoon together and arrange to meet again that night. Paula wants to watch Richard's rehearsal.

Richard goes back to his home to get some notes for another training. This training is spiritual in nature. Suddenly, two angelic beings appear in his living room. They are tall and dressed in robes, but Richard isn't startled. He's elated to see them. They gently escort him out of the house and then fly through the air, carrying him a great distance with incredible speed. Richard is thrilled by the experience. He soon finds himself in an exhilarating environment. He is now on the seventh rung of the fifth astral plane and standing in front of a beautiful building called The Temple of Instruction. Other magnificent buildings are nearby as well.

This temple is large and elaborate. It's a busy place and there's a lot of excitement. The angels usher him to a gate protected by angelic guards. The guards recognize the angels accompanying Richard and he is permitted to enter the building, supported by the angels. He walks into a classroom with many other students and sits at an assigned seat as he has been coming here for a while.

The instruction begins. One by one, celestial beings discourse on various metaphysical and spiritual subjects. The main emphasis is how to work with spiritual energy. Once the instruction is over, the angels disburse and work with the students one-on-one. An angel comes to Richard and teaches him a new technique to work with the Divine Light. He is given an assignment. When the class is over, there is no socializing. The two angels who brought Richard take him back to his home, where Richard relaxes by reading.

The sun is setting and night is approaching, but it's still easy to see everything. Richard leaves for his rehearsal and float-walks to an auditorium in town. Paula is there as well as various cast members and the rehearsal begins. The theme of the play is a story about life in the high sixth astral plane. The music is enchanting, and the cast members feel as if they are on the sixth plane as they perform. Afterwards, Paula and Richard say their goodbyes and separate. Richard comes home once again after a full day and goes into his relaxation/sleep period before beginning a new day in the astral worlds.

The Temple of Healing : ILLUSTRATION 7.1

In this illustration, the young woman shown is being taken to The Temple of Healing which is located on the seventh degree of the fifth astral plane. She has been in the astral worlds for some time. In her latest incarnation, she was of Ethiopian descent. She had difficulty with her father, who was not kind to her. He, too, has been on the other side for a long time and is living on the fourth astral plane. She was recently taken to the fourth plane to meet with him as there were still unresolved issues. Unfortunately, the meeting did not go well. Even after all this time, antagonism remained between them. He was still in an unkind place with her, and she found herself resentful and unforgiving. This surprised her as she thought she was past such strong negative feelings. The experience revealed that she has issues with forgiveness. She sees the pattern that when she feels wronged, she holds a grudge and can't let it go.

She knows these emotions are not aligned with the wonderful life she is living. To help, her angelic teacher takes her to temples for emotional healing, first The Temple of Healing and then others, especially

The Temple of Love, to be instructed by the angels. She is excited to be going to the temples, as she knows she needs help and is hopeful that she will be able to strengthen this character weakness. They float-walk to a pathway that takes her to the entrance of the temple. She sees many people entering the temple for healing and relief.

The Temple of Healing is a remarkable place—three high stories, and rectangular with a grand main entrance framed by beautiful pillars. A path lined with flowers leads to white marbled steps that take her to up to a pair of huge blue doors of a deeper shade than the walls. A magnificent golden dome sits in the middle of the building. Inside are many healing rooms as well as a large auditorium that sits under the dome. The temple was not built by human hands but by angels, and is of an architecture not found on Earth. It is not as ornate as some others but is still impressive. The marbled walls are a light blue color, and a pale pink and blue aura surrounds the structure. Hues of blue color and light are found throughout the temple, as the color blue, especially sapphire blue, represents spiritual healing energy. The golden dome in the center has exquisite designs on it and stunning windows. In this illustration, a beam of light from the Higher dimensions blesses the dome and all who are inside.

This temple is in an astral city. You see other buildings and temples in the background as well as a mountain range in the distance. The building is strategically situated near an ocean of green-blue water. The magnetization of the water is very healing. Behind the temple and looking toward the ocean is another remarkable feature of this, and many, temples—pools of light. They look like Olympic-size pools, but they are not for swimming; they are for floating as part of the healing process. Each pool is of a different spiritual color and offers its own quality of support: peace, love, healing, vitality, prosperity, harmony, or strength.

Interspersed throughout the grounds near the pools are fountains of varying sizes, colors, and energy rays where blues, purples, pinks, greens, and silvers radiate in beautiful water patterns. You don't just admire these fountains; you go in them as well! The rush of the water, filled with spiritual energy, is exhilarating and helps to enliven both the body and consciousness.

REACHING THE HIGHER SELF— THE SIXTH ASTRAL PLANE

Your evolution quickens as you ascend through the sixth astral plane. You have built your power and character to a level that you are now on strong spiritual ground. The journey through the sixth astral plane is about dethroning the dominance of the lower nature and resurrecting one's higher, divine nature.

On the sixth astral plane, civilization becomes more refined and sophisticated. Astral towns and cities are more spacious and spread out. While civilization on the fourth and fifth planes strongly reflect life on Earth, civilization on the sixth astral plane looks less like the way we know it. It has more of a timeless quality with traits unique to the astral realms. There are many more temples on this plane that cover a wide variety of training and guidance. The landscape and scenery are more expansive, colorful, and radiant. The God presence is becoming stronger and felt wherever you are.

On this plane, you refine your talents and reach a new level of proficiency. You improve your ability to float-walk, which helps you move freely about the astral world. The sixth plane is a peaceful place; a lot of the dramas of the lower human nature have passed. You come to experience a tranquility of spirit—what the mystics call "the silence of peace." This helps you turn inward to better understand your spiritual nature. You contemplate God in a new way, and the divine life becomes a deeper part of you. On the fifth plane, you still had a lot of personal intentions, but on the sixth plane, your mind and heart are turning more fully to God. You come to feel the oneness of life and start to experience how everything is interconnected and that all life works together. You feel the unity of the flowers, trees, animals, and nature. You discover the spirits who support and thrive in nature and delight in their presence.

On this plane, there is a balance of the active and contemplative life. You spend more time alone—alone but not lonely. In solitude, you feel more alive than ever. Some have difficulty at first in the solitude and have to learn to better tune into their own inner nature. On the sixth astral plane, you find special training centers. These are like the mystery schools and ashrams on Earth. You live in these centers for periods of time to develop your spiritual skills. During this type of monastic life, souls learn to better control their mental, emotional, and instinctual natures. You are taught new facets of the arts and sciences which open new doors in your understanding of life.

Throughout the sixth astral plane, your intuition and inspirational mind are further developed to prepare for the spiritual glories that lie ahead. You start to have visions which stimulate the ethereal part of you. Special angels are assigned as a type of tutelage to help in your spiritual growth. There is more interaction with the celestial hierarchy, and you start interacting with aspects of beings you weren't aware of before, some even more glorious than the archangels.

With all this power and support, you more fully refine your character and let go of your attachments to the lower nature. There are tests and challenges on this plane to make sure the soul has mastered the lower self, but it's worth every sacrifice, every effort. The lower self will fight back as it still wants to dominate and hold onto the objects of its attachments: people, things, and even ideas. These internal dramas can be demanding. As you work through them, there are battles to win. The good news is that spiritual momentum is strongly in your favor.

On this plane, there is discipline and sacrifice. You learn to give your life force to serve the Divine. You realize that this is where the life force comes from and, in giving back, you are exponentially developing your spiritual life. Your activities and service on this plane take on new meaning. You come to the understanding that the joy of life is not in the taking but in the giving. Compassion for yourself and all life expands. Self-serving interests and self-aggrandizement slowly drop away.

As you ascend through the various sub-planes of the sixth astral plane, you build your power until you are ready to be tested on your willingness to surrender the dominance of the lower nature. To pass this test, the aspirant to the higher life must go through an ordeal in which the Higher takes you to dark regions known as the netherworlds. Souls in the netherworlds have devolved to such a point that they are not able to participate in the evolutionary process until they get back on track. These souls are consumed by uncontrolled, tormented, and dark behaviors expressed with reckless abandon. The test is to see if your lower, animal nature can withstand the stimulation without being affected or succumbing to it. It is not an easy test. If you do not pass, it means the soul has more work to do. Yet another opportunity will come along in the future to try again.

If you do pass this test, it means you are ready to sever the attachment to the Personality Ego. This is done in a sacred ceremony. While there is no death in the astral worlds, detachment from the lower nature is the closest thing to it on the other side. Again, this is not the annihilation of the Personality Ego; it is the severing of the attachment, which can feel like death.

After dethronement of the Personality Ego comes enthronement of the Individuality Ego—the real, higher self that overshadows the lower self. This is a glorious moment that occurs when the soul has reached the top of the sixth astral plane. The golden light of individuality is bestowed on the auric field, further preparing you for the glories of enlightenment and beyond.

Dropping the Personality Ego : ILLUSTRATION 7.2

In this illustration, the candidate for the higher life is going through what mystics call the crucifixion, or surrender ceremony. This is not a literal crucifixion but the detachment from dominance of the lower self. To prepare for this moment, this man has gone through a series of trainings that includes instruction, reflection, meditation, sacrifice, surrender, tests, and trials. He is in a sacred temple sanctuary. Within the temple, he is in a prayer room with intricate designs on the walls and ceiling like the interior of a mosque. There is an area for an audience, as this is a major event and the candidate is being supported by friends and loved ones.

The candidate is wearing white robes and lying down on an altar. The mood is solemn and a little funereal. There is a sense of grief as the persona is released. His friends are happy for him because they understand what this means, yet there are mixed emotions, as it feels like they are losing an old friend. His soul mate is there, offering support and also happy for him, but she knows this is a turning point in their relationship as the personality chord is cut. It is a rite of passage, a change of season in the relationship, so there are feelings of loss and sadness before a new phase in the relationship begins.

Angels surround the candidate as they perform the ceremony. They are all wearing golden robes. Radiant white light fills the room as everyone is in meditation and prayer. You watch as the angels dissolve a mental image of the person's Personality Ego and "cut the cord" of this energy. It doesn't mean the persona is no longer there; it is, but its dominance has come to an end. Some in the audience are crying tears of compassion as the image of the persona self is lifted. The old life is gone. Soon, he will undergo the resurrection ceremony where he will claim his higher nature. His true self will gradually take dominance, and a new day in his evolution will begin.

Chapter 8

THE REALM OF ENLIGHTENMENT—THE SEVENTH ASTRAL PLANE

The road to salvation is through truth.
—Swami Vivekananda

Y OUR ASCENT TO the seventh astral plane is a marvelous culmination in your astral journey. You enter this radiant realm attuned to your higher nature—the pinnacle of your astral experience. The landscape and scenery are beautiful in every way. Souls have continued their incarnations on Earth and have now reached an extraordinary place in their spiritual unfoldment. In this realm, there is a graceful awakening to the mystical nature. The spiritual path that started in earnest on the fourth astral plane blooms as you unfold your mystic nature. Of the many wonders to experience in this realm, it is here that you pull together all you've learned in your astral/physical journey to take the great step of enlightenment.

What is enlightenment? This is when you bring all aspects of your consciousness into maturity. It's a fundamental shift in awareness when you "pierce the veil of matter" and experience the inner nature of life. With enlightenment come many spiritual gifts and abilities that have come to be associated with souls who are spiritually advanced. Most important of all, through enlightenment you experience God. In your seeking and striving, it is in this spiritual dimension that you experience God directly through what is called the "God Within Experience." You now know God exists; God is real. And while this is not the same experience of God you will have when you return to your celestial Home, it is the inner compass that guides you through the higher realms.

Each sub-plane of the seventh astral plane is a profound experience. There are initiations to pass which are not easy to do. On the lower planes, there is some grace given to help in your growth. On the seventh astral plane, you have to master each sub-plane before you go to the next. The Book of Revelation speaks of seven seals that must be broken open. These seals—think of them as gates—are rites of passage that each soul must cross to complete their ascent through this plane, complete their astral journey, and reach the great goal of enlightenment.

As you begin your journey through this realm, you realize how far you have traveled. What an accomplishment to dethrone the personality ego! And how necessary that was to handle the unfolding powers and talents experienced in this realm. The wisdom now accessible is amazing. You are taken to temples and places where you have access to vast resources of knowledge. It takes some acclimating to stay balanced with such universal intelligence is at your fingertips. As you learn to keep your thoughts steady through this grandeur, the intellect relaxes and the inspirational mind takes center stage. Marvelous creative ideas start to flow. This creativity can be applied to any aspect of life: artistic, scientific, business, education, and so on. This is an exciting time as everyone on this plane is expressing their divine creativity in their area of expertise. You delight in your interactions with other souls. There is creative expression on every astral plane, but the seventh astral plane is a nucleus of creativity.

As you build up your creative powers, a door opens to enlightening the mind—the prophetic gift experienced by sages throughout the ages. It is the Holy Spirit, the Ruach HaKodesh of the Hebrew mystics. Once this happens, your intellect has been illumined by Divine Mind. You live your life by that illumination which gives you a direct connection to eternal mind. The brilliant philosopher of the Middle Ages, Moses Maimonides, beautifully expressed the spiritual requirements for Ruach HaKodesh:

> *Such a person must work on himself until his mind is constantly clear and directed on high. He must bind his intellect on the Throne of Glory, striving to comprehend the purity and holiness of the transcendental. He must furthermore contemplate the Wisdom of God in each thing, understand its true significance, whether it be the highest spiritual entity or the lowliest thing on Earth. The individual who does this immediately becomes worthy of Ruach HaKodesh. When he attains this spirit, his soul becomes bound up to the level of the angels...and he becomes as a completely different person. He can now understand things with a knowledge completely different than anything he has experienced previously.*[1]

Once you reach this illumined mental state, you are taken to where the great work of administering the divine plan on Earth is undertaken. While the heaven worlds are the spiritual headquarters, the seventh astral plane is the administrative center for executing this plan. You are shown the bigger picture of how well—or not—humanity is progressing. There is a lot of prayer work for souls on Earth. Even if things on Earth are chaotic, the plan continues for everyone, and the spiritual

---

[1] As quoted from *Meditation and the Bible* by Aryeh Kaplan.

hierarchy works every day to help realize that plan individually and collectively.

You participate in sending Divine Light and inspiration to souls who are in need—those who have lost their way and are suffering or distressed, as well as those who are doing important work to improve conditions in the world. You see that there are advanced souls on Earth pursuing important missions. Many of them are from the heaven worlds and working quietly to serve the Divine. As you work with the suffering, your heart opens, and a new level of compassion awakens. You see that enlightenment for its own sake is a vain enterprise when barren of genuine service. You learn of enlightened souls who gave their life's blood in service to humanity. A great inner revelation about the path of service is revealed to you. You feel a tremendous sense of devotion and love for others. When the inner workings of the divine life open up, it's a miraculous moment—a moment that fills your heart till it overflows with joy.

As you awaken deep compassion, the Holy Ones help you to understand your own soul. This leads to the experience of your soul as an individualized spark of eternal life. This is a compelling and dramatic experience. The sacredness of this intimate moment cannot be effectively expressed in words. It is an experience of your own immortality. You are given a glimpse of who you really are and begin to recognize the eternal spark of life in every soul. This leads you on a journey to more fully understand and experience the soul and its relationship to all life, which you will do in the dimensions that yet await you.

With the experience of your own soul, you awaken your mystic senses, which, until now, have been latent and accessible only through intuition. That which you have experienced in part before, you now experience in full. With this mystic clairvoyance, you can pierce the veil of matter and see into the spiritual operations of life. You experience

Divine Light directly and see auras around people and things. Through the mystic senses, you can hear the divine voice and the music of the spheres, which dazzle the mind and heart. You have been initiated into the inner sanctum of nature.

You interact with others who also have the mystic talent, and you relate to people in a new way. You go deeper in your work with Divine Light. These emerging talents drive you toward an irresistible new level of attainment; you *have* to know God. Nothing else matters. Everything you have experienced up to this point, as wonderful as it has been, points you to this great goal. Before you can attain success in this most crucial phase of your ascent, you must pass the toughest test you have ever had to face: the test to see if there is a character blemish, fear, or temptation that can still turn you away from the Divine Light. This is the test of evil.

To pass this test, you are taken to a place of unimaginable darkness—the demonic worlds. These realms are not fantasy or science fiction; they are chillingly real. They are different from the netherworlds, where you were tested before reaching your higher nature on the sixth astral plane. The demonic worlds are far worse. Here is where you find those who are consciously breaking spiritual laws and doing all they can to thwart the divine plan for their own selfish ends. It's a place of indescribable gloom. Vile and degrading things are committed with the deliberate intention of destroying anything that is good. There are demonic initiatives to pervert every divine principle in a vain and stubborn attempt to bring down other souls. It is a truly terrifying experience to know that such things exist and that free will could be so misused.

You are escorted through these realms by the angels, for you would not last long there on your own. Even with divine support, these demonic energies test you to your very core. These evil spirits are intelligent and clever. They will attempt to find any flaws in your character—the slightest weakness to exploit—and if there is one, they will find it. They will try to terrify, seduce, and tempt you. Your intellect alone will not keep you centered in such a place. Only the pure of heart can withstand the test of evil.

If the soul has withstood this demonic crucible and stands holy and pure, it has proven it is ready and returns to the seventh astral plane a victor. With this great achievement, you go on a pilgrimage to a secluded area. Here, in the silent glory of nature, is where the God Within you awakens and you attain enlightenment. You have been searching, serving, and loving, and now you finally know God. You rekindle the knowing of the Creator who bore you. You are no longer the spiritual infant of long ago. Now you walk the path in conscious cooperation with God. There is bliss, joy, and communion in this culmination of an amazing journey. Everything you have done in your life has led to this. All of the lifetimes, trials, hurts, sorrows, joys, adventures, relationships, careers, and missteps have led to this moment. You are not yet in your eternal Home, but God is awake in you and you are awake in God.

You are granted extraordinary visions. There is celebration and rejoicing. You have almost completed your astral evolution, but not quite yet. There is one more step: Awakening your awareness of the higher worlds beyond the astral. With enlightenment, you begin what is called "spiritual planetary travel." You knew there were greater worlds, but now, with the support of the angels, you will visit these greater realms. It takes your breath away to behold such wonders and know such beauty exists. Your triumphs are tempered by humility, compassion, and divine service. With the crowning achievement of enlightenment, you experience *samādhi*, a Sanskrit word for bliss—absorption into the divine oneness. In some ways, this samādhi is the final good-bye to the astral worlds. Now your soul is set for the next great adventure in your journey back to God—ascending through the interplanetary worlds that lead to heaven.

Every spiritual step you take in the inner worlds must also be accomplished in physical life—including enlightenment. As you build your illumination, compassion, clairvoyance, and enlightenment in the inner worlds, you accomplish the same feats back on Earth, bringing all you have manifested in the spiritual worlds to outer expression in the physical realms. This process "cements" the experiences, making it an eternal expression of the soul.

Enlightenment and the Temple of Love : ILLUSTRATION 8.1

This illustration shows the culmination of individual powers and talents developed in the long, majestic journey through the seven astral planes. To get to this place, this soul evolved through many life experiences in the astral and physical worlds. She has matured her character and awakened many spiritual gifts to reach enlightenment.

This woman has reached the seventh degree of the seventh astral plane— the highest plateau in the astral worlds. She has been in the spiritual worlds for some time and has fully integrated her spiritual powers into her astral consciousness. She has awakened her mystic powers, her telepathic abilities, and her clairvoyance. She went through many tests and initiations to reach the place of direct experience of the God presence. From here, she has one final test—to reawaken these same powers in her next earthly incarnation. If she can accomplish this feat in physical form, she will be ready to move into the interplanetary worlds and prepare for her ascent to heaven.

In this depiction, the awakened initiate is standing on a veranda that overlooks the Temple of Love: an elaborate structure resembling the glory days of ancient Greece with exquisite architecture and impressive columns. Divine Light is flowing everywhere in radiant hues of pinks, violets, and blues. Surrounding the courtyard in front of the temple are stunning roses of a variety not found on Earth. They radiate living Light; delightful nature spirits drink from the nectar of their spiritual essence. Even the trees are glowing with Divine Light.

The Temple of Love is the embodiment of celestial love and compassion. The angels of love work from this temple to send love and Light to others. The temple receives Divine Love from the heaven worlds and transmits that loving power to the astral planes and to Earth. Great lessons are learned in this temple. This woman has just come from inside another temple where she was conducting a healing and is taking a moment to reflect and recharge. One of the greatest gifts of being enlightened is that you become part of the spiritual hierarchy and give of yourself in service to help others in their evolution.

We see her enlightened aura. It has a pointed oval shape with an outer glow indicating her advanced spiritual status. She has mastered her instinctual nature and is now guided by Divine Spirit. The energies of her aura ascend all the way to the flower-like radiance above her head. This is her opened crown chakra indicating awakened and mature mystical powers. Her heart center is particularly vivid with spiritual power indicating she has experienced the God presence and walks with the Divine from a place of knowing. It took her a long time of faith and devotion to get to reach such inner awareness. Her heart is firmly centered on God, and no one can shake her dedication to the Divine.

As she looks out to a stunning vista of extraordinary beauty, this woman is receiving a vision from the divine of the planetary systems, depicted by the diamond-studded spiral. As the planets and solar system are spiritually alive, she is now a conscious participant in the cosmic order of life. As part of her enlightenment, she has the gift of planetary travel and can consciously move in higher spiritual dimensions. The vision brings her into a state of spiritual ecstasy where she exalts in the fruits of her long labors and joins in the oneness of life.

Enlightenment is something we will all eventually experience. Whether it happens in this life or a future incarnation, it will happen. Our job is to do what is needed to prepare for the greater life that awaits.

Chapter 9

PREPARING FOR HEAVEN— THE INTERPLANETARY WORLDS

Where the Mystery is the deepest is the gate
of all that is subtle and wonderful.
—Lao Tzu, Tao Te Ching

O NCE YOU HAVE completed your ascent through all seven astral worlds, you have reached a marvelous place in your spiritual evolution and grown enormously in the Divine Light. But before you can enter the heaven worlds, there is yet another glorious spiritual mountain to climb—*the spiritual interplanetary worlds.* The job of these dimensions is to prepare you for the ascent to Heaven. In these realms, you gather the many experiences of all your incarnations in the physical/astral worlds while unfolding new spiritual powers.

Various metaphysical traditions have included the interplanetary worlds as part of their spiritual cosmology. They have used varying terminologies which can make the study of these realms difficult. Regardless of the terms employed, these are powerful, enlightened realms: mystical, mysterious, and exciting. Because of their extraordinary quality, some associate them with Heaven and speak of them in that way. The interplanetary worlds do have a majesty even more magical than the astral realms. And as with the astral planes, they are actual locales that souls inhabit as well as planes of consciousness to experience. Visionary and supernatural experiences are hallmarks of these realms.

Three grand realms comprise the interplanetary worlds. Each realm serves its own purpose in the divine process. In the interplanetary worlds, you develop your powers of enlightenment further. You bring together all aspects of your spiritual nature and auric composition; in a sense, you bring all parts of you together. You unite the accumulated wisdom gleaned from all your lifetimes on Earth and all the experiences from your long astral climb to fully express the gifts and talents you have earned. In these realms, you resolve your karmic debts to reach the mystical marriage that ushers in your new life in Heaven.

BUILDING YOUR FULL SOUL POWER

To understand how these realms are part of your spiritual evolution, some insight into the dynamics of the soul and its connection to the process of reincarnation is needed. As we have seen, one lifetime on Earth is not enough time to accumulate all the wisdom and experience the soul needs. Your soul incarnates many, many times to evolve to the heaven worlds. Each time you incarnate, your soul brings with it the spiritual power you have earned.

Yet when you incarnate, you do not bring *all* the soul power you have accumulated. It is simply too much. You bring a portion of the total spiritual power you have earned; the portion you don't bring stays in the spiritual worlds. More specifically, you only bring a quarter of your full auric power into an incarnated life. The other three quarters of Divine Light the soul has earned stays in the spiritual worlds.

Why doesn't the soul bring its full power all at once? There is so much for the soul to learn and develop that it can only focus on certain aspects of soul expression in any single lifetime. For example, let's say a soul incarnates with extraordinary musical skill, a talent learned in previous lives. It will naturally gravitate to a career in music and do well. If this person lives a full life and completes everything he or she was meant to do as a musician, the incarnation is considered a success. Yet there is still more for the soul to learn. Maybe it wasn't good at business or managing money or negotiating with publishers and promoters. It might not have been good relating with people as all its attention went to its music. Maybe it wanted to have a family but didn't because that wasn't part of the life plan.

So, while this soul completed everything it was meant to as a musician, other areas needed attention. In a future lifetime, this person's musical talents might be held back to develop other parts of its consciousness and talents and explore other facets of soul expression. Otherwise, if the soul returns with the same musical talents, it would naturally gravitate to music again and might ignore other parts of its nature that need work. By reserving some spiritual power, it can focus on other aspects in order to develop a well-rounded character. The musical creative power is still there, just on hold for the time being.

In the next life, this person may be born with a love of music but would not be a great musical talent. He or she may play the piano or sing well but nothing like the previous lifetime, and decide not to pursue a career in music. As a result, other aspects of the soul's spiritual energy will incarnate. This new auric configuration may, for example, steer the person into a life of business and family, giving the person the opportunity to build new skills and talents. Through the experiences of this new incarnation, another aspect of the soul's spiritual power is being expressed. The soul is developing new facets of its character and nature.

As the soul learns the lessons in this new incarnation of business and family, that aspect of its soul power blossoms. Once that life is finished and hopefully successful, that spiritual power will be added to the greater soul expression. Eventually, the soul will bring together all the various facets of its experiences and spiritual powers: musical, business, social, spiritual, and so on. This happens while the soul evolves through the spiritual interplanetary worlds.

This principle teaches us not to worry about trying to do everything in a single lifetime; it simply can't be done. Focus on the essential things that you know need taking care of. At the right time, you will bring together all the qualities of your soul's nature.

THE MENTAL WORLD

The first dimension above the astral is called the *mental world*. Theosophy calls this realm *devachan*. It has also been termed "the shining land." The mental world has been described as a type of heaven, although this is not true Heaven. In fact, many people who have reported out-of-body experiences of being in Heaven were, in fact, in devachan. Nevertheless, the mental realm is a fascinating place. There is a bliss connected to the mental world that is difficult to describe.

You enter the mental plane as an enlightened soul. In this realm, you explore your enlightened powers, especially the enlightened mind. On the mental plane, you gain deeper insights into the inner workings of the mental process and your relationship with Divine Mind. You learn about the structure of mind, and experience how everything which takes form and substance begins with mind. Your body, the world you live in—all are creations of mind acting on matter. You discover how the universe itself is a mental construct. You receive true pictures of

Divine Mind without the veils those images must wear in the astral and physical worlds. You learn how mind permeates all dimensions of life at every level, from the most primitive to the most enlightened.

One of the things that makes the mental world so unusual and exciting is that you are no longer in an astral body. You are in a body made up of *etheric atoms*. This body has form and looks like you but has more spiritual power than the astral. This shift is dramatic as it does feel like you are in a more heavenly state. You are able to perceive forces of nature you previously could not.

When first evolving into the mental world, there is a period of adjustment. You are taken to a place known as the Rose Room. In the Rose Room, you sleep for a while. This helps you adjust to being in this exhilarating environment. Once you adjust, life on the mental plane really begins. The soul continues to bring together the accumulation of knowledge it has been gathering through its many incarnations on Earth and in the astral planes. It's a glorious experience to tap into the greater part of your mental self. Imagine accessing all the inspired ideas you developed in all of your various incarnations!

The mental plane is where thoughts become things. Here, you gradually learn the incredible ability to manifest things directly through the power of your mind. This ability is truly extraordinary. I had an experience in the mental world where I was able to manifest a beautiful ruby ring through the power of mind. The experience was thrilling! As part of manifesting, you also discover the extraordinary power of tone and speech. Spiritual tone activates ideas, stirring them into motion. Because of this, speech in the mental world is sacred. People are careful what they say as they understand the power of words.

Your telepathic powers greatly increase. This intimacy of thought deepens your relationships with others. You meet incredible people and share more with others than you ever have. You have nothing to hide. You can see others for who they are, and they can see you for who you are.

During your evolution through the seven levels of the mental world, you are still incarnating in physical life. For example, I once had a visitation from the spirit worlds of Thomas Troward. He was a pioneer in the mental sciences and New Thought movement in the late nineteenth and early twentieth centuries. He appeared to me in his etheric form to offer some inspiration for a lecture I was preparing on the spiritual dimensions of the mind. He had a wonderful vibration, and I could tell from his aura he was coming from the mental plane.

With all the mental stimulation that happens here, it can be easy to forget that the true lessons of the mental plane—as with all spiritual dimensions—are the lessons of the heart. What helps you graduate through the various mental levels is your ability to live the spiritual truths you have been learning.

Mind over Matter : ILLUSTRATION 9.1

In this illustration, the robed man is standing in front of a magnificent pyramid called the Temple of Spiritual Tone. It has white marble sides, dramatic entrances, and triangular windows. It's in a beautiful pastoral setting on a mountain plateau surrounded by smaller buildings. Various light rays move in and around this grand structure. In this temple, souls learn to use the power of speech as an instrument of mind to materialize things. This enlightened soul is using his mental powers to manifest a book he has conceived. Angels of music stand on both sides of him. One is playing an unusual instrument that looks like a small harp; the other is singing. The musical tones are exquisite. As they perform, the vibrations of the music are helping him build his powers of manifestation. He is deep into a process of spiritual creation bordering on a state of reverent ecstasy.

THE CAUSAL WORLD

———

The next realm above the mental world is the causal world. Here is where the soul comes to terms with its own identity and its cosmic history. Some of the great mysteries of the soul are revealed on the causal plane.

To inhabit this realm, you are in a causal body. The causal body and world are made up of more rarified etheric atoms than in the mental world. All the spiritual realms from the mental plane up through the heaven worlds are made up of varying degrees of etheric atoms, each ascending realm more rarified. The atoms of the causal world are not as rarified as those of the heaven worlds, but they bring in a lot of power.

Some metaphysical schools teach that the causal plane is an extension of the mental plane. Theosophy called the mental world the plane of *concrete* thought and the causal world the realm of *abstract* thought. In Hindu metaphysics, the mental plane consists of two parts. The lower part is known as *swarglok* (heaven) and the upper part as *maharlok* (the causal plane). The Indian mystic Sri Aurobindo emphasized the power of the causal plane when he called it "the super mind plane." The causal world is where archetypal thoughts reside. In the causal world, you accumulate more mental abilities and your powers of manifestation increase. You become adept in your enlightened powers yet more humble because you know the source of your power is not coming from you; it's coming from the Divine.

An extraordinary feature of the causal plane is the way you experience life. Life is all about experience. Some experiences affect you deeply, others not so much. Sometimes, you aren't really present for what is happening in the moment, as you may be preoccupied elsewhere. Or you simply don't realize the significance of what is happening. On the causal plane, you are very present and keenly aware of the significance of everything that takes place. Your interactions and activities are deeply meaningful as you recognize their inner significance.

A new level of devotion unfolds. Your experiences with others are more profound. You discover just how rich the bonds with other human souls can be. You love more deeply and give more of yourself. You are keenly aware of areas of your character that still need work. Even though you are enlightened, there is always room for improvement. There is tolerance for others—their strengths and weaknesses and where they are in their spiritual evolution.

Reincarnation and the Causal World

As part of the soul expression, the causal world is deeply involved with the process of reincarnation. Reincarnation involves many realms of life, but a lot of the strategic planning and review work happens in this realm. In the causal world, key elements of preparations for a new incarnation take place.

The causal plane is the plane of the soul. One of the most important objectives while evolving through the causal world is coming to terms with the experiences of your many past incarnations, both good and bad. In your spiritual ascent to the heaven worlds, you review the breadth and scope of your long karmic history. You begin a reconciliation process where you view past lives to get a first-hand account of your cosmic story. You view lifetimes when you did wonderful things. You see yourself in your best and highest incarnations. You see how you have succeeded in many facets of human experience. This reinforces your confidence in the strong spiritual heritage that is your soul history, giving you courage and hope.

In the same way, you review difficult lifetimes where there was suffering and struggle. You see how much you've endured. You realize that no effort is ever lost. Even if your actions didn't bear fruit in a particular lifetime, the good eventually came around. Your past sufferings may have seemed bewildering at the time, yet they served a higher purpose. You were never really alone. Even in those difficult lives, God was there.

Then you review incarnations when you took the wrong road or lost spiritual ground by doing terrible things, even evil things. There are lifetimes where you cheated, stole, connived, murdered, or delved in the dark arts. It is difficult to view these lives and see the pain you caused others and how you offended the Divine. There is remorse that you were capable of such despicable acts. It opens your heart to know that truly we all have a checkered past, that these experiences are an inevitable part of spiritual evolution. This is all part of the reconciliation.

You then go through a period of asking God's forgiveness for past sins, purging your soul of any vestige of these ancient remnants. Through this process, you are purifying, cleansing, and uplifting your soul. The Lords of Karma show you what you worked through, karmic areas you still need to complete, and karmic debts you owe. Even having evolved to the causal plane, you have not yet worked out all your karma. But now you are more than motivated to do everything necessary to reconcile past errors.

As you reach the culmination of your evolution through the causal world, you gain a much greater understanding of who you are as an immortal soul. You have worked through many remaining unresolved karmic issues and come to terms with your long karmic history and the lessons that history offered. You are now ready to bring together all your accumulated talents, experiences, and spiritual power as a grand whole in preparation for the leap to the heaven worlds.

Reconciling Past Lives : ILLUSTRATION 9.2

This soul has evolved to the causal world and is going through the process of reconciling his past lives. He is with the Lords of Karma in a viewing room in a magnificent temple. On a table is the Book of Life; it is open to his page. On the pages, the letters of the sacred words are alive with Divine Light. On the wall is a viewing screen. On this screen, the man sees a scene from a past life when he was of service and sacrificed much for others. He views the scenes like a movie, but this movie is in three dimensions. He feels part of the scene, experiencing the true motivations of what he did and felt in that life. His experience is objective, void of personal coloring. He is happily surprised he was capable of such goodness and it motivates him to do more.

THE ETHERIC WORLD

Now we come to the top of the spiritual interplanetary realms—the etheric world (not to be confused with the heaven worlds of Spiritual Etheria.) By the time you reach this plane, you are more heavenly than earthly. It is a plane of spiritual advancement and splendor that is only surpassed by Heaven itself. In this realm, all aspects of the soul come together in final preparation for the heaven worlds.

This is a very mystical plane, full of visions and spiritual experiences. There is great joy as you celebrate your achievement in reaching this stage in your spiritual unfoldment. You feel accomplished and profoundly grateful. There are exciting celebrations. You join conclaves and meetings with advanced spiritual beings and work more closely with the spiritual hierarchy who reveal secrets about themselves they could not before.

In this realm, you are in a powerful etheric body. Your spiritual senses are more refined, and you can see into the mystical life with greater detail. Your enlightenment powers are at a peak. Most of all, this body is so strong and resilient it can contain the full power of your soul. In this etheric form, you bring together all the facets of who you are—all the lessons and talents accumulated during your long spiritual journey—into one cohesive whole. What you felt in part before, you now feel in whole. You are the renaissance person, expressing multiple talents.

On the etheric plane, you finally resolve all your remaining karmic debts. You have been dealing with karmic conditions throughout your evolution. Now, you wipe the slate clean before ascending into the heaven worlds. There is a tremendous sense of completion and freedom, knowing you have finally righted all your wrongs and resolved any wrongs that others committed toward you.

You reach a new place of personal expression. The radiance of your divine self overshadows everything else. You attain a new level of selfless service. You are industrious and involved with many projects. You have learned to cast off the delusions of the lower self and operate from the divine you. This has been building from the time you reached the seventh astral plane, but now it has reached its full flowering. You receive many spiritual visions, especially visions of the Divine Plan. You are shown potential future events based on dynamics that are in motion. You see how all the realms you have been growing through weave together, and how physical life depends on the spiritual worlds. At the same time, you see how physical life affects the spiritual worlds; they are all interconnected.

There is much preparation for Spiritual Etheria, the first of the seven heavens. All spiritual, religious, and metaphysical teachings inspired from the heaven worlds reside in the etheric world. The archetypes of the great world religions and metaphysical traditions are orchestrated in this realm. You see how heavenly emissaries such as Buddha, Krishna, Moses, Muhammed, Jesus, and Confucius worked from this realm to objectify their divine teachings on Earth.

The incarnations you have from this plane are the most sacred you have ever had up to this point in your spiritual journey. While this realm is not as populated as other spiritual planes, each soul is preparing for its final ascent. Of course, it's not only you; everyone in this realm is at the pinnacle of their achievement. They share with you their story and you share yours. There are friendships experienced here that have gone on for ages. Your relationship with nature and animals reaches a new plateau. The beauty of the ethereal realm surpasses anything found in the astral, mental, or causal worlds. You experience the livingness of all things.

Reaching the pinnacle of the etheric world is the culmination of an extraordinary journey of adventure. At this level of spiritual maturity, the soul has brought together into one great whole all it has learned and developed and is now ready to enter Heaven. To honor this great achievement and give the soul the power it needs for what lies ahead, it receives *The Mystic Marriage*.

Various religious and spiritual traditions have interpreted the mystic marriage as a union with God and the Divine, a union with Christ, a union with various aspects of human nature, or a union with the soul mate. These are all wonderful interpretations, but in terms of the soul's evolution to Heaven, the mystic marriage means the union of Divine Spirit with the human soul. Many equate spirit and soul as essentially the same thing, but metaphysics makes a distinction between the two.

You *are* an immortal soul. It is your soul that has been going through the evolutionary process we have been exploring. The Divine Spirit is different; it's the part of you that is already in a state of perfection and has been guiding the soul all along. We hear people say what a strong spirit someone has or how spiritual they are. What we are really saying is that this person has learned how to work with the spirit, together with its soul, to increase its power and eliminate from the soul the flaws it comes in with. As your soul grows, you are learning to be "of the spirit." While the Divine Spirit has always been with you, it does not become a part of you until you are ready for the heaven worlds. With the mystic marriage, it is time to unite with the Divine Spirit, so spirit and soul can work together as the soul enters Heaven as a celestial citizen.

The Mystic Marriage : ILLUSTRATION 9.3

In this scene, the initiate is going through the ceremony of the union of spirit and soul. The ceremony is held outdoors in a sacred, secluded area with beautiful scenery. The woman is in the middle of a circle of angelic beings. Everyone wears formal robes. Leading the ceremony is a being of unimaginable splendor: the Lord of Wisdom Light. The Lord of Wisdom Light is blessing this woman in holy power. Above the woman, an ethereal form has descended from above her head. This is her Divine Spirit. It has taken form to be recognizable. It is radiant in Divine Light, with so much power you mostly see white light. With this union, the anointed soul is ready to enter the celestial realms of Heaven.

Chapter 10

THE GLORY OF HEAVEN

Arise, shine, for your light has come,
and the glory of the LORD has risen upon you.
—Isaiah 60:1

W HEN I BEGAN my metaphysical teaching career, it was an exciting time. I had been under spiritual training for many years building my clairvoyant skills and knowledge, and now I was ready to help others in their evolution. This was in the early 1970s. The metaphysical field was wide open as there weren't many spiritual teachers. I was becoming known for my clairvoyant work with the aura. As soon as people knew I could see the auric field, they were interested. I quickly built up a large following giving lectures and workshops and conducting spiritual healings and aura readings. I also set up ongoing, weekly metaphysical training classes. This allowed students to delve more deeply into the work. I met some wonderful people in those days who became life-long friends.

During this time, I had a celestial experience that changed my life. While traveling to the inner planes, I found myself with an archangel in a magnificent celestial pine forest in a heaven world called The Kingdom of Light. An ethereal apricot light permeated the atmosphere. The pine trees were vibrant, tall and lush with needles and of a variety I had never seen. The scent of pine was the sweetest I had ever experienced. As we walked through the forest together, I tuned into the spirit essence of the trees. They were aware of our presence—especially the presence of the archangel—and were communicating in their own way. Somehow, in consciousness, I could communicate with them as well in a way they understood. Such an intimate experience with nature was new to me.

There were areas of the forest where the Divine Light was so strong that I could hardly distinguish the trees from the Light. Then the archangel led me to a clearing in the forest. He indicated for me to look up. When I turned my attention upward, I saw a dazzling display of spiritual light, like a sea of multicolored lights suspended in the sky. At first, I thought it might be an unusual formation of clouds, but it didn't move like clouds. The archangel told me this was a gathering of divine consciousness, created by celestial beings and was how they blessed nature with Divine Light.

The next thing I knew, drops of Divine Light were falling from this celestial sea of light! They didn't just touch my clothing and skin; they permeated into my body. It was refreshing and invigorating. All around me, nature was absorbing and enthralled by the Light. As we kept walking in this heavenly rain, I felt more and more elevated. Eventually the rain subsided, and we approached the grounds of a magnificent temple—ornate, elegant, and radiating a pink Light.

I was led inside to a beautiful prayer room. In this room were other extraordinary celestial beings. These divine ones started talking about the spiritual teachings I had been trained in. The leader started showing me how it was my mission to help spread these teachings to others. Inez had already prepared me to go on a public lecture tour. Now the Holy Ones were showing me more fully how these teachings originated from

The Kingdom of Light and their purpose in helping souls ascend to the heavens. This celestial being said that I was not the only one being prepared for such work.

They then showed me a holy book with countless names of souls who were ready to begin their journey to The Kingdom of Light. These were their celestial names, written in a celestial language. It would take lifetimes of spiritual growth for many to reach this goal, yet the time had come for each to begin the journey. The divine ones said that even those whose names were not yet written would eventually start the journey as all souls are destined for Heaven. I started to get the bigger picture of the divine work. There was a magnificent plan for humanity—a new revelation of spiritual truth as part of the natural growth and evolution of civilization—and the Higher was working diligently to make things better for us all. As exciting as all this was, I wondered what I could do. The Holy Ones said they would guide me. They gave me confidence that with their help, I would do my part. I received a blessing and told them I was ready to serve.

In this chapter, we will explore the magnificent journey into the heavens. Once a soul has become a citizen of Heaven, what now? Is the spiritual pilgrimage complete? Are you finished incarnating on Earth? Do you see God? The mystic Helena Blavatsky was asked about what happens when a soul reaches such a spiritually advanced state. She answered, "You grow from perfection to perfection." Life is not static; it is dynamic and expressive. As beautiful as Heaven is, it's not the end of your spiritual journey because it's not your ultimate destination. Reaching Heaven is an enormous accomplishment; it means you have reached a state of perfection. Yet the full unfoldment of your human potential is not complete. With the accumulated spiritual powers you have earned, you will build on that perfection. You will now perfect yourself as a human soul through Heaven. So not only do you grow *to* Heaven; you grow *through* Heaven! And there are seven heavens to grow through.

You may say, "Wonderful! But that sounds so far away. How could Heaven have anything to do with my life here?"

A lot.

As we have been exploring, Heaven is not just "out there" somewhere. Heaven is also within you. You are partaking and receiving from the heaven worlds every day. They are sustaining and inspiring you. The goal is to connect more directly with a presence that is already part of you. Every time you pray and meditate; every time you put others before yourself; every time you are loving and kind without thought of return; every time you show generosity for the joy of giving and not receiving; every time you make your spiritual life your priority. In each instance, you are partaking of the heavenly vibration. Your earth life is not a digression from your spiritual life; it is an intrinsic part of the spiritual life and offers every opportunity for attaining the divine goals you seek. Truly you bring Heaven to Earth in the way you live.

When you first graduate to Heaven, there are celebrations. This is a time of joy and adventure as you acclimate to the heavenly vibrations. You meet other heavenly souls—some are newcomers like yourself—while others have been part of these worlds for a long time. Your relationships with others take on new dimensions of expression. You learn there is so much to love, how love holds the universe together, and how entire spiritual planets are dedicated to love. Culture, art, music, science, philosophy, religion, and government all exist in extraordinary ways in the heaven worlds.

The heavens are places of Divine Light and spiritual power. The God presence, divine mind, and the heart of spiritual love are everywhere. Virtue and holiness are natural states of being. The heaven worlds are prototypal realms where divine ideas first take shape before being objectified on Earth. The heavens are the headquarters for the spiritual hierarchy. This is where the guidance, Light, and inspiration we receive originate. In the heaven worlds, there is creative expression beyond compare. Your talents and skills reach new heights. There is wisdom of staggering proportions. Now that you've awakened your spiritual powers, it's time to fully use and express them.

Each of the heaven worlds is an opportunity to unfold new levels of divine awareness. You step into a deeper understanding of what life really is—a fuller understanding of you as an immortal soul. You gain deeper knowledge of the Holy Ones and work more closely with them in their co-creative process. You integrate and participate in the divine plan. Yet even here, in the midst of all the grandeur, there are personal challenges and tests, and sometimes there are missteps. Even in Heaven, your ascent is not a straight line upward.

Everything in Heaven is on a grander scale than you have ever experienced. Nature and life take on qualities both glorious and unique. Each heaven world has its own set of laws and yet is bound by the same universal laws. It is stunning to realize how much there is to the laws of life and how dynamic nature can be. You directly tune into the inner essence of nature all around you including flowers and trees and communicate with them. In a sense, the inner life becomes the outer life.

You have a heavenly body made of the material of the heaven you are in. This heavenly form is extraordinary. As Saint Paul states:

There is a natural body, and there is a spiritual body…as we have borne the image of the man of dust, we shall also bear the image of the heavenly man.[1]

In your heavenly body, your soul finds a much greater range of expression. Imagine a violinist playing the best Stradivarius violin while

---

[1] *1 Corinthians 15:35-49*

creating the most exquisite music. Your body has an expansive auric field, and while it does have form, it is often referred to as a "pure body of light" because of its radiant qualities. Your celestial eyes behold divine colors that do not exist in physical life. Your celestial ears hear tones and harmonies that can only be heard in Heaven. You drink of celestial ambrosia. You commune with the bounty and manna of Heaven.

Some depictions of Heaven illustrate an austere image of our divine nature. Yet the truth is that you have a broad range of emotional and mental expressions. You are still very much human, so you have the "normal" range of human emotions. Free will is also very much in play, and you can still make mistakes. Yet your range of emotions is of a truly celestial nature. Your heavenly body accommodates this greater mental and emotional life.

Do you experience God in Heaven? The God presence is everywhere, and you have already had the God Within experience in your ascent. In Heaven, this experience is greatly deepened. The heavens themselves are a direct creation of The Kingdom of God, so everything about them speaks of the divine Creator. Yet as grand and inspiring as these experiences are, they do not compare to the actual experience of standing before the glory of God. That is reserved for your ultimate ascent to The Kingdom of God. As you experience the wonders of the seven heavens, there is always something urging you onward and upward to the source from where you came.

THE SEVEN HEAVENLY PERFECTIONS

———

Reaching Heaven means you have attained a certain state of perfection. Yet this is not the end of the spiritual road. The soul evolves through *seven* heavens. As it evolves through each one, you unfold even more of your soul potential. As there are seven heavens, there are also what are known of as *The Seven Perfections* that you develop in your evolution through these celestial realms. As you perfect these sacred attributes, you truly unfold the fullness of your divine self.

You may wonder why, after traveling so far to reach Heaven, attaining enlightenment, and unfolding so much of your spiritual potential, it isn't enough! What more is there to accomplish?

In our evolution through the astral and interplanetary worlds as well as our many physical incarnations, the soul is learning and developing many things to reach the stage of perfection that earns its way to Heaven. But that perfection is not the completeness of understanding. The wisdom earned needs to go through a seven-step perfecting process. As we ascend the heaven realms, we will revisit these life lessons (along with many new experiences) to enrich the soul in understanding and wisdom in ways unimaginable before. Helena Blavatsky spoke of turning the key of wisdom seven times to truly understand and embody that truth.

Each heavenly perfection is related to a particular heaven world. One builds on the other, so you accumulate perfections as you evolve. These qualities are no strangers to physical life. We are all expressing them to a degree even now. The Seven Perfections and their associated heaven realms are:

The Perfection of the Eternal Self—Spiritual Etheria
The Perfection of Eternal Life—The Kingdom of Light
The Perfection of the Creative Spirit—The Kingdom of Creation
The Perfection of Holiness—The Kingdom of the Gods
The Perfection of Service—The Kingdom of the Inner Light
The Perfection of the Infinite Spirit—The Kingdom of the Spirit Light
The Perfection of Humility—The Kingdom of the Seven Spirits

Robed in the aura of divine love and divine mind, you do not need to reach Heaven to start embodying these spiritual qualities. By doing your best to express these attributes now, you are preparing for the glories yet ahead.

THE HEAVENLY INCARNATIONS

When the soul reaches Heaven, is it finished incarnating on Earth? The Hindu tradition describes the completion of the reincarnation cycle as "getting off the wheel of necessity." Souls incarnate to experience life—to learn and spiritually grow. Lifetimes on earth are like grades in school. So, the real question to ask is, "When the soul evolves to Heaven, has it completed its spiritual education on Earth?" The answer is: not yet. The earth has more to teach the soul! By the time a soul has reached Heaven, it has awakened its spiritual power and talents. Its spirit eyes are opened. Now the soul can spread its spiritual wings and experience life on Earth to its fullest. The job of the soul is to now take its hard-earned talents to new heights of expression.

In Heaven, a new cycle of incarnations begins. These are known as the heavenly incarnations. Your heavenly expression on Earth encompasses the most exciting, mysterious, and fulfilling lifetimes you will have in physical form. You understand the physical world in greater depth and make your most profound contributions. Humanity's greatest thinkers, musicians, artists, leaders, theologians, scientist, philosophers, metaphysicians, and inventors were all born of the heavens and brought in that power to serve the greater good. Some heavenly incarnations are exalted while others can be quiet and humble. This opens the consciousness to some of the deepest expressions of compassion and understanding for the human condition.

Heavenly souls incarnate on Earth all the way through the third heaven—The Kingdom of Creation. By the time you evolve through the three heavens, you have learned all you can as a human soul on Earth. Countless souls have passed through these doors. At this point, the soul has earned its way "off the wheel of necessity" and is ready to go onto the higher heavens.

SPIRITUAL ETHERIA—THE FIRST HEAVEN

The first heaven is a mystical realm called Spiritual Etheria. This is a place of indescribable beauty and glory. An ethereal blue light pervades this realm, which may be the reason for its name. There are scenes of pastoral splendor and holy temples of great power and learning. There is no darkness in Spiritual Etheria. Everything is filled with light and love. There is wonderful celestial music—the true "music of the spheres." You experience an extraordinary sense of freedom and creative expression.

When a soul first becomes a citizen of Spiritual Etheria, there are celebrations. You meet other heavenly souls; extraordinary exchanges and friendships develop. A beautiful facet of Heaven is that you enter Spiritual Etheria with your soul mate! You are taken together on spiritual voyages through celestial planetary systems. The scope and grandeur of the heavens takes your breath away.

After a period of enjoyment, adventure, and relaxation, the angelic beings meet with you to talk about what is next. They discuss your future heavenly incarnations on Earth. You are shown the divine plan and arc of your coming incarnations through the heavens and how much you will accomplish. If you have talent in science or the arts, you may build that talent to the level of an Einstein or Mozart. Not all your upcoming lives with be grand, however. During many heavenly incarnations, you will work quietly, without fanfare, to serve the divine plan, sometimes without conscious awareness that you are part of the heaven worlds. The angels will show you visions of where humanity is headed so you better understand the world you will be incarnating into and how you will best contribute.

You begin your heavenly ascent by working on the first heavenly perfection—*The Perfection of the Eternal Self.* This is a deeper experiencing of your immortality. During the process of incarnating, that truth became camouflaged. Physical life is mortal: You are born, you live, you die. Yet this is not the eternal you. There is a part of you that has never been born and will never die—your immortal soul.

As part of building this perfection, the Holy Ones show you some of the Akashic records related to your evolution. Let us pause for a moment to understand what the Akashic records are. The word *akasha* comes from the Sanskrit for "open space" and is often used synonymously with the word *ethers.* The concept is that the universe is pervaded by a primordial material, out of which everything is made. Metaphysics calls this primordial material Spirit-substance or the akasha. The atoms of your body, the atoms of all nature and the planets and stars, are made up of this primordial material. When you express a thought, action, emotion, or word, you impress the akasha, creating a type of record. So, everything you are doing is getting recorded in the fabric of life!

These spiritual impressions can be viewed or played back like a movie. *The Book of Life* that we explored earlier is part of the Akashic records. Yet the Akashic records show even more. They have the record of your entire arc of evolution, even before your incarnations on Earth, when you were in much more primitive states. This explains why, contrary to popular understanding, no one can view the Akashic records while they are on Earth. You can only view them when you become a citizen of Heaven.

Once in Heaven, the Holy Ones show you the length and breadth of your spiritual pilgrimage. Even in your earliest primitive stages, you can see the mark, the character, of your own soul! You identify with and see yourself in various states of evolution and realize it was the same immortal soul that went through all these experiences. You understand in new ways what it means to be an eternal being going through the evolutionary cycles of life.

Spiritual Etheria is a prototypal world. As the fourth astral plane is the staging area for many of the things that will be objectified on earth, Spiritual Etheria is a type of staging area for celestial designs from the higher heavens and The Kingdom of God. The divine plan is beautifully laid out in this heaven. From Spiritual Etheria, much Divine Light and inspiration flow to our humble earthly realm. Truly, we are blessed by Heaven every day.

As you evolve to the higher reaches of Spiritual Etheria, you unfold a celestial enlightenment. As each heaven is a chance to unfold each of the seven perfections, each heaven is also a time to deepen your enlightenment. As you reach the culmination of your evolution through the first heaven, you embody the power of Spiritual Etheria, unfold new talents and abilities, and expand your love flow. Best of all, you gain a deeper understanding and experience of God. Once you reach the enlightenment of Spiritual Etheria, you are ready to graduate to the second heaven—The Kingdom of Light.

Physical life benefits from all the heavens, but Spiritual Etheria is most closely connected to life on Earth. Organize and align your life to this great realm. Spiritual Etheria is the realm of consciousness we are all aspiring to reach on our journey to the fountainhead of life.

Entering Spiritual Etheria : ILLUSTRATION 10.1

This scene depicts the triumphal entry into Spiritual Etheria. The location is a celestial city specifically built for those new to the heaven worlds. There are a variety of architectural styles, including representations of the cultures on Earth.

The two beings in yellow robes are soul mates who have graduated to Heaven. One of the most beautiful parts of evolving to Heaven is that you do so with your soul mate. If one soul has climbed the spiritual ladder a little faster than the other, it waits until joined by the other so they can enter Heaven together—an act of true love. In this union of love is felt the cosmic love that brought them together at the beginning of their spiritual pilgrimage. It has been a long journey to get to this place, and they are thoroughly absorbing the holiness of the moment.

They are greeted by a group of heavenly souls who are citizens of this realm. There is song and dance as they rejoice in greeting the new arrivals. They are all in a courtyard with exquisite roses and flowers. In the middle of the courtyard is an ethereal tree. Mystics have symbolically called this The Tree of Life because it brings in the ethereal, eternal vibration—the fruits of spirit.

Behind this celestial couple is a grand building known as The Cathedral of the Soul that resembles one of the majestic cathedrals of Europe. It is made of white alabaster with various colored light rays radiating from within. On Earth, a cathedral represents a seat of ecclesiastical authority. In Heaven, this cathedral is non-denominational. It represents the seat of the soul—the wisdom the soul has gained through experience.

In the sky is a temple suspended in the air with people float-traveling to it. This temple is blessing the inhabitants of the city with energies from heaven worlds that lie beyond Spiritual Etheria, inspiring their heavenly climb.

THE KINGDOM OF LIGHT— THE SECOND HEAVEN

Each Heaven brings a new revelation of the divine life. As the soul graduates from Spiritual Etheria to The Kingdom of Light, new worlds open up. The Kingdom of Light is more vast than Spiritual Etheria. In this heaven world, an ethereal apricot light permeates the atmosphere. Life moves at a quickened pace. You discover new facets of your spiritual make-up and unfold even more of your character and talents. As beautiful as life is in Spiritual Etheria, it is even more exquisite in The Kingdom of Light. Your experience of nature and your understanding of the spiritual hierarchy and God continue to deepen. At this evolutionary level of development, souls are continuing their heavenly incarnations on Earth, but nearing the culmination of these experiences as they make some of their biggest spiritual strides, bringing their gifts to all facets of society.

As the name implies, this heaven is where the Divine Light is gathered and organized from the celestial source and then projected to Spiritual Etheria and from there, to us here in physical life. There is profound education on what the Divine Light really is and how to harness that power. In The Kingdom of Light, you truly come to experience how Divine Light and consciousness walk hand in hand. This opens the door to experiencing consciousness in new ways. For example, there is a metaphysical principle that states: *You are where you place your attention.* This means that regardless of where you are at a given moment, if your attention is somewhere else, a part of your consciousness connects with where you have placed your attention. For example, if you are sitting in your chair at home reading this book and start thinking about your favorite beach or forest, part of your consciousness actually goes to that place.

This "directing your consciousness" to places other than where you are takes on new expression in The Kingdom of Light. For example, say you want to connect with someone in The Kingdom of Light but aren't able to go there in your celestial body. You can direct your consciousness to them, and if they wish to respond, they will direct their consciousness back. The two of you can then have a "merging in consciousness," interacting and engaging as if you were actually together. It's an amazing experience and changes your perspective of space and distance. You realize how the angels and archangels can do so much for humanity because of their profound skill in utilizing consciousness to support you even from a great distance.

In The Kingdom of Light, you also develop the second heavenly perfection—*The Perfection of Eternal Life*. Like a veil that has been lifted, you can see how alive everything is around you. You understand the vastness of eternity itself, the immensity of it all. You learn how to tune into the eternal pulsation of life. Your compassion for life awakens to the most profound level you have ever experienced because it's not just you who is without beginning or end; it is everyone and everything. Life itself is without beginning or end. These experiences are thrilling beyond compare. Your respect for life in all forms multiplies exponentially. In this Heaven world, you come into a deeper revelation of the source of all life—the Unknown Root of Existence. Whereas you experience the eternity of you as an immortal soul in Spiritual Etheria, here you experience yourself as the "drop" in the ocean of life.

In this holy realm, your celestial body is even more magnificent and powerful than the one you inhabited in Spiritual Etheria. In your

Kingdom of Light body, you deepen your understanding and awareness of God and The Kingdom of God. So much time and energy has been directed at getting to Heaven, to awakening the spiritual powers and latent talents within. Now that you have awakened and are expressing these powers, the time has come to start focusing your attention on the ultimate goal. For the first time since beginning your spiritual climb, you are given the clearest picture yet of what The Kingdom of God is all about. You are now setting your sights on that which is beyond even the seven heavens. You receive visions and understandings that stir the deepest parts of your soul. And somewhere in the back of all this is the remembrance, the familiarity, of the source of your origin. A love of God never before experienced awakens.

There are twelve great divisions in The Kingdom of Light. They represent twelve attributes of the divine life the soul must embody to work its way through the second heaven. These attributes are reflected on Earth as cultures of civilization. Throughout our many incarnations, we experience and express all the cultural attributes and develop the divine powers they embody. This is why it is so important to honor and respect the various cultures of the earth and the people who are part of them. They make up the fabric of divine life. In the second heaven, there is a great diversity of human expression. Here you experience the twelve cultural attributes in their essence as this is where their expression originated.

As you reach spiritual maturity in The Kingdom of Light, you reach the second celestial enlightenment. You are now ready to enter the third heaven where you will earn the crown of life.

THE KINGDOM OF CREATION—
THE THIRD HEAVEN

Human souls who incarnate from this realm are reaching the full maturity of their earthly experiences and making important contributions to society. Earth's greatest spiritual teachers, artists, scientists, inventors, and political leaders have incarnated from The Kingdom of Creation.

As the name implies, The Kingdom of Creation is a place of extraordinary creative power. A diaphanous light of many colors permeates the atmosphere of this heavenly realm. The landscape, scenery, and buildings pulsate with inner life. There is civilization here, but it takes on new qualities. The cultural streams that were so beautifully expressed in The Kingdom of Light and are reflected in the cultures on Earth, merge in the third heaven into a unified whole. In The Kingdom of Creation, there are no cultures as we think of them. Third heaven souls have mastered the cultural influences and the divine attributes they represent and now bring those powers together. While there is magnificent diversity in The Kingdom of Light, in The Kingdom of Creation, souls are unified in the divine oneness. There is a cooperation, unity of thought, and purpose that brings you closer than ever to your brothers and sisters in Light.

This is the realm where infant souls, descending from The Kingdom of God, are brought to prepare for the evolutionary process they will soon begin. There is a beautiful exchange between developed souls ascending and infant souls descending. Here we learn that God did not give birth just to our own "life wave" of souls; there were human life waves born before us, and births of human life waves continue after us. Both younger and older souls incarnate on Earth, and each is serving its part in the divine plan. One isn't better than another; each is at differing evolutionary levels depending on when it began its spiritual pilgrimage. All are equally precious and bear the spiritual mark of their evolutionary birth in their auric framework. These varying evolutionary streams are "sorted out" in The Kingdom of Creation.

Many extraordinary experiences await in The Kingdom of Creation. As in all the heavens, there is a "central sun." Central suns are found throughout the universe and work together to form the energetic backbone of the cosmos. They are the celestial hubs from which all dimension of life—spiritual and physical—receive support. Even the sun of our own physical solar system receives support from the hidden central sun. In physical life, the sun is made of physical material, which gives light and warmth that keeps physical life going. This same principle holds true in the spiritual realms. In the astral worlds, there is an astral sun illuminating astral planets; in the causal worlds, there are causal suns; and so on.

Yet the sun that illuminates and nourishes The Kingdom of Creation does not consist of the same celestial material found in the third heaven; it is made of a primordial, divine material that provides much more than just heat and light. It radiates great spiritual power that fuels the evolutionary process and the many spiritual activities that go on. Just being in the presence of this central sun makes you feel as if you are in the hub of creation. I had the honor of being in The Kingdom of Creation and beholding its central sun. This sun was like no other. Dazzling flows of Light and energy radiated from it. I could look at this sun without damaging my eyes and see the celestial fires it emanated.

A key theme in the third heaven is "the fire of spirit." We consider harnessing fire as one of the first signs of civilized living. We know how essential it is to life on Earth. In The Kingdom of Creation, you experience fire in a new way. External fire is a reflection of the fire of the creative spirit—the fire that does not burn. You recognize that this creative fire dwells within you. Yet like any fire, it must be tended. The creative fires within can be dimmed through discouragement and misuse but never extinguished. In this realm, you discover the eternal pulsations of the creative spirit, the spirit that brought the universe into being. It flows through creation as everything is imbued with creative power.

In The Kingdom of Creation, you develop the third perfection— *The Perfection of the Creative Spirit.* The expression of this creative spirit is sometimes known of as the "gifts of the magi." The term magi is Persian and refers to Zoroastrian priests who were reputed to have supernatural powers. In the ancient days, magi were thought to perform miracles. From the metaphysical perspective, the gifts of the magi refer to practices that enable someone to consciously harness divine powers in service to God. They aren't miracles but the expression of universal laws operating at high levels, reflecting an understanding of how spirit influences life on all planes of physical and spiritual expression. Those who harness these powers for good do wondrous things. Great mystical powers are developed in the third heaven.

As you evolve through the third heaven, you experience the source of the creative spirit as part of life—part of you. Truth, understanding, wisdom, and love find new expression while you cultivate these fires of spirit. You are tested to make sure that you don't make the fatal mistake of taking personal credit for such powers, that instead you recognize you are not the source but the vessel. And because you are still a reincarnating soul on Earth, your job is to take these holy powers and express them in physical life. This emphasizes the importance of being creative and expressing your creativity for the joy of it. You are learning to harness the eternal principles of life within and bringing those principles to outer expression. As you master the mystic powers that are part of this heavenly experience, you eventually reach the third heavenly enlightenment.

The pinnacle of achievement in The Kingdom of Creation is to earn The Crown of Life. This crown is bestowed not by conquering lands and peoples but by unfolding the powers of life that dwell within. You cannot usurp or steal this crown. You earn it through your own effort, sacrifice, love, and service. When you attain The Crown of Life, you get "off the wheel of necessity." This is the final chapter in a long pilgrimage through many realms of life, through countless ups and downs, successes and failures, adventures and accomplishments. You have now finished your physical lifetimes and left your indelible mark on Earth. The Crown of Life ushers you into the higher heavens and glories yet to unfold.

Chapter 11

THE HIGHER HEAVENS AND THE CELESTIAL LABORATORIES

Only a person who has passed through the gate of humility
can ascend to the heights of spirit.
—Rudolf Steiner

B EYOND THE FIRST three heavens are the four higher heavens and the vastness of the cosmos. In the higher heavens, we experience creation in ways that would make science fiction stories pale in comparison. You are stepping into the grandness of the cosmos and its stars, planets, and moons. To graduate into these realms, you have reached the pinnacle of human achievement on physical Earth. Yet you are still very much human in its noblest expression. And you experience being human in new ways as you draw ever closer to the divine source.

I hesitate to write about the higher heavenly realms for fear they might sound far-fetched. Also, there is a fundamental challenge in writing about realms beyond the third heaven because, despite what you might read or hear, there are limits on what human souls on Earth can experience, no matter how spiritually developed they may be. What I share about these realms is partly based on my experiences but largely based on divine revelation. The only word that can come close to expressing the wonder of these realms is, "incredible."

To start our exploration, I will ask a question: If graduating to the higher heavens means completing the process of physical incarnations on Earth, what is life really like without being part of our beautiful Earth? You have been part of the Earth experience for so long—done so much, gone through so much. What does it feel like to finally say goodbye to this beautiful part of your evolutionary journey?

Though it may sound strange, the initial reaction is mixed. When you reach the higher heavens, you are excited with what you've accomplished. Yet there is a certain nostalgia, a longing, perhaps even a celestial melancholy that sets in. You are no longer attached or dependent on Earth but that doesn't mean you don't have feelings. The soul has built a deep bond with Earth that is very different from an attachment. While you will continue to serve Earth in some way as many souls in the higher heavens do, the process is different than incarnating. Completing the earthly cycles of incarnation and entering the higher heavens is a little like leaving a loving home and childhood to find your own way in life. You know you are doing the right thing and everything is as it should be. Yet you will experience emotions and a sense of bewilderment while finding your way. A greater career and personal life may lie ahead, but that life is not yet built, and you have left a part of your life you loved.

As you acclimate to your new heavenly environment, your earthly incarnations become the memory of extraordinary experiences—an indelible part of your evolution that you will always keep in your heart. Now, you deeply contemplate the ultimate destination. With the freeing of your earthly incarnations, there is no other path to take but the one that leads Home. You turn completely to the goal of God. There are no more ups and downs in the journey. There is no turning back. There is only one direction: up! No matter what it takes, whatever the tests, trials, or initiations you will need to go through, your sights are set on The Kingdom of God.

What do you do in the higher heavens? For one, you start to participate in the grand cosmic processes. The celestial laboratories are the realms of creation that orchestrate the activities of the universe. Science would have you think that the universe is randomly created, without reason or purpose, and that life is a lucky concurrence of organic matter. Of course, there are natural laws in motion, but those laws are governed by divine intelligences. Nothing comes into expression without heart, intelligence, and intention. There must be a desire to do something, a willingness to focus on a task to completion, and creative intelligence to figure it all out.

In the higher heavens, the camouflage of creation is not so strong as the presence of eternity emerges even stronger. More and more, you see through the created and into the eternal. You are introduced to celestial beings so titanic in scale that you feel you are in the aura of the gods of Olympian myths or the triune of the Hindu pantheon. You truly understand that you are one part of a staggeringly grand cosmic plan. Yet rather than feeling insignificant amidst all this majesty, you feel an intrinsic part of it.

FOCUSING ON GOD

In the higher heavens, the soul comes to terms with the Creator. Of course, God has been with us all along. Every step in the spiritual pilgrimage has been attended to by the Divine. In reaching enlightenment, the soul awakened the experience of the God Within. This was not just extraordinary in its own right; it became the compass for climbing the higher spiritual realms. Now, the soul is preparing for the experience of the Glory of God. The excitement, the beauty, the grandeur, the splendor of the higher heavens is bathed in the radiance of the Divine preparing the soul to stand before the Creator.

At this magnificent stage in our evolution, we embody the most important attributes of the divine life: *God is the constant throughout the everlasting.* God is there in your most intimate thoughts and feelings. God always sees you in your highest and best self as the eternal soul that you are. The more you align with God, the more you feel godlike. This is not in an egotistical sense but in the sense that you truly feel like a son or daughter of the divine parents. In the higher heavens, everything and everyone around you is immersed in the same holy radiance. As you participate in celestial processes, you understand that this is your training to become a co-creative being.

Take inventory of your own understanding and attitude about God. For a subject that is so important, there have been many ideas about who and what God is throughout history. In some spiritual traditions, God is seen as the One: an all-encompassing presence, the source of everything. Yet there are also traditions of many gods, your god, and my god. In some traditions, God is the ultimate principle, the ultimate reality. Others present God as anthropomorphic, like a wise Father or Mother sitting on a throne. God has been given many names to describe in human language that which is not human or describable. There is the worship of God through human incarnations in such noble figures as Jesus and Krishna. There has even been a tradition of describing what God is *not* in an effort to understand what God is. Some say God can never be understood, that the Divine is eternally beyond our grasp to comprehend and can only be taken on faith.

We can study revelations given by God-illumined souls and the various spiritual traditions for guidance and insight. And while there are those who can inspire, teach, and guide, no human can reveal God to you, as God is not an argument or intellectual discourse. In trying to understand the principle of all principles, you have to use your reason, intellect, and your judgement. Equally important, you have to use your heart, intuition, and divine sensing that lies within you. Unshakable belief and faith are needed to give substance to the mystical life before it is seen and experienced. Yet belief requires reason to stop it from becoming superstition.

Ultimately, we each have to define God for ourselves, knowing that our definition will change as our growing understanding and experience evolves. If God is the most intimate experience we will ever have, it's up to us to use the wisdom of those who have gone before us, as well as our own innate sense, to guide our illumination and understanding.

We begin to understand God by opening our minds to divine intelligence and our hearts to infinite love. God doesn't "tell you what to do" like a stern parent. God reveals, inspires, and empowers you to understand life. Spiritual principles ultimately aren't told; they are experienced. If the only reason you do something is because you are told to, it will have little meaning because you don't understand it for yourself.

To truly experience the Divine, you have to align with the Divine. It's a relationship. Some wonder why God doesn't seem to answer their prayers or allows bad things to happen. God hears every sincere prayer and is constantly working on our behalf. Yet the Divine has to leave room for us to grow. God doesn't do the growing for us; we have to do that for ourselves. The Divine has to allow us to make mistakes—big ones at times—for this is how the soul grows.

The Indian poet Kabir, speaking about God, says:

How difficult it is to know, how easy it is to love Thee. We debate and argue, and the vision passes us by. We try to prove, and kill it in the laboratory of our minds, when on the altar of our souls it will dwell forever.[1]

---

[1] Jn or In. X:30

Sometimes we don't want to accept God. We think we can figure everything out on our own. Our ego can refuse the intimacy, love, and infinite intelligence of the Creator. Eventually, life teaches that we cannot outrun our destiny. We can resist the currents of life for a time, but eventually we are all swimming toward the same divine source.

As the Bhagavad Gita teaches:

Thou art the Imperishable, the Supreme, the One to be known. Thou art the Supreme Refuge of this universe. Thou art the ever-unchanging Guardian of the Eternal Dharma. Thou art I know The Ancient Being...By Thee alone the space between heaven and earth and all quarters is pervaded.[2]

THE KINGDOM OF THE GODS—
THE FOURTH HEAVEN
(NOT TO BE CONFUSED WITH THE KINGDOM OF GOD)

Entering The Kingdom of the Gods opens a new chapter in the evolutionary life of the human soul. The Kingdom of the Gods has been said to be the outer court of The Kingdom of God itself. This realm is overseen by hierarchical beings of such glorious proportions, they feel like gods themselves. In the spiritual realms, these divine beings are known as the *devas*. The term has been used in reference to angels and other holy beings, but the devas themselves are in a hierarchy all their own. Like all hierarchies, they are of differing levels of development[3]. While from our perspective, they seem to have a certain impersonal quality, you are captivated by their power, compassion, and intelligence. These "gods" are regents of grand splendor.

---

[2] *Bhagavad Gita,* Chapter 11, verses 18, 20
[3] The book *The Kingdom of the Gods* by Geoffrey Hodson has some beautiful illustrations of devas based on Hodson's clairvoyant observations.

In reaching the fourth heaven, you have earned The Crown of Life and graduated from incarnating on Earth. Now, new wonders of creation are revealed. The temples continue and are grander than ever. Your interactions with other ascending human souls deepen as they are in the same extraordinary place as yourself. You share experiences and develop new bonds of fellowship. You spend precious time with your soul mate and continue to develop your talents and skills.

Here, you truly begin to participate in the celestial laboratories of creation. This starts by understanding the spiritual dimensions of organic form. You witness how organic form first comes into spiritual expression before it is clothed in physical material. These forms are not just for you and me but for every living thing that is under the domain of this realm. You discover how the genetic code of organisms is a spiritual blueprint long before it becomes part of a living organism. You are taught in more detail how the body is an expression of the spirit and that parts of the body have specific spiritual attributes. In my experiences in this sacred heaven, I have witnessed areas where the great devas are working on the spiritual prototypes of organic forms. Truly, you are learning divine biology.

These archetypal forms are organized according to levels of consciousness and evolutionary status. For example, while humans share many physical qualities with animals, they are in a completely different kingdom spiritually from the animal kingdom. The design of form for a human soul is different from that of an animal soul.[4] As part of this division of evolutionary kingdoms, the fourth heaven is where the energetic orchestration of humanity and of each individual kingdom of nature takes place. We see how species share in collective levels of expression: birds migrate in groups, fish organize themselves in the schools, and humans share certain collective activities that are unique to being human. While instincts play a part in these activities, it goes

---

[4] For a detailed description of the kingdom of nature from the metaphysical perspective, please see our book, *Communing with the Divine*.

deeper than that. There is a celestial coordination that is essential to support evolving life within a kingdom of nature.

A beautiful part of your experiences in this heaven world is your work with souls who are getting ready for a new lifetime on Earth. Even though you have graduated from the process of physical incarnation on Earth, you help souls who are still bound by that cycle. In addition to physical pregnancy, there are spiritual preparations that go on once physical conception takes place to prepare the incoming soul for the body it will inhabit. And you participate in that process.

In The Kingdom of the Gods, you develop the fourth heavenly perfection—*The Perfection of Holiness*. What is meant by this? The dictionary defines holy as coming from the word "whole" and meaning "dedicated or consecrated to God or a religious purpose; sacred." When something is holy, we give it veneration. In this heaven, we come to embody the truth that life—by its inherent nature—is holy. Here you are granted visionary experiences that bring you into the direct experience of the sacredness of life.

From the metaphysical perspective, holy means *that which is incorruptible*. This is saying not only that life is, by definition, holy, but that it cannot be otherwise. Life cannot be defiled, degraded, or corrupted no matter what we do. Life can only be life—eternal, everlasting, pure, and divine. Yet, we may ask, "Why is there degradation in this world?" People can do terrible things. They corrupt themselves and those around them. We speak of depraved and evil souls. And here we need to be careful how we speak. Of course, people can do terrible things. The energies of the aura can become degraded and corrupted through misuse. But these degradations are a result of our own actions and attitudes; they are not the essence of who we are. One of the great metaphysical mysteries is that no matter what the soul does, the essence of it remains pure. The reason we don't experience that is because we cloud our understanding of the holiness of life with weights and burdens of our own making. And if we don't value life, we can end up moving in destructive directions.

In expanding our creative nature, part of what we're doing is striving to bring that which we create into a reflection of life's holiness. We purify what is unclean to make clean. We sanctify to make our creative expression a reflection of life's sacred nature. We speak of the angels and archangels as Holy Ones. This is not just because they are in higher spiritual kingdoms than we are; it's because of the divinity of their service and how they reflect the divinity of life. In our evolution, we are at different times the saint and the sinner because we are learning, experimenting, and growing—falling off the path but then getting back on. It is thus essential to treat life with reverence even if those around us do not.

As you reach the culmination through the fourth heaven, you have irrevocably consecrated yourself to the Divine. Everything you do, big or small, has intrinsic value. You are ready to serve God even more deeply, and you will get that chance as you evolve to the fifth heaven world.

THE KINGDOM OF THE INNER LIGHT— THE FIFTH HEAVEN

As the soul enters The Kingdom of the Inner Light, it enters a phase of evolution that becomes difficult to describe. Life is even more splendid and refined in this sacred place. You interact with even grander celestial beings and spiritual processes.

In the fifth heaven, you experience how planetary processes begin, both in the spiritual and physical realms. Planets by spiritual definition are *fields of evolution*. They are conscribed areas of space dedicated to spiritual growth. You're amazed at how alive the universe is and how much planetary work goes on. There are celestial beings who guide planetary births, evolutionary growth stages, and eventual planetary deaths when the spiritual cycle of a planet is complete. Planets have their own divine attributes, specialties, and purpose. There are spiritual planets dedicated entirely to love, creativity, intelligence, and so on. When you visit some of these planetary systems, their grandeur leaves you speechless.

Even more staggering are the celestial intelligences building and governing these systems. You now encounter what are called "planetary spirits" who orchestrate how the varying evolutionary streams work together. The auras of these beings can embody an entire planet. It is nearly incomprehensible to realize that our planet Earth has its own loving planetary spirit guiding over it. You could say that this being is the "celestial principal" or "dean" of schoolhouse Earth. This planetary spirit oversees all the many evolutionary kingdoms connected to Earth, from the microbial through the plants, animals, humans, and on through the angels, archangels, and other grand celestial beings, orchestrating how these kingdoms coordinate and work together. We are all interlinked in the great chain of life because we are all playing a collective part in the divine plan. This interactive alignment is administered in The Kingdom of The Inner Light.

Through all these experiences and revelations, you gain much more confidence in your own talents and creative power because you understand even more deeply how much creativity there is in the universe.

In this heaven, you develop the fifth heavenly perfection—*The Perfection of Service*. The spirit of giving and philanthropic work on Earth is strongly supported by the inspiration and support of the fifth heaven. The perfection of service is "the law of giving." Spirit by its nature gives. Physical life is completely dependent on the life of spirit to survive.

Awakening to the Higher Life : ILLUSTRATION 6.1 (page 104)

The Temple of Healing : ILLUSTRATION 7.1 (page 118)

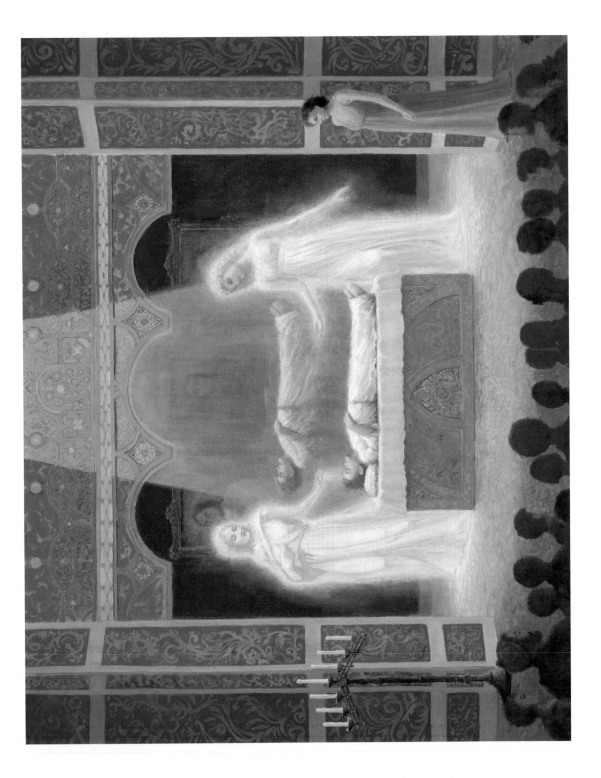

Dropping the Personality Ego : ILLUSTRATION 7.2 (page 123)

Enlightenment and the Temple of Love : ILLUSTRATION 8.1 (page 131)

Mind Over Matter : ILLUSTRATION 9.1 (page 140)

Reconciling Past Lives : ILLUSTRATION 9.2 (page 144)

The Mystic Marriage : ILLUSTRATION 9.3 (page 147)

Entering Spiritual Etheria : ILLUSTRATION 10.1 (page 160)

Spirit gives; the physical takes. You experience how this spirit of giving is inherent in all life, but not everyone expresses selfless service equally because there is free will. One must choose to give out of love, not by force or coercion. The story of the Archangel Lucifer who became the Satan transgressed because he refused to be of service and wanted to be his own god. This story reveals that you can never take the act of service for granted no matter how spiritually developed you are.

As you climb to the pinnacle of the fifth heaven, you are in many ways the divine being you were born to be. You are aligned with the infinite life and immersed in the divine presence. As you are prepared for the sixth heaven, you will continue the work you have been doing in ever more beautiful and grand ways.

THE KINGDOM OF THE SPIRIT LIGHT—
THE SIXTH HEAVEN

As the soul ascends to the sixth heaven, the glory of spirit evokes new revelations. With the achievement of five heavenly perfections, you are ever more confident in what you are capable of doing. In this realm, your work with the angels and archangels deepens. They have been such an indispensable support all along. You could not have reached this point without their steadfast help. The more you get to know the spiritual hierarchy, the more wondrous and mysterious they become. Your relationships with your fellow human travelers mature even further. You are constantly surprised at the beauty and grandeur of the human experience.

In this heaven, the power of love becomes an overriding theme. More than ever, you recognize that love, in its infinite variety, is the driving force of creation. Love is life itself, and here you enjoy life more than you ever have. You can hardly wait to embark on the next spiritual adventure.

Now you delve into even grander aspects of the celestial laboratories. You become aware of how suns are created, both spiritually and physically. Behind these suns are the great Central Suns. Tremendous spiritual powers emanate from these suns. With the support of the angels and archangels, you work with celestial beings of such majestic proportions, their very presence is almost incomprehensible. These great ones are called the Solar Logi—regents who embody entire solar systems! Even the planetary spirits take their direction from the Solar Logi. Through the coordinated efforts of the Solar Logi, suns, stars, planets, and moons relate to each other energetically and rhythmically on the physical and spiritual levels. The countless kingdoms of evolutionary life that thrive within a solar system receive love and support from the Solar Logos. The sixth heaven helps coordinate interaction between these many realms.

The name of this heaven—Kingdom of the Spirit Light—refers to the power and mystery that the Solar Logi embody. Their Spirit Light, sometimes referred to as the Elohim, stimulates creative drive. The mystic and clairvoyant Geoffrey Hodson beautifully expressed the majesty of these beings:

> *The Solar Logos is omnipresent and omniscient throughout His solar system…The Logos is power, wisdom, love, beauty, order, glory, knowledge immeasurable…The Sun is His chief physical manifestation, though the whole visible solar system is His physical body… the Solar Logos is also transcendent…sitting above His system…This Supreme Being is referred to by such names as The Most August and Sovereign Lord of Life and Life and Glory…The Inner Ruler Immortal.*[5]

---

[5] *Basic Theosophy: The Living Wisdom*, pages 452-454

In this heaven, you develop *The Perfection of The Infinite Spirit*. This is where the mystery of Spirit is revealed. By now, you have already experienced a profound connection with Spirit through the mystic marriage of spirit and soul, which ushered you into the heaven worlds. Now, a deeper understanding of spirit life emerges that encompasses how your human consciousness is an aspect of Spirit itself. When you were born of God, your immortal soul was clothed in human consciousness. You will be human throughout your evolution, but your human experience does have a beginning, middle, and eventual end. Your soul lives forever, but your soul will not be in a human consciousness forever. One day, the human experience will end and you will enter a higher state of consciousness. So, it is in this heaven that you finally come to terms with the full grandeur and inevitable limitations of being human.

As you ascend to the top of the sixth heaven, you have learned new sacred powers, perfected yourself, and fully embodied the spirit presence that makes you human. This leads you to the pinnacle of the heaven realms.

THE KINGDOM OF THE SEVEN SPIRITS— THE SEVENTH HEAVEN

The seventh heaven oversees and regulates cosmic order and the activities of all the heavens, as well as life on Earth. It is the door to The Kingdom of God. Much has been written about the seventh heaven, some equating it with The Kingdom of God. As grand as this realm is, it is still not Home.

One of the most essential activities of the Kingdom of the Seven Spirits is to organize and distribute the spiritual power rays that guide and direct evolving life. These powers are known as The Seven Rays of Life. The mystic Alice Bailey wrote a great deal about the seven rays. They are the energetic foundation of the evolutionary plan. They flow into every aspect of manifested life. The angels and archangels are empowered because of the hierarchy of Light emanating from the seven rays. While the source of the seven rays is a place greater than the seventh heaven, it is from this heaven that these holy powers are administered.

In the seventh heaven, you bring together all that you have learned and experienced into a grand synthesis. The power is so strong; you have accomplished so much. In the seventh heaven, you experience yet another class of spiritual beings—The Seven Spirits before the Throne. These are seven great celestial regents who govern this realm. Each of these grand spirits embodies one of The Seven Rays of Life. As you evolve through the seventh heaven, you are vested one by one with the holy power from each of the seven rays, which is needed in order to enter The Kingdom of God.

In this heaven, you develop the seventh heavenly perfection—*The Perfection of Humility*. It is a touching tribute that as you ascend to the height of heaven, humility is the cornerstone. Humility is often misunderstood and misinterpreted to mean low in importance. Yet if we are all essential to the divine plan, how can anyone be low in importance? From the spiritual perspective, humility means knowing your place in the cosmic order of life. Life has a hierarchical design arranged by levels of consciousness. The amoeba and the archangel both have the same immortal spark of life, but the archangel has a far more developed level of consciousness. Yet, both have their essential place in the divine plan.

We often fall into the ego trap. We inflate or deflate our importance. We sometimes think we are better than or not as good as others. When we do this, we are not expressing the quality of humility, which throws us out of spiritual alignment. The first great sin humanity committed is said to have been pride. This is when we marveled at our own accomplishments without understanding what made those accomplishments possible. Of course, we want to acknowledge our own efforts, but we need to keep them in perspective. It is the divine presence within us that makes all success possible. When we are prideful and claim the credit, we cut ourselves off from our divine source.

There will always be people further along the path than you and those who are not as far along as you. As the "Desiderata" so beautifully puts it:

If you compare yourself with others, you may become vain or bitter, for always there will be greater and lesser persons than yourself.

In the days of ancient Rome, when a conquering general would parade through the city in triumph and celebration, a slave would stand behind him as he rode in his chariot, holding a golden crown over his head and whispering throughout the procession, "Remember, you are mortal," reminding the hero that all temporal victories are fleeting.

Your talents and accomplishments happen because of your dedicated efforts, but they are not your own. They are the glory of life flowing through you. You cannot claim them as your possessions. If you glorify yourself, you cut yourself off from the Tree of Life and your victory will be short-lived. Glorify God, do the work of life, and the glory of life will flow through you. Humility is one of the greatest virtues because it perpetually connects you to the divine source.

In the seventh heaven, you accumulate the spiritual power needed for taking on the co-creative talents you will express in The Kingdom of God. Your spiritual training and the pilgrimage you have been on are coming to their culmination. In the majesty of your accomplishments, you humble yourself before the Divine, and a spiritual peace deeper than you have ever felt envelops you. You are ready for Home.

Chapter 12

RETURNING HOME—FROM HEAVEN TO GOD

There is a river, the streams whereof shall make glad the city of God, the holy place of the tabernacles of the Most High.
—Psalm 42

ONE MUST LAY down the pen in humility to speak of The Kingdom of God—the fountainhead and wellspring of life. Understanding this kingdom is beyond anything a book can describe, yet we will let divine inspiration be our guide to begin to conceive and understand our return Home.

As vast as the spiritual realms we have explored are, they are all contained within The Kingdom of God. As the prophet Muhammed describes in the story of his night journey to the heavens, "When I gazed upon the throne [of God], then all of what I had seen of God's creation next to the throne became small of mention."[1] The Kingdom of God is the source for all creation. All the streams of life, human as well as all the hierarchies, draw their spiritual nourishment from this realm.

---

[1] *Muhammed's Night Journey,* primitive version.

As you enter Home, you are now in the heart of love. You are the prodigal son and daughter returning to your parents' house from distant lands. You find yourself in an environment that can only be described as royal, noble, and majestic. There are hallowed halls, sacred palaces, and holy realms. The laws of nature flow in their primordial state, and you experience nature's inner sanctum.

All the hierarchies come together in joyful oneness. There are celestial regents and hierarchies who are the immortal ministers of God. The originating designs for creation, including the design for humanity and the master architects of human civilization, are found here. You are at the fountainhead of life, the holiest of holies, where creativity issues forth, where Divine Light issues forth, where spiritual tone issues forth, where Divine mind and Divine love issue forth.

You inhabit this kingdom in the most glorious celestial body you have ever had. This is the body you had before you left The Kingdom of God to begin your pilgrimage. It has waited for your return and supported you along the journey, connecting you to Home no matter where you were on the path. All seven perfections you worked so hard to attain, the enlightenments, the talents, the union with spirit now pay off in untold ways. You realize you needed every step of your spiritual ascent to become a citizen in this kingdom. You now understand why it took so long and why you suffered and made many mistakes. All the things that seemed incomprehensible are now comprehensible. You dreamt of this moment and now you are here. There's an inner song of creation. You are in the most beautiful, loving place you have ever experienced.

You enter Home with your soul mate—the love of your life. The reason the Divine brought the two of you together was to share in the pilgrimage so that you wouldn't be alone. In the great adventure, you both loved and supported one another. You shared the joys, sorrows, successes, failures, tragedies, and triumphs. Now that the pilgrimage is coming to its completion, your time together has come full circle. You understand that union with God will mean the end of your relationship as soul mates. There is a touch of sadness, even here, because you know there are other experiences, other souls, and other adventures to go on. You are meant to experience other bonds of fellowships and relationships. Of course, your love for each other will always be there, yet the cycle of union has completed itself. You go through a type of farewell while also preparing for the ultimate glory.

THE DIVINE REUNION

Once acclimated to this divine place, you are prepared for the great moment of meeting God. The angels and archangels are with you for support. To begin, you are ushered into what is called The Throne Room of God. This is a term for a conscribed area of space where you can make direct contact with Deity—a place where a portion of God can descend upon you. The throne is said to be of a beautiful emerald-green color indicating balance and harmony. This throne is like the hub of a wheel; all the Divine Light we have been receiving emanates from The Throne of God.

You enter the outer sanctuary of the Throne with many others who were part of your life wave and have reached the ultimate state as you have. Now you are back together to share in the glory. They are your brothers and sisters in Light. In the outer sanctuary of this Throne, there are celestial hosts in prayer, worship, and song. You join in the singing. This song will forever stay in your heart from this moment forward: It is the song of God.

When the moment of moments, the goal of goals, the ultimate culmination of your entire pilgrimage happens, you stand before The

Throne of God. A portion of God then descends upon you and you behold the Ultimate. This intimate, one-on-one experience of God is not initially perceptual or mental even though you are one with God-mind and its inspirational flow. You do not see or hear God, yet your celestial senses are keenly alert. You experience the glory of God's presence and the beingness of God and life. This is love eternal, and through love, the inner true consciousness and essence is communicated to you and you communicate back. A new relationship with Deity is born, forever engraved on your soul. The experience of being embraced by God envelops the entirety of you. The mystery of the infinite is revealed. It is the greatest moment of your life.

As you orient yourself in the sublime moment, you delve deeper and merge into the mind of God. As the Divine describes it, you experience the mental workings of the Creator (as much as human consciousness will allow). This leads you to a sense experience of God. You are seeing the source of seeing, hearing the source of hearing. Light, sound, and form merge together in a unified whole. Through this merging into the mind and heart of God, a secret of consciousness is revealed. Your spiritual ascent was a journey in consciousness, which brought you to this ultimate understanding.

As you complete what cannot be put into words, you realize that you were always part of God but now in a more conscious and direct way. This presence will never leave you, even after you leave the Throne Room. Wherever you go, whatever you do, this presence remains. You have "seen" God. You are anointed. The seal of God is emblazoned in your aura. It doesn't matter where you go in creation to serve; you have attained the glory of being human, the glory of being made in God's image and likeness.

Eventually, you leave the Throne Room to bask in the celestial beauty of what you have experienced. You will return to this throne room again to deepen even further your experience of God. This union with the Divine completes the spiritual ascent Home. Yet, your human experiences are far from over. Upon your celestial anointing, you are now a co-creator with the Divine. As a co-creator, you will begin a new phase of service. You will experience deeper aspects of the heart and mind of God and new dimensions of the Divine Light. The possibilities are infinite.

WORKING WITH SOULS
FROM THE KINGDOM OF GOD

It has been a great honor to clairvoyantly work with human souls from The Kingdom of God. They play an important role supporting us here in physical life. I have worked with many of these souls over the years. These Immortal Ones have seen the glory of God and realized the fullness of their human potential. They have traveled the spiritual path we are travelling on now and have reached the spiritual pinnacle we are striving to reach. Their perfection is inspiring but can be intimidating as you realize how much further you need to go in your spiritual journey.

When I teach classes, I can clairvoyantly see the Higher working with students even though they aren't consciously aware of what is going on. In one memorable session, I had a student who was new to metaphysics. He was interested in learning about the spiritual life but had a problem with the topic of God. He had challenging experiences in the religion he was bought up in, so he resisted anything that sounded religious. During this session, a magnificent being came into the room. She had exquisitely beautiful features, wore powder blue robes, and radiated extraordinary, brilliant Divine Light.

As I tuned into her aura, I saw the sacred signature of God. I knew this was a human soul from The Kingdom of God. While she blessed all the students, she focused on helping the man who was having trouble accepting God. She came close to him, sending spiritual light to his heart chakra. He was unaware of what was happening. I didn't say anything, but it was clear he was feeling the Light. She stayed for a while and then gracefully left. This marked a turning point for him. Over the next weeks and months, he had a turnaround in his attitude. He began to separate his distressing experiences of the past from his unfolding spiritual power and started to redefine God for himself.

ASSIMILATION AND THE GREAT REBIRTH

What is the ultimate? After untold ages serving the Divine co-creatively in The Kingdom of God, when your services are complete, God ushers you back to the source you came from before you were born as a human soul—The Unknown Root of Existence. The cosmic story comes full circle. You are reabsorbed into the Sea of Life for rest and assimilation, eventually to prepare for another cosmic day, another pilgrimage, on a higher level of existence. The Hindu mystical tradition refers to this rest time as *pralaya* or dissolution. Yet this is not a dissolution into nothingness. Your soul—the individualized spark of life that is you—goes on during this period of rest from the activities of life.

After an eternity of pralaya in which the soul has rested and replenished itself and absorbed all that it went through, it will be ready to reemerge in a new cosmic birth. The cycle will begin anew, but not in a human consciousness. Our soul will eventually be reborn in a higher state of awareness and bring everything it accumulated in its human pilgrimage into a new adventure in the consciousness we call angelic.

New horizons in eternity await, new wonders to behold. We will discover new ways to live, love, and create. The glories of life will reveal yet deeper mysteries to solve.

Praise God for this glorious path, praise life, praise all that is good. You are part of this immortal process. Do everything you can to live a sacred, holy, noble life. It will lead you to glories yet untold.

PART

3

_____

Pitfalls on the Path

Chapter 13

YOUR ASCENT IS NOT A STRAIGHT LINE UPWARD

If you don't know where you're going, any road can take you there.
—Alice in Wonderland

As you climb the spiritual ladder, it is hoped that the ascent is smooth and steady. And more often than not, the soul is making spiritual progress and evolving through the various dimensions of life. Yet there are times when the soul resists the divine impulse and ends up losing rather than gaining spiritual ground. We have all had lifetimes when we evolved beautifully, but also have had lifetimes in which we didn't. This is an inevitable part of the growing process. The big picture of your ascent looks a little like a stock market graph—up and down. This goes on for some time until the soul fully commits to the spiritual ascent and makes the consistent effort to do what it takes to grow to the heaven worlds.

In this section, we look at what can throw off your spiritual growth, what happens when you lose spiritual ground, and how you can eventually reclaim your spiritual heritage.

We all start an incarnated life vibrating on a spiritual level that corresponds to one of the spiritual dimensions we have explored and earned. For example, a soul may incarnate on the vibration of the sixth degree of the fourth astral plane. As the soul fulfills its purpose and potential, it will finish its incarnation with more spiritual power than when it started. This spiritually evolves the soul. But if a soul creates a life of heartache and misery for itself and others, it may lose enough spiritual power to unintentionally step downward and complete that lifetime at a *lower* spiritual level than when it started.

Some people do a better job of cooperating with the plan than others. There are some who don't even call themselves spiritual and yet are doing a good job spiritually because they are *living* truth with integrity. There are also spiritual egotists who think they are better than others because they have acquired some spiritual knowledge but aren't actually living those truths. Ironically, those souls are not spiritually progressing. The objective in any incarnated life is to pursue the spiritual path with conscious intent *and* live your truth with integrity. You are not forced to walk the spiritual path; it's something you choose to do.

WHAT CAN CAUSE YOU TO
FALL OFF THE SPIRITUAL PATH?

———

In broadest terms, you fall off the path when you seriously break spiritual laws. You may not always be consciously aware of these laws, but all of us are bound by them. Spiritual laws are not arbitrary or created; they are impartial and self-existent. Break these laws and we fall out of step until we learn and correct those mistakes. In the aura, breaking a spiritual law is clearly visible. Any thought, emotion, action, or word that creates unenlightened energy in the aura is destructive and counter to spiritual laws.

Sometimes, we want rationalize missteps because we want to keep doing them. Maybe we enjoy what we're doing and don't want to stop. Yet, we are all answerable to the same laws of life. As a spiritual aspirant, you want to know the truth. You want to understand your motivations for your actions. You want to see things clearly, uncolored by your own opinion. Even if the truth stings at first, that is temporary. Truth will set your feet on the upward path Home. So, take responsibility for your own actions, right or wrong.

The following conditions can cause a soul to lose spiritual power and possibly devolve:

1. Actions that create unenlightened energies in the aura.
2. Actions that create unenlightened energies and destructive karmic conditions.
3. Actions that create unenlightened energy and karmic conditions.

We all make mistakes. No one is perfect, and most of us have auras that are mixed with both enlightened and unenlightened colors. This doesn't mean one is devolving. For example, if someone gets very angry, they will generate a vitiated red energy in their aura. This is not a pretty color to clairvoyantly see. it does cause that person to lose valuable Light, but it doesn't mean they are devolving. it just means they have to let go of that anger and release that negative energy.

Actions that create destructive karmic conditions are different. This occurs when someone initiates a destructive action but feels the effect at a later time. For example, let's say someone was mean and hurtful in a romantic situation. Perhaps they were good-looking or in a socially advantageous position and seemed to "get away" with their hurtful actions. Because they didn't immediately feel the effects of their misdeeds, they kept doing it. This generates negative energy in the aura but also creates a destructive effect in the fabric of life. Then years later, they find themselves in a very different situation. Maybe they've lost some of their looks or their socially advantageous position. Now they may be genuinely looking for romantic love—longing for it, even—but cannot find it. This could be a karmic condition presenting itself to teach the soul the value of love and affection.

Actions that devolve the soul take destructive outcomes to a greater extreme. Generally speaking, intentional, accumulated, and sustained negative actions over time start the downward spiral, especially if there is no recognition or contrition. In these situations, the destructive actions are causing the person to consistently lose spiritual light. And without the needed spiritual power, the person can lose spiritual ground. It isn't easy to fall off the path; it requires a stubbornness in a negative direction over time. Usually, a single destructive act won't cause enough spiritual light to be lost to devolve unless it's particularly heinous. Those who commit cold-blooded murder, for example, can start the process of devolving, especially if they don't see the error of their ways and do nothing to redeem themselves.

Fortunately, we have had many more progressive lifetimes of growth than lifetimes of missteps. The problem is that when we do go through the experience of losing spiritual ground, it takes time to recover. These situations can be dramatic, such as tyrants or ruthless leaders in any field of endeavor who exhibit sustained cruelty, murder, and so on. Those who have more modest spiritual falls can redeem themselves more quickly. Either way, the key is whether the aura reaches a "tipping point" that then creates the devolving situation.

RECLAIMING YOUR SPIRITUAL HERITAGE

No matter how far a soul may fall, there is no such thing as eternal damnation. While a soul may do terrible things, it is still the same eternal soul. No matter how misguided or evil certain actions may be, the core of the soul remains intact. The inherent divinity and goodness are always there, even if camouflaged for a time. Because of this inherent goodness, all souls eventually turn back to the Light even if it takes a long time to get there.

This is the nature of compassion: the ability to see the divine spark in yourself and those around you regardless of the face a person may wear. While it's a disturbing truth that one could lose so much Light in a single lifetime, the saving grace is that not all is lost. At some point after a soul falls, it "wakes up" to the truth and begins the slow, sometimes painful process of retracing its footsteps and reclaiming lost spiritual ground. This is the process of redemption back into the Divine Light. As it starts its evolutionary climb once again, the soul draws on its spiritual heritage and gradually reclaims it former status. Fortunately, retracing one's footsteps back through the spiritual realms is a much faster process than when first climbing the ladder, because the soul is reigniting spiritual steps already taken.

You may know of someone who is taking the wrong road in life and doing things that create negative energy for themselves while hurting others. Pray for them. See them as the divine beings they are and do what you can to lend a helping hand. Encourage them to turn their life around—it's never too late to start. If you recognize destructive actions or behaviors in you, don't despair. Refuse to condemn yourself. You can rebuild your spiritual energy at *any* stage of your life. Rather than rationalize wrong actions, take responsibility and correct those actions. Do everything you can to set things right.

A Story of Spiritual Redemption

To illustrate the process of losing spiritual ground and redemption, I will tell a story shared by the Higher from *The Book of Life*. The story takes place ages ago during the dynastic period in Egypt around 2000 BCE about a woman who incarnated from the causal world. She was a spiritually developed soul and was born into a mystical family. Her parents were part of a mystery school—training centers in the ancient world where aspirants were educated in the "mysteries of life." At that time, Egypt had some of the best mystery schools in the world. She was born with awakened spiritual gifts such as clairvoyance but had not yet learned to harness those powers. In addition to being spiritual, her family was wealthy and had connections to the royal court. She had brothers and sisters but seemed to be the most talented, spiritually speaking. While she had many interests, she knew from an early age that metaphysics was her life path. She began her esoteric training early and grew up to be an attractive, smart, and creative woman.

This was a difficult time in Egypt as groups had sprung up that practiced black magic. Their aim was to subvert the use of spiritual power for anything good and to misuse that power for their own selfish gain. Some of these black magic groups had infiltrated the Egyptian priesthood and held influence in the court of the pharaoh. Ruthless and ambitious, they would stop at nothing to achieve their goals.

As part of their subversive work, they were always on the lookout for young, talented souls they could seduce and use. They spotted the woman in our story as a candidate for the dark arts. She was in her early twenties and had not yet gone through the spiritual trials for her enlightenment. At this point, there was a proud side to her as she had fallen into the trap of thinking she was better than others. She also had a weakness for glamour and was attracted to the power of the royal court. She saw her parents being passed over for important positions because they wouldn't compromise their ethics. This bothered her, and she thought she could do a better job of outsmarting the royals at their own game. She realized that by following the path of her parents, she would live a life of service and never hold temporal power.

One of the leaders of an influential black magic group approached her one day. He began to flatter her and was able to find her emotionally vulnerable areas. He understood her angst and started to weave his black magic on her. She knew who he was and thought she could handle him, but he was too clever and she fell under his spell. He promised her power and prestige—more than what the mystery school she was part of could give. She didn't share what happened with her parents or anyone in the mystery school, although they picked up that something was troubling her.

Though it may sound strange, even one who has climbed the spiritual ladder can fall prey to the temptations of the personality ego. One can enjoy the inflated ego and the seduction of the "Left Hand Path" while not understanding the dire consequences. When you step into these dark waters, they quickly envelop you, giving you no time to think clearly. Such decisions have no rationale because the illumined mind is not in charge.

Her spiritual fall happened quickly. She soon made the fatal decision to leave the mystery school and join the black magic order. Her parents were shocked, but she was now hypnotized by the black magician. Her family could do little to stop her, and they were heartbroken. After she was initiated, her spiritual descent quickened.

This dark order was close to the pharaoh and she gained the trust of the royal court. She became intoxicated with power and started using her talents to disrupt, make sick, or even kill perceived opponents. She was good at this, well-trained by the evil souls she had partnered with. And because she was still young with a charming demeanor, few suspected she carried such evil intentions. She continued to attain influence and power but completely lost touch with her family. Those who dealt with her understood how rotten she had become. She didn't live long in that incarnation and was eventually killed by an enemy while still in her thirties.

Where does a soul go after such a devolving lifetime? In her case, she had lost so much spiritual power that she plummeted from the enlightened causal world she came from to the netherworlds. These are regions in the lower astral worlds where devolved souls go who cannot be part of the normal reincarnation process until they learn their lessons and work their way out of those dismal places. The netherworlds aren't hell, but they have a hellish feel to them.

In this fallen state, she was not initially aware of her own misdeeds. Her mind was still saturated by the evil that had engulfed her. Making matters worse, she was surrounded by others who had also lost spiritual power and fallen. One of the most poignant moments in the evolutionary story happens when a soul reaches a spiritual height, falls, and eventually sees the Light again while still in its self-created darkness. This is one of the hardest lessons a soul can go through: You can never put ego above God.

Once the woman began her climb back into the Divine Light, she began again to incarnate on Earth. Because of the heavy karma she created, the first couple of lives were miserable. In one, she was born a slave into harsh conditions and was mistreated. It was a short life, but during the incarnation she was shown a vision of her previous life as the black magician and understood why her life was so difficult. In another life, she was born into poverty but had loving parents and a family. Despite such difficult lives, she was starting to pay back her karmic debts and regain spiritual momentum. She then went through several lifetimes to pay back karma to specific people she had hurt.

Then it came time to rebuild her talents and gifts. She had creative lifetimes to express herself, which gave her a lot of joy. When she regained her character and strength, she was ready to rebuild her mystical life. This took a couple of more lifetimes. In one incarnation, she joined an ashram in India to start developing herself spiritually. She eventually reached a point when she was ready to reawaken her mystical powers and build her energy all the way back to the causal world.

The redemptive life that brought her back into her spiritual status was once again in Egypt during a better time in Egypt than in centuries past. In this incarnation, she came back as a male child into a good family of merchants who were well off but not wealthy. She wasn't born with clairvoyant powers, but she did have spiritual visions. Eventually, as a young adult, she was asked to join a mystery school. While her parents in this life were not particularly spiritual, they recognized the value of the mystery tradition. She took to the teachings quickly without any yearning for temporal power or influence. She was very happy learning as much as she could about metaphysics, serving, and helping those less fortunate than herself. She became known for her goodness and trustworthiness. It took many years, but slowly she began to rebuild her mystical powers, finally regaining her clairvoyance as an older individual. She lived a long life and was able to pass the initiations she failed so many centuries ago. As part of those rituals, she had to confront evil once again to prove she could not be seduced, and this time passed her trials beautifully.

She completed her incarnation honored and revered. People would say she never complained and was always ready to lend a helping hand. Not only did she reclaim her spiritual power; she became a more beautiful soul than she had ever been, looking forward to the spiritual journey that lay ahead.

FALSE PROPHETS

Not everything labeled "spiritual" is, in fact, spiritual. Part of your job on the spiritual path is to recognize true mystical teachings/teachers from false ones. As more people are interested in spiritual development, more false teachings will pop up. You must be discerning.

False prophets are souls who profess to help you in your spiritual climb, but in truth are either self-deluded or out to take advantage of you. The Bible warns of those who pretend to come in the name of God to mislead souls: "Beware of false prophets, which come to you in sheep's clothing, but inwardly they are ravening wolves. Ye shall know them by their fruits."[1] Unfortunately, such people are flourishing today and many of those searching for the Divine fall prey to their influence.

There are different kinds of false prophets. Some are simply out for monetary gain. They use their charisma and will power to wield influence. Then there are those who have spiritual talents but misuse them. Sometimes, this is done unintentionally. They are under a self-delusion that they really are a spiritual teacher when they aren't. The worst kinds of false prophets are those who have spiritual talents and use that talent to deliberately mislead souls with malicious intent.

Why do people get caught by false prophets? There are many reasons. Some are lonely and looking for company or community. Others may be weak-willed or want to prove something. Still others may have experienced difficulties or tragedies and are in a vulnerable place. False groups can give those with low self-esteem an inflated self-image of themselves. And still more may be looking for a quick and easy way to enlightenment. The list is endless.

---

[1] *Matthew 7:15*

When looking to study a teaching or work with a spiritual teacher, it's essential to first look at your own motives for pursing a particular path. Once you understand your motivation, look at the teachings and teacher. My advice is to always put a spiritual teaching to the test. Refuse to accept things at face value. Honor the spiritual teacher but recognize that a teacher, no matter how good, is still human. You will attract a teaching according to your own vibration. Ultimately, you best honor the teacher by honoring the teachings through your own applied experience.

An Encounter with a Trance Medium

I have always been cautious when encountering things of a psychic nature. There are those who are good and sincere in their psychic skills and others who are questionable. People often think of me as psychic because I can see auras. While I do have awakened psychic senses, I tell people I'm not a psychic. I use *mystic* clairvoyance when reading an aura, which is completely different from the psychic.[2]

Years ago, I had a student, young and impressionable, who was enamored with psychic phenomena. Unfortunately, she misunderstood my talents and thought they were psychic. She was hoping that I could teach her to be clairvoyant. Even though I emphasized the importance of spiritual development, she only half heard. I cautioned her of the dangers of the psychic world, but my words did not make an impression. One time, she invited me to join her to see a popular trance medium who was conducting an evening event at a spiritualistic church in Pasadena, California. She wanted my clairvoyant opinion as to his integrity and skill. I reluctantly agreed.

---

[2] For an explanation of the difference between the psychic and the mystical, please see our book, *Communing with the Divine.*

A trance medium is different from a psychic medium. A psychic medium is someone who receives thoughts, images, or messages from the psychic world and relates those messages to you. He or see is often in communication with a spirit from the other side, acting as the medium through which those messages are transmitted. In this scenario, the medium is consciously aware and in control of what he or she is saying.

A trance medium takes things a step further. The psychic goes into a trance state and isn't conscious of what is going on. During the trance, a spirit from the other side takes control of the medium's bodily functions including the voice and physical movements. It is now the spirit, or "the control" as they are called, who is speaking through the medium. The idea is that you are talking directly to the spirit through the medium. There can be a dramatic transformation, as the voice and physical mannerisms of the medium change as the spirit takes over. The challenge is that you don't really know who or what you are dealing with because you can't see the spirit. When the session is over and the medium comes out of the trance, he or she usually isn't aware of what happened and must be told by others.

And so I went with my student to observe the trance medium. The church was packed, as this figure was popular. He was a tall, good-looking man in his fifties with a charming way about him. He wasn't married, and women clearly liked him. He had been doing this for several years and developed quite a following. He claimed to be channeling an enlightened soul from the days of Atlantis.

As the evening began, the medium went into trance and spirit took over. The medium's mannerisms and speech patterns changed. Then the spirit began talking of various spiritual topics, coming across as fairly reasonable and logical, which I'm sure was part of the appeal. He was animated in his speech and presentation. The audience was galvanized. The medium had an assistant who was helping to orchestrate the session.

After a while, the medium started answering personal questions from audience members. He seemed to have a psychic awareness of people's lives. He knew about their relationships, jobs, and financial status, which left everyone—including my student in awe.

At events like these, my habit is to sit in the back of the room in case I need to leave before the session is over. The session had been going on for about thirty minutes when I decided I wanted to know who the control was. Who was the spirit working through this man? I have a way of sending spiritual light, so I could then clairvoyantly see what was happening. As I focused the Light on the medium, I tuned into the spirit who was standing next to him and, instead of an enlightened soul, I saw a grotesque, lowly soul with menacing light around him. It is always regrettable to clairvoyantly see things like this because you want to see the best in people, yet I wasn't surprised. This was not my first time seeing such entities. He was a masquerading spirit pretending to be someone he was not.

As I was shining the Light on the entity, he became aware of what I was doing and became clearly distressed. A few minutes later, to my great surprise, the medium got up while still in full trance and under the control of the entity and walked all the way down the aisle to the back of the room where I was sitting. No one had any idea what was going on. He leaned over close to me so no one could hear and, speaking through the medium, whispered, "Withdraw your light. What do you expect coming from a drunkard like this?!"

I could hardly believe what I was hearing. This entity understood who and what he was, and he was telling me that the medium was no saint. His tone showed that he had no respect for the medium he was working through. Obviously, I couldn't stay and left with my baffled friend. Later, I described what had happened. I shared with her that while these masquerading spirits can know something about you, their aim is not to help. Their deceptions, half-truths, and outright lies aim to draw you in. They do this to filch spiritual energy from the audience. The entire show is a diversion from the spiritual path, what I call "the circus floor." She was dumbfounded but understood and fortunately realized that one must be very careful in dealing with psychic matters.

A Tragic Story of a False Prophet

In another encounter with a false prophet, I knew a woman, Claire, who was involved with the infamous Jim Jones group. The drama of Jim Jones and the "Jonestown Massacre" is an especially tragic event in modern America history and one that still baffles people today. Jones was a cult leader who became influential in the San Francisco area. He started a group called the Peoples Temple by practicing what he called an "apostolic socialism." He gained popularity, but stories gradually leaked out about his maniacal behavior and mistreatment of followers. To avoid growing pressure, he relocated his group to Guyana and started a communal living group known as Jonestown. While proclaiming utopia, the actual living conditions were far from ideal, and life there spiraled from bad to worse. Concerned relatives and mysterious deaths prompted California state representative Leo Ryan to inspect Jonestown. While in Guyana, he was killed by members of the cult. Knowing that the authorities were closing in and in a deteriorated mental and physical state, Jones ordered his followers to commit "revolutionary suicide." Nine hundred men, women, and children killed themselves by drinking cyanide-laced punch.

Claire, who was married with three children, attended my classes in Los Angeles. She told me she was part of the Jim Jones group; at the time, it was still based near San Francisco. She talked about him and the group in glowing terms. As she did, I was looking at her aura and could sense something seriously wrong. I wasn't familiar with Jones at the time, but I could see that she was in trouble. She invited me to travel with her to San Francisco to meet him. I was getting the inspiration to help her and so I accepted the invitation. The drive from Los Angeles to San Francisco takes hours, so I planned to stay at a local hotel while she stayed with family in the area.

We went to his gathering which was more like a rally. There were hundreds of people and a lot of excitement and anticipation. When he walked onto the stage, I took one look at his aura and could hardly believe the dark and menacing energies around him. He clearly had been involved in bad things, including murder, and I immediately understood why I was inspired to take this trip and help Claire get out. As he started his talk, he began to create a hypnotic energy in the room bordering on the hysterical. As a clairvoyant, I'm sensitive to vibrations, and the wild chaotic energies he was projecting were more than I could stand. I didn't tell her what I was seeing but said I needed to leave and asked her to join me. I just couldn't comprehend what Claire saw in him. Bewildered and embarrassed, she decided to stay, so I left on my own.

As I was walking out, a guard at the door was blocking my exit. In an intimidating voice, he exclaimed, "Nobody leaves a Jim Jones rally!"

I looked at him straight in the eyes and said, "You wanna bet? Watch me!" And I marched right out of there.

I went back to my hotel room. Later that night, Clair and I talked on the phone. I didn't quite know how to explain what I saw, so I decided to just be loving and direct. I told her how much I cared for her and wanted what was best. I warned her that Jones was not what he seemed and implored her to take her children and husband and leave. She respected me as a spiritual teacher but was surprised and offended at my impression of Jones. She was under the spell Jones had cast and completely rejected my advice, saying, "You don't know what you're talking about, Barbara!" I pleaded with her again to think about her children and what was best for them. She would have none of it.

I had no choice but to drive back to Los Angeles alone. Once back, I tried reaching Claire but never heard from her again. She stopped taking classes and stopped all communications. Not long after, Jones took his followers to Guyana. When the tragedy happened, it made the news. I was worried and tried to reach her again to see if she was okay. I couldn't get a hold of her but did make contact with a friend who told me the tragic story.

Claire did go down to Guyana with her family, and what's worse is that she convinced a friend and her friend's family to join the group. While Claire was in Guyana, her aunt died, leaving her an inheritance. Jones directed her to go back to the States so she could collect the money and bring it back. While back in California, the tragedy happened. Claire's entire family—her husband and three children—and the family she introduced to Jones, all died by taking the cyanide-laced drink.

How can reasonable people fall prey to such deception? In the case of Claire, she was a good person, but I think she couldn't conceive that such evil could exist. She was naïve and put blind faith in Jones— essentially letting someone else do the thinking for her and then lacking the willpower to break loose when the evidence told a different story. A type of hypnosis takes over that can be hard to break.

No one is immune to these temptations. God allows these pitfalls to exist as a challenge and a test. The Divine wants you to learn to recognize the true from the false through first-hand experience because the dangers are very real. When dealing with spiritual matters, don't "rush in where angels fear to tread.[3]" Evolution is a *gradual* process, not

---

[3] Alexander Pope, *An Essay on Criticism*.

an overnight phenomenon. Anyone who promises otherwise is either misinformed or a false prophet. Your job is to do the best you can to see through these spiritual traps and tricks. When you do, you gain a tremendous spiritual advantage and progress even quicker along the path.

Chapter 14

THE NETHERWORLDS

No human being is so bad as to be beyond redemption.
—Mahatma Gandhi

*I*N MY WORK as a spiritual teacher, I am often given specific assignments by the Higher to help those on the other side. In a way, I live two lives: as a teacher in physical life during the day and as a teacher in the spiritual worlds at night. Early in my career and during one of these nighttime, inner world travels, I was taken to a place I had never been before. I was in a modest building, and while it wasn't a temple or a training center, it was clearly a place of the Holy Ones. The Divine Light was there but also a melancholy vibration. The celestial being who brought me here said they had taken me to the netherworlds and that this was a sanctuary where they helped souls spiritually wake up. I knew these were dark and dismal regions and I was apprehensive, but the celestial being told me not to worry. He put a cloak of Light around us to protect and conceal our energy so we wouldn't disturb the people who were here and then took me outside to show me around.

We were in what appeared to be a simple, small-town setting. (I was to later learn that these structures were built specifically for netherworld inhabitants to give them a place to live.) It was nighttime and there was little light to illuminate our way. Now outside the safety of the sanctuary, I could feel the sad, tragic nature of this place much more intensely. People were wandering around in a sort of preoccupied daze. In their semi self-awareness, there was also a type of social order as some of the souls were interacting with each other. Some interactions were mildly affectionate while others were confrontational.

As we walked about, my celestial guide took me into one of the structures: an opium den! Here was a group of people indulging themselves and clearly enjoying their intoxication without reservation. The feeling in the room was oppressive. My celestial guide saw my incredulous look and told me these souls had been consumed by opium on Earth and were continuing their activity here on the other side. They identified with the patterns of behavior that brought them here.

The tragic feeling this place evoked is hard to describe. My heart went out to these people. They were souls like you and I, and it was distressing to see such conditions exist. I asked what could be done to help them. My guide said that these souls weren't doomed to stay here. The Holy Ones were working diligently to wake them up, but it was a difficult task. They often don't want to be awakened and resist any effort, sometimes violently. Some only stay a short time, while others have been here a while and need more time. Moments later, the visit ended, and the divine one took me out. While this first trip to the netherworlds was about learning the dynamics of such a place, later I would be taken back to help uplift these souls. I understood how difficult the task was and yet how valuable and essential.

In order to understand the spiritual realms and all they encompass, we must also turn our attention to the netherworlds, also called the "astral hells." The word "nether" means *down* or *under*, so netherworld is a term for what the ancients called the underworld. From a metaphysical perspective, the netherworlds are where souls go when they have lost so much spiritual light that they have forfeited the right to participate in the normal evolutionary process. One devolves to these realms because of serious misdeeds. Souls who find themselves in the netherworlds aren't being punished; they are there because they don't have enough spiritual power to go anywhere else. You might call the netherworlds a type of spiritual holding area where the angels help them understand what has happened, to help them get back on spiritual track.

No one stays in these astral hells forever. There is no such thing as eternal damnation without hope of redemption. This is a necessary but unnatural situation that cannot last indefinitely. No matter what the soul has done or how far it has fallen, eventually it will find its way back home.

THE ANIMAL, BEAST, AND BRUTE NETHERWORLD KINGDOMS

There are three netherworld realms in descending order of vibration: the animal, beast, and brute kingdoms. Based on the destructive actions and the spiritual light lost, souls can find themselves in any one of these three kingdoms. They relate to the first three lower astral worlds. However, netherworld souls don't participate in the normal evolutionary flow. They aren't among the group of younger souls who are evolving through these astral realms. The netherworlds are partitioned off areas and of a very different vibration.

The Animal Netherworld Kingdoms

The first of these descending realms is the *animal netherworld kingdoms*. The term "animal" in this context has nothing to do with animals. Animals are in their own kingdom of evolution and have nothing to do with the netherworlds. Being an animal is their nature. The animal netherworlds refer to humans who have regressed into their lower instinctual levels. These netherworlds correlate to the third astral plane and their various sub-planes. You will recall that the third astral plane is where we developed our instinctual nature.

Souls who devolve to these levels have retarded their spiritual growth. They have negated the rational, thinking mind and given in to reckless abandon and their lower instinctual passions. Though consumed in the unbridled dark side of human emotions, they still retain their self-awareness. This makes their situation all the worse as they are consciously directing their thinking to the lowest part of their nature.

In the animal netherworlds, there is the semblance of a social order—almost tribal-like—provided by the Divine. People interact with each other, but feelings of sorrow and hopelessness are pervasive. Sanctuaries are provided by the Higher to help these souls wake up, but it's surprising how often they don't respond to the spiritual call. Sometimes, the Divine will take them to higher realms to try and remind them of where they came from, but this can have a disturbing effect, as they don't identify with who they were before they fell. When a soul does start to see the Light again, there is shock, grief, and remorse. These are the painful yet healing signs that the soul is coming to terms with what it did and ready to begin the journey upward again. There is steady, loving support for as long as it takes to bring these souls back home.

As there are seven sub-planes to each astral plane, there are seven realms within the animal netherworlds. A soul can fall to any of these realms depending on how much spiritual light is lost. When a soul is finally awakened, it is taken out of the netherworlds and the rebuilding process begins. It gradually begins to respond to its own higher nature and the support of the Divine. However, when souls refuse to wake up, they continue to lose Light. This can cause them to fall further down the spiritual ladder—a terrible situation.

What actions can cause you to fall to these realms? In *The Divine Comedy*, Dante went to great efforts correlating specific crimes to specific realms in his conception of hell: the Inferno. Certainly, some actions are more destructive than others. Stealing a loaf of bread is not the same as cold-blooded murder. From the metaphysical perspective, the *depth* and *persistence* of the offense and the amount of Divine Light forfeited determine where one ends up in the netherworlds more than the offense itself.

Watch your emotional nature carefully. Giving in to destructive impulses can literally open yourself up to a hellish vibration—igniting old instinctual energies and doing things you never dreamed you would do. This happens with people who have unquenchable appetites for lust, money, power, and so on. Those who persistently act on these lower impulses lose a lot of spiritual light. And once they transition in this heavy consciousness, they can end up in the animal netherworlds.

The Beast Netherworld Kingdoms

Below the animal netherworlds are the *beast netherworld kingdoms*. These realms correlate to the second astral plane. Souls naturally evolving through the second astral plane are in a beautiful, idyllic innocence.

Those who end up in the beast netherworlds are in a very different situation. This realm is hard to describe. It doesn't resemble the fire and brimstone of traditional pictures of hellish worlds, but it's certainly dark and dreary. There is a lot of suffering as these souls feel the extreme frustration of their actions yet don't comprehend what they have done or why they are there. When souls have fallen this far, the angelic beings have a more difficult job lifting them out.

Those who find themselves in the beast netherworld kingdoms are caught in a type of persistent nightmare. On the second astral plane, you naturally live in the dream mind state. This allows for freedom of mental expression without much consequence. But with devolved souls, the dream state reverts to a nightmare. The reason they call it the beast kingdom is because of the wild, unchecked behavior that happens in this disturbed dream-mind state. There is a perpetual feeling of hopelessness. As with the animal netherworlds, there is a social order and interactions with others and people live in primitive structures. Yet even here, in such darkness, the Divine shines the Holy Light to awaken and uplift.

The Brute Netherworld Kingdoms

Descending from here are the lowest and darkest places of the netherworlds—the *brute netherworld kingdoms*. These realms correlate to the first astral plane, where we started our astral journey eons ago. Young souls in this realm do not yet have an astral body. But for souls who have devolved to the brute kingdoms, the astral body is retained. Those who end up here have exhausted their instinctual lusts and passions and are weighted down by the darkness they've immersed themselves in. They are in an almost comatose state, consumed by the dark vibrations they've accumulated. Yet even here, the Divine is helping souls awaken out of these states and rise up out of these dismal conditions.

THE DEMONIC REALMS AND THE DARKEST PLACES IN CREATION

Are the netherworlds as bad as it gets? Unfortunately, there are worse spiritual realms. The goal here is not to dwell on such darkness but to give a fuller picture of the spiritual journey in all its shades and colors. If ever there was a hell, these regions are it. They are known as *the demonic realms*, below even the lowest astral worlds. Like the netherworlds, they are not part of the divine, evolutionary process. They are partitioned off areas to give space for these souls to work through their evil behavior.

These are the regions of the fallen angels and others who were once high Holy Ones. Just as there are humans who refuse to cooperate with the divine plan, there are angels who refuse to cooperate with the divine plan. These fallen angels have lost an enormous amount of spiritual energy yet still retain their inherent angelic intelligence. And since they have fallen from a greater place than you and I can imagine, they are particularly dangerous.

What can cause someone to fall this far down the spiritual ladder? There is no correlation with the demonic kingdoms to our human character and spiritual growth, which means these souls have connected in some way to demonic, non-human characteristics. If you consciously align with evil during your incarnation and do the bidding of the demons, you can lose so much Divine Light that you find yourself for a time in the demonic realms. Such an experience is truly a fate worse than death. It would teach you to never again take your life, your Divine Light, or your spiritual path for granted.

Souls caught in these realms are essentially "in league with the devil." They are under the control of the evil ones. In these realms, you do not wander around aimlessly; you become part of demonic initiatives. While the netherworlds are chaotic, disorganized places, the demonic worlds are organized and vicious. There is even an organized "inverse" hierarchy of evil souls based on ruthless ambition. The Kabbalah speaks of Qliphoth—The Tree of Death. As The Tree of Life is the path to our eternal home, The Tree of Death is the downward spiral.

The demonic worlds are ruled by overbearing pride, hate, cruelty, and desperation. They are a complete perversion of the creative principle. These souls are so devoid of spiritual light, they have to constantly steal light from others. They are, in a sense, spiritual vampires, constantly usurping Divine Light from anyone they can get to. These fallen ones are cunning. They use everything they have to pursue their demonic initiatives as they have lost their moral compass. The more time souls spend here, the more desperate they become as they start to realize the ultimate futility of their efforts.

Yet again, even here, the same spiritual principles remain. As fallen as these souls are, they are still eternal sparks of life, part of the whole. God still sees them as the divine beings they are despite all the horrible things they do. The way Home is still there for them. Even though they are doing everything they can to thwart the divine plan, to destroy all good in life, they cannot win. For a season, they can seem invincible. But their work is hollow and artificial, and that which is artificial cannot last. Eventually, "every knee shall bend."[1] The Holy Ones have quite a job awakening fallen angels and humans who have found themselves here, yet the Holy Ones have pulled countless souls from these demonic realms, for goodness reigns supreme.

---

[1] *Romans 14:11*

For all those caught in such utter darkness, the light of truth will eventually shine through. The long, long night for those who have self-imprisoned themselves in these regions will end, and the dawn of a new understanding will come. The roots of evil go deep, but in the end, they are like weeds to be cleared out of God's garden. Suffice to say, the very existence of these lower realms reveals how precious our evolution is and how long and hard we have worked to get where we are. It is a privilege to be on the spiritual path—a privilege we can forfeit if we turn our face away from the Divine. Be grateful, then, for all you receive, and never take your spiritual growth for granted. Give thanks for everything in your life, and for all the spiritual opportunities being given to you.

PART

4

Exercises to Accelerate Your Spiritual Development

Chapter 15

YOUR PASSPORT TO ETERNITY IS THE LIGHT YOU EARN

"Do not be afraid of your difficulties. Do not wish you could be in other circumstances than you are. For when you have made the best of an adversity, it becomes the stepping stone to a splendid opportunity."
—H.P. Blavatsky

A
S YOU EXPLORE the incredible journey of your spiritual ascent, you naturally start to wonder where you are in this process and if you are doing all you can to fulfill your potential. These are important questions as it is through your own efforts that you facilitate your spiritual climb. In the spiritual worlds, it's clear where you are in the great ascent. Yet in physical life, such knowledge is generally camouflaged until one awakens the spiritual understanding within. It is by *not* knowing where you are in the journey that you are tested and strengthened in your character and talents. Slowly, through humility, patience, and persistence, the divine life emerges, and your cosmic story unfolds.

There is a key that unlocks your spiritual evolution—the Divine Light. The Divine Light you have earned will carry you through all the ascending planes of consciousness. The most precious thing you possess is your Light; the most important thing you can do is to earn

Divine Light. The more Light you earn, the higher in consciousness you climb. Here in physical life, you are vibrating at a certain level of consciousness based on how much Divine Light you have developed. That vibratory level correlates to a realm which exists in the spiritual worlds. When it's time to cross over to the other side through the portal we call death, you gravitate to the spiritual plane you have earned the right to be on by how much Divine Light you have earned. This is neither a punishment nor a reward—it is like attracting like. If you lived a life of deceit and cruelty, not only have you hurt others and yourself, you have lost spiritual power and won't find yourself in a high spiritual realm on the other side. If you have spent a lifetime serving others, being creative and constructive, then you are earning Divine Light and may find yourself in a higher spiritual dimension. The plane of consciousness you are vibrating on right now is where you presently are in your spiritual ascent.

Here on Earth, there are souls of a wide variety of evolutionary levels, from the spiritual beginner to the mystically advanced. Most souls on Earth today are somewhere on the fourth astral plane, and yet there are souls vibrating on the fifth astral plane and all the way through the third heaven. The key is not to compare yourself with others. Your ascent is not a race; you are on your own spiritual ladder. The goal is to do the best you can for yourself.

If Divine Light is the key to your ascent, how do you build up that Light? There are two basic ways to earn Divine Light. One is through every good word, thought, act, and deed. Every positive, constructive thing you do, recognized or unrecognized, is building up power in your auric field. This power is fueling your spiritual evolution. All the great spiritual traditions emphasize the importance of the quality of one's life. These include The Four Noble Truths and The Eightfold Path of Buddha, The Ten Commandments and The Golden Rule of the Bible,

The Five Pillars of Faith of Islam, Karma Yoga or the law of right action of the Hindu faith, and the Chinese philosophical tradition of Taoism. The common thread that runs through all of them is the importance of personal conduct and integrity. The way you live your life matters. You can't buy your way or talk your way to Heaven. You have to earn it.

The other way to earn Light is by meditating with Divine Light and effectively applying that Light in your life. Through sincere prayer and meditation, you can access the universal life force and draw that energy into your auric field. If you are looking to build your love flow, you can call on the spiritual energy of love, which appears as a beautiful rose-pink light. As you draw that energy into your aura, it blesses you with the consciousness of love. Then as you apply that love in your life, it becomes part of you, and you have strengthened your auric field.

In this chapter, we'll explore some keys to building spiritual power through the way you live your life. Then, in the following chapters, we will offer highly effective meditations to help accelerate your spiritual growth.

First, we will explore the following four qualities. Cultivating each one facilitates the building of divine power in your spiritual journey.

1. Make spiritual growth your priority.
2. Apply truth in everything you do until it becomes wisdom.
3. Pursue quality spiritual education.
4. Transform distresses into blessings.

MAKE SPIRITUAL GROWTH YOUR PRIORITY

The key to success in your spiritual pursuits is motivation and desire for the higher life. When the soul spiritually awakens, a beautiful aqua blue light appears in the auric field. This is an inspiring and uplifting energy. As the awakening soul pursues the spiritual path, this Light brightens. Some people awaken but choose not to follow their spiritual aspirations. They may be afraid or content where they are. This is a shame as a golden opportunity is lost.

You have to make room for the spiritual life to unfold in you. Like starting a new garden, you must clear new ground to plant new flowers. If your life is too busy or you are too preoccupied, it's more difficult for the spiritual life to unfold. As with any goal, you have to set priorities. Make spiritual growth the centerpiece of your life and watch how everything else falls into place. When first acclimating to the spiritual path, there is a "honeymoon period" when you are exploring and having fun in the spiritual playground. In this mode, you are adapting the spiritual life to accommodate the world you know to make it more beautiful and harmonious. Then, as you continue on the spiritual journey and deepen your commitment to the Divine, you learn to adapt your personal life to the divine life. Slowly and gracefully, your life becomes the reflection of the divine life.

A woman in one of my training classes wanted to know how much importance to give to physical activities and how much to spiritual activities. What does that question reveal? An assumption that the two are separate? They are not! There is no physical life and spiritual life; it's *all* spiritual. If you see your spiritual life and earth life as separate things, you are dividing your energy and consciousness. All your activities are part of the great whole: your career, your relationships, even your finances are part of your spiritual journey. Pursue them with equal zeal, and you will build up tremendous spiritual power.

Keep life simple. There are too many choices today and too many things you can do. You have only so much time and energy to expend. A busy life does not necessarily mean a productive or fulfilling life. You want to be economical, accomplishing the most with the least amount of effort. Pace yourself for the long journey, not the quick ride. You will need the full arc of your incarnated life to accomplish all you came to do.

Some people think they have to drop everything to pursue the spiritual life. This is not true. Your spiritual life is with you now. Start right where you are, bettering yourself in your character, relationships, jobs, and activities. You bring your Light wherever you go. As you pursue the higher life, your work life may change as you change. Sometimes friends change as you climb the spiritual ladder. Handle everything with love, common sense, and intelligence. Be kind and considerate. And be ready for the unexpected. Part of the beauty of the divine life is that it's an adventure. And as with any adventure, the best part is that you don't always know what's around the corner!

APPLY TRUTH IN EVERYTHING YOU DO UNTIL IT BECOMES WISDOM

As you walk the spiritual path, many truths will be revealed. This opens the mind to new possibilities and inspirations. Gathering mystical knowledge is exciting, but as the philosopher and mystic Abu Hamid Muhammed al-Ghazali so famously taught, "Knowledge without action is useless." It's essential to illuminate the mind, yet until you actually go through the experiences that knowledge presents, your soul will not grow. The soul only grows through *experience*. As you learn the lessons of experience, they turn into wisdom. Wisdom is earned experience.

To build up spiritual power and ascend, your soul must embody many spiritual truths. This takes time, patience, and persistence. When faced with new opportunities or challenges, it's not always clear what to do. You will inevitably make both right and wrong decisions. Through it all, the soul is absorbing those experiences. As you reach genuine success, you will have learned essential lessons that brought you to that point of accomplishment. You will have gained wisdom in a part of your life, and that wisdom becomes part of the soul. You then carry that wisdom in your heart through the rest of your life and on into the hereafter.

Truth is not truth until it lives in your heart. Focus on living an intelligent, heart-centered life. Even if you are not openly rewarded for the good you do, do good anyway. It will brighten your aura and bless your life. You will bear spiritual fruits according to the degree of your efforts. These fruits are worth every labor and sacrifice as they multiply your joy and fulfillment.

PURSUE QUALITY SPIRITUAL EDUCATION

Today there is a strong desire for spiritual knowledge. With so many people waking up to the spiritual life, there is a thirst for illuminated understanding. The question is how to acquire such knowledge. Like any demanding pursuit, if you want to be successful and good at what you do, you seek skilled training. You go to a school or study with an expert in the field. The same is true for metaphysics. At a certain point in the spiritual climb, when the soul has achieved what it can on its own, it needs the guidance of a qualified spiritual teacher—one who has reached the summit the aspirant is striving to reach.

The question as to whether an aspiring soul needs a spiritual teacher in physical form is a contentious point for many. In today's world, there is a distrust of authority, as it seems to go against the independent spirit. As a result, there are many who are trying to climb the spiritual ladder on their own. They draw knowledge from many different sources and try to forge their own spiritual path. You can do your own growing, yet at a certain point on the spiritual journey, you need a qualified teacher.

The practice of spiritual guidance is a time-honored tradition in all the great metaphysical traditions. In the East, these teachers are called *gurus*. The ancient Greeks called these souls *hierophants*—or revealers of mystic knowledge. These enlightened souls have not only reached a high mystical state, but through long effort, purity of heart and mind, selfless service, and unwavering devotion, they have built a direct communication with the Divine and are ordained by the Divine to serve as spiritual teachers.

A genuine spiritual teacher does not just share knowledge; he or she facilitates spiritual transformation. Under the direction of the teacher, a student learns to awaken the cosmic forces within. Such spiritual training is rigorous. The soul has to be purged of personal ambitions and appetites. The aspiring soul has to gradually loosen and release personal attachments so it can unite with the Divine. There are disciplines to master to prepare the soul for the demands of the enlightened life. There are initiations to pass. Gradually, the aspiring soul passes its tests and achieves illumination and enlightenment. A glorious new life emerges. In my own personal journey, even though I was born with spiritual gifts, I would not be where I am today in my own growth and as a spiritual teacher without the training I received from some exceptionally gifted souls. There is simply too much to learn, too many transformations to go through, for us to patchwork it ourselves.

How do you discern a quality spiritual education? You must use your own best judgement, common sense, intelligence, and intuition when seeking out spiritual training. There are many spiritual teachers and practices, but they are not of the same quality. Some are of a high and inspired order while others are not. Some are outright false and misleading. Ask yourself the following questions: Do these teachings agree with your own moral code? Do they inspire you and bring out the best in you? Your own experience of the teaching will reveal the veracity of their value.

Look also at the integrity of those who present themselves as spiritual teachers. Do they practice the things they are teaching? Do they tend to glorify themselves rather than focus on helping you? Do they make unreasonable demands of your time and resources? Then look at the teacher's background. What was his or her spiritual training? These days, there are many "half-baked" teachers. They have some innate talent or have learned a few things and suddenly decide to present themselves as teachers. Beware of those who say they woke one morning and were spontaneously enlightened. It takes *decades* of training—even with inborn gifts—to be a true spiritual teacher.

Equally important: look within yourself. How dedicated are you to the spiritual task? The Bible teaches, "For many are called, but few are chosen."[1] No matter how great the teachings or how qualified the teacher, if the student isn't dedicated to the task, little progress will be made. Check your motives. Are you pursuing the spiritual path to escape from something, to feel somehow better or more privileged than others? Or are you doing so out of a sincere desire to come closer to the Divine? You will attract a spiritual teacher according to your own intentions and readiness.

---

[1] *Matthew 22:14*

TRANSFORM DISTRESSES INTO BLESSINGS

Healing means change—changing from one condition to another. Healing is one of the cornerstones of the spiritual life. At some point, we all need healing in mind, body, or soul. If some facet of your life is troubled, face that situation and heal it. Don't let troubles linger. The process of transmutation is essential to spiritual growth. You cannot climb the spiritual ladder without the art and science of spiritual healing.

Throughout your evolution, there will always be a need for healing and transmutation. You may not think of yourself as a healer, but if you are walking the spiritual path, healing is a part of that path. So it's important to learn the skills, both physical and spiritual. This doesn't mean you need to become a doctor or a professional healer, but it does mean that you need to understand and apply healing principles. The first step is a willingness to change, not just physical conditions but any conditions you are presented with. Forgiveness is key in healing. Far too much precious time has been wasted holding onto grudges, regrets, angers, and hatred. Become adept at the art of forgiveness. It matters not who made the mistake. By genuinely forgiving, you are freeing yourself of the energy that distressed you.

When there are troubles in our lives, many people tend to look the other way or hide. We see that part of us as unpleasant and to be avoided, not realizing that while this may be a weak link at the moment, it has the potential to become a strength. Refuse to think that there are problems too great to overcome. There is no part of your life that you cannot transform into a blessed experience.

TEN KEYS TO SUCCESS
IN YOUR SPIRITUAL GROWTH

———

When I first started teaching, I was asked by students to outline some keys to growing spiritually. Of course, there are many keys, but if your heart and mind are set in the right direction, you start the momentum of building spiritual power. I have used these keys for many years in my classes. In wrapping up this chapter, I offer them to you to facilitate your spiritual journey.

1) *Imagination*

The ability to imagine is one of our greatest gifts. Imagination is not fantasy; it is the power to envision something that does not yet exist on the physical plane. Through imagination, you can envision your highest self and set the ideal you aspire to.

2) *Intense Spiritual Desire*

Your desire must be strong to succeed on the spiritual path. If your desire is weak, your job is to fan that desire and, over time, make it stronger. Even if you take just one step a day in the right direction, you are moving on the upward spiral of evolution.

3) *Knowledge*

As we have explored, there is a lot to learn about the spiritual life. You need a steady flow of knowledge to be successful. Don't ever be fooled into thinking you have learned it all; there is always more to learn. Mystical knowledge, as well as knowledge in all fields of human endeavor, enriches the soul. We are all perennial students of life.

4) *Affirmative Will*

Willpower is the stabilizer of thought. It holds an idea in place until that idea becomes an expression. If you feel you cannot reach your spiritual goals or that you are somehow not worthy of God's attention, intentionally change that attitude. You have a spiritual potential in this incarnated life. Your attitude needs to be, "I know I will get there!!"

5) *Perseverance*

This is the ability to continue despite difficulties and opposition. Refuse to allow anything to obstruct your determination. Too many on the path get a faint heart and don't go as far as they are capable of. They quit too soon. Take the long view of your spiritual unfoldment. Perseverance leads to results.

6) *Inspiration*

Inspiration is the act of receiving guidance from Divine Mind. It flows like beautiful music. Inspiration is indispensable as you don't walk the path alone. You are constantly being led by the Divine and need to stay open to that guidance. Maintain a state of relaxed readiness for that unexpected moment of divine upliftment.

7) *Enthusiasm*

In addition to desire and will, cultivate enthusiasm to facilitate your spiritual growth. This helps in those moments when situations or others try to discourage you. Enthusiasm is not a blind euphoria that quickly melts away; it is the ability to do the work that lies before you with a cheerful heart. Enthusiasm is infectious; it encourages others on their spiritual journey.

8) *God Confidence*

Confidence says that you know you are a child of the Divine. When you work with God, how can you not succeed? To maintain steady confidence, include God in everything you do. Your cooperation with the Divine process will unlock the secret of confidence.

9) *Dynamic Action*

One could say that dynamic action is the first law of the universe, as it manifested Creation itself. Dynamic action generates the vigor and vitality you need to bring something into being. You can desire the spiritual life, but if you aren't putting that desire into action, you will not get the benefit. Your spiritual growth cannot just stay as a wonderful idea; you have to be actively involved in bringing it to life.

10) *Divine Love*

In your spiritual quest, you will need to express a great deal of love and compassion. Love is the unifier of life. When you are in your spiritual love flow, you are in the oneness and goodness of life. To build your love flow, let go of selfish actions and embrace unselfish acts.

Chapter 16

MEDITATIONS TO CONNECT WITH THE SPIRITUAL WORLDS

Meditation brings wisdom; lack of meditation leaves ignorance
—Buddha

EDITATION IS THE cornerstone of metaphysical practice. Many things are part of the evolution of the soul, yet the foundation of your spiritual work is meditation. You cannot climb the spiritual ladder without regular meditation. Since Divine Light is the fuel of your spiritual ascent, meditating with Divine Light will greatly increase the spiritual power in your aura to accelerate your spiritual growth. Make meditation a daily practice and you will greatly enhance your spiritual unfoldment.

What is meditation? There are many different types of meditation practices to suit the needs and temperaments of the individual. Meditation is, in essence, *receiving from the Divine.* It is your one-on-one time with God. During meditation, you are temporarily withdrawing from the activities of life. You are physically still yet keenly alert. During the meditative state, you are receiving spiritual energy and inspiration from the Divine to renew and refresh your consciousness. Once the divine power is received, you are meant to take that power and employ it. If you have meditated upon the divine qualities of compassion and love, for example, then it's your job to be compassionate and loving.

Complementing meditation is prayer. If meditation is receiving from the Divine, prayer is petitioning the Divine—the sending *out* of energy. Many mistakenly think prayer is about getting something from the Divine. The role of prayer is not to receive but to give. The Divine is well-aware of our needs, but many times we disconnect in consciousness from the divine flow. We get too immersed in our personal cares and lose spiritual perspective. Prayer keeps us connected. The first job of prayer is to connect with God for the joy of being one with the Divine. Once you are in the divine oneness, then you can petition the Divine for guidance and inspiration. This is not to demand but to let the Divine into your life. Once you see things from the divine perspective, you will know what to do.

Your work with the Higher also involves the use of *meditative prayers*. In this type of supplication, you are making a specific request to strengthen a divine connection with some aspect of your life such as building your love flow or sense of spiritual confidence. You then receive the blessing that the Divine wishes to give you. The beauty of meditative prayers is that you are focusing your mind and consciousness on the spiritual quality of what you are requesting, which keeps the mind alert and focused.

THE HIGHER SELF MEDITATION

The meditations offered in this book are part of a practice called The Higher Self Meditation.[1] No meditation can instantly bring you enlightenment, and there are no shortcuts to the evolutionary process. Yet effective meditations can greatly support your spiritual journey. From

---

[1] For a comprehensive description of the Higher Self Meditation process, please refer to our book, *Change Your Aura, Change Your Life*.

my work with the auric field and following the tradition of The King-dom of Light Teachings, I have focused on the practice of meditating with Divine Light to strengthen the auric field and, through the aura, all facets of consciousness. In these meditations, you will be envisioning Divine Light flowing to your auric field.

The key to this meditation is the Higher Self. Your Higher Self is the bridge to Heaven. In the auric field, your Higher Self is clairvoyantly seen as a golden chakra point about two feet above the head, appropri-ately called The Meditative Pose (See Illustration 16.1). Your Higher Self is part of your divine nature—a guiding light to your soul that you can depend on during your spiritual journey. It stays in perpetual commu-nion with the celestial realms yet is keenly aware of what is going on with you. Divine Light and inspiration from the celestial realms flow through the Higher Self point to reach you.

To begin your Higher Self meditation, start by finding a quiet place where you will be undisturbed. When you meditate, you want your full attention on your meditation, free of outside distraction. In meditation, you are calming the mind, body, and emotions and stepping back from the activity of life. It is recommended that you sit upright in a comfort-able chair with your back straight and your feet flat on the floor rather than sitting in a lotus position. In this type of meditation, spiritual power is flowing down from above like an electrical current, so you don't want to "cross wires" by crossing your legs or inhibiting the flow of energy in any way.

While sitting physically still, reflect on what it is you are requesting of the Divine. Each divine attribute comes in on its own power ray, so by being specific in your request, you will be more effective in the results. In starting out, it is recommended that you work with three or four of the recommended meditative prayers (described below) in one sitting to give yourself time to absorb these powers and implement them. If it isn't clear what to request of the Higher, ask divine intelligence to guide you.

Start your meditation by relaxing. Take a couple of deep breaths to feel your body moving in rhythm with your mind and soul. Then, envision a golden bubble of protection all around you. It is important that you are spiritually protected when doing any type of meditation. Then put your attention on your Higher Self point about two feet above your physical head. See this point as a radiant golden-white sun. As you place your attention on the Higher Self point, let go of any worries or concerns. They do not exist in this divine place. You are on sacred ground. Know that a part of your consciousness is in that Higher Self in joyful reverence.

As you put your attention on your Higher Self point, recite out loud this invocation (memorize it for future meditations):

Invocation to Connect with the Higher Self Point

༚

Heavenly Father/Holy Mother God, I raise my
consciousness into Thy consciousness where I become
One with Thee. I ask to receive that which I need and
that which I need to know, now.

From your Higher Self, you are ready to begin your meditative prayers. You can follow the ones offered in this and the following chapter or use your own. Please remember that meditative prayers are requests, not commands. You are *asking* for this holy power, but it's always up to the Divine as to what spiritual power you need. In your meditative prayers, open your mind and speak your heart to God. Verbalize the meditative prayer in reverence and love. Envision the Divine Light that you are requesting "down-raying" from the divine source to your Higher Self point. Then, from the Higher Self point, envision this

The Meditative Pose : ILLUSTRATION 16.1

light down-raying to you and bathing your aura, your body, and your chakra points. Give permission for this Light to touch into every part of you: your thinking, feeling, speaking, and activities.

Hold still to feel the Light blessing you. Feel your consciousness being raised up by the spiritual quality you are requesting and the boundlessness of your spiritual expression. You know in your heart that with God and the Divine ones, you can accomplish anything.

In finishing your meditation, express your gratitude for what you have received. Feel refreshed and grounded. Use the power given to support your evolution; make it a part of your life. When starting out, meditate fifteen or twenty minutes a day. Eventually, the Higher recommend that you expand the time to thirty minutes or more. Equally important is the depth of your meditation. When you finish a meditation, you should feel differently from when you started.

In these meditations, it is not expected that you will see the Divine Light, but you *will* sense or feel its presence. Meditation is an experience in divine consciousness.

The Four Key Spiritual Centers (Chakras)

There are seven spiritual centers or chakras that are part of your spiritual anatomy. While Divine Light will flow to all aspects of your aura, it especially flows to four essential chakra points (out of the seven), as they are strong receiving and transmitting stations of Divine Light. Envision the Light flowing down to each of these four centers and uplifting you. The centers look like golden spheres of light with beautiful light rays moving out of them.

1) *The mental center:* Located in the middle of the forehead, this is the nucleus of your conscious thinking self.

2) *The throat center:* Located in the middle of the throat, this spiritual center is the nucleus of your creative tone.

3) *The Hermetic center* (also known as the *heart chakra*): Located in the middle of the chest, this center is the nucleus of your personal world affairs. Everything that is going on in your active life is making an energetic connection in this spiritual center.

4) *The emotional center:* Located in the abdominal area near the navel, this is the energetic nucleus of your emotional nature.

RECEIVING SPIRITUAL INSPIRATION

Every day, we are blessed by the Divine, but too often we get mixed up in our own concerns and don't respond to the divine impulse. The following meditative prayers will help you to better orient yourself to divine inspiration. You cannot command inspiration, but you can set up an environment that is conducive to making you more receptive. Work with the prayers as you feel the need.

The spiritual energy of inspiration clairvoyantly appears as a beautiful powder-blue light. When calling on this energy, feel its ethereal power opening your mind and consciousness to the divine flow.

Meditative Prayer for Inspiration and Attunement to the Divine Realms

Down-ray the powder-blue ray of inspiration to help
me tune into the creative vibrations of the spiritual
worlds. Inspire me to objectify all the creative power
I have earned. I ask to be in attunement with the
guidance and direction that flows from the heaven
worlds, and to do my part to bring into physical
expression that which has been manifested in the inner
worlds for the betterment of myself and all around me.

To receive from the Divine, you need to connect with the divine part of you. The more aware you are of your inner spiritual nature, the more you will be open to inspiration. The purple ray of peace helps you to quiet your consciousness so you can hear what the Divine is saying to you.

Meditative Prayer to Awaken the Mystical Nature

꙳

Down-ray the purple ray of peace to still my
consciousness that I may feel the eternal life
that dwells within urging me upward in divine
creativity and expression. May the Divine Light
bless my powers of intuition to awaken my
inner spiritual nature and better understand the
spiritual forces working within me.

The silver ray of divine intelligence is essential for helping to clear the mind so you can better discern the difference between spiritual truth and your own subjective thoughts.

Meditative Prayer for Spiritual Discernment

꙳

Down-ray the silver ray of divine intelligence into
my mental center to help me know if the ideas I am
receiving are my own or truly inspired from
the Divine. May this holy light keep my
mind clear, sharp, and objective.

ACCELERATING YOUR SPIRITUAL GROWTH

There are many qualities of the divine life to embody. Through countless experiences, tests, trials, successes, and failures, we accumulate wisdom and evolve. Look at all your opportunities and challenges as learning and growing experiences. These meditations are designed to help build more inner strength to enhance your spiritual unfoldment.

In the following meditative prayer, you are asking the Divine to help orient your consciousness to make spiritual unfoldment your priority. The golden ray of wisdom light is a dynamic spiritual energy that gives the needed inner strength to walk the spiritual path with courage and confidence.

Meditative Prayer to Make the Spiritual Path a Greater Priority

Down-ray the golden ray of wisdom light to give
me strength and courage to make my spiritual
evolution the number one priority in my life. Help
me take bold steps in my spiritual unfoldment
so that I may overcome any apparent obstacle or
discouragement and reach my highest spiritual
potential. May I be a blessing to all around me
in all my interactions and activities.

The spiritual energy dedicated to spiritual growth shows up in the aura as a beautiful apple-green color. It is often seen above the head and indicates that the soul is making progress in its spiritual ascent. This meditative prayer is targeted to draw this energy into your aura to support your spiritual unfoldment.

Meditative Prayer for Spiritual Growth

❧

Down-ray into my spiritual centers and aura the apple-
green ray of spiritual growth and renewal to support
my soul in its spiritual unfoldment. Help me to be
flexible and adapt my life to the divine life. May I feel
refreshed in my spiritual journey.

You won't travel far on your spiritual journey without love and compassion. True compassion is the ability to see the divine spark of life
in yourself and in those around you. When you or others do something that is hurtful or unkind, it can be difficult to see that, regardless of the action, the divine spark is still there. It cannot be tarnished
or corrupted, even if our aura darkens through misdeeds. Compassion
elevates you and has the effect of elevating anyone you hold in a compassionate light. In the auric field, compassion shows up as a beautiful
pink light.

Meditative Prayer to Build Compassion

❧

Down-ray the deep rose-pink ray of spiritual love
into my spiritual centers and aura to fill me with
compassion for others and myself. Inspire me
to honor the divine spark in everyone I interact
with. Help me to understand that we are all born
from the same spiritual source. May I show kindness
and understanding even if others do not return the
kindness. May I feel the joy of spirit and express
gratitude for being on the path of spiritual growth.

Devotion is a fundamental part of building spiritual power. In your evolution, the bond you are building is directly with the Divine. You have your earthly responsibilities, yet ultimately, your only obligation is to God. The royal-blue ray is the spiritual power of devotion and dedication. It is the "true blue" energy in the aura that demonstrates you are sincere in your efforts.

Meditative Prayer to Strengthen Devotion
ॐ

Down-ray the royal-blue ray of devotion into all levels
of my consciousness to deepen my dedication and
devotion to God and the divine process. Help me to
release divided areas of my consciousness that have
not yet aligned with the divine impulse. Through this
divine power, may I make a stronger connection with
God and be true to my own divine nature.

There is a lot to learn about our spiritual evolution, and as with any worthwhile endeavor, metaphysical education and training are essential. The lemon-yellow ray of concentration is wonderful for focusing consciousness when learning new things and supporting you in the accumulation of spiritual understanding.

Meditative Prayer for Spiritual Knowledge
ॐ

Down-ray the lemon-yellow ray of concentration to
quicken my mind to be more receptive to spiritual
understanding. Illuminate me to discern quality
spiritual education from false or misleading teachings.
In its divine time, may I find a true spiritual teacher
who can support me in my spiritual ascent.

OVERCOMING TESTS AND CHALLENGES ON THE SPIRITUAL PATH

Walking the spiritual path is the most exciting adventure there is, but that doesn't make it easy. While rewarding and wondrous, there are also challenges, both within and without. The environment around you may or may not be conducive for spiritual growth. You may have internal conflicts where you recognize the value of the spiritual path yet find it difficult to follow through on the demands that any worthwhile endeavor will inevitably make.

This meditative prayer is designed to help you connect with your spiritual roots. Every soul on Earth is part of the divine process regardless of where they are on their spiritual journey. Knowing this helps you to understand that you are always supported spiritually. You are never alone. The white light keeps you connected to the Divine.

Meditative Prayer to Connect with My Cosmic Origins

Down-ray the pure white light to help me sense my
celestial origins out of which my spiritual potential
and divine purpose were born. May I feel the support
of the Divine through every aspect of the journey
and know I am never alone—God is always with me.
Help me make my contribution to the greater creative
expression of life in its infinite beauty and variety.

Sometimes we are our own worst enemy. We can unintentionally inhibit rather than accelerate our spiritual growth. The Personality Ego is most often the culprit. Be honest with yourself about your shortcomings.

In your ascent, you are working through your imperfections, and to do that, you need to see them for what they are. If you see a fault in yourself, pay attention to what needs to be done to correct it. The silver ray of divine intelligence will help you to think and see things more clearly.

Meditative Prayer to Be Released from Delusional Thinking

૨઴

Down-ray the silver ray of divine intelligence to
reveal any ulterior motives I have that are hindering
my spiritual journey. Release me from any spiritual
egotism thinking I am better than anyone else and
any false thoughts that I am further up the spiritual
ladder than I really am. Help me to use good sense
and reason to see clearly where I am in my spiritual
unfoldment and the next steps to take.

Humility is fundamental to spiritual success. Some mistakenly think that being humble is a sign of weakness when, in truth, it is a sign of great strength. When you are humble, you understand your place in the cosmos and the part you are playing in the divine plan. Through true humility, universal powers open up for you to accomplish that which will best serve the higher good. The emerald-green ray of balance and harmony helps to keep you in rhythm with the divine pulsebeat.

Meditative Prayer to Tune into My Place in the Cosmos

૨઴

Down-ray the emerald-green ray of balance and
harmony to orient me in the divine plan of evolution.
Grant unto me humility to understand my place in
the cosmos. May I recognize that I am essential to

the divine process and am making an indispensable
contribution to the divine plan. My heart sings out to
the Divine to unite with the celestial order of life.

As this book has made clear, healing is part of the spiritual life. At
different points in our evolution, we need healing and transformation.
The blue-white fire is an essential energy ray for healing the body, mind,
and soul. See this spiritual fire bathing every part of your consciousness,
soothing and healing distressed areas. This is an excellent prayer to uplift you if you are feeling depressed.

Meditative Prayer for Spiritual Healing
※

Down-ray the blue-white fire of renewing life force
so it flows into every level of my consciousness,
healing me in mind, body, and soul. Transmute
any unhealthy areas of my life and restore
them to health and wellness.

Spiritual unfoldment is not an overnight process. The soul learns
through experience, and it takes time to go through those experiences.
Sometimes we are impatient. We want things to happen on our time
and not divine time. We can push too hard, creating stress for ourselves
and others. Be diligent in doing the things you need to do but leave the
rest in the hands of the Divine. If you are doing your part, your spiritual evolution will unfold in its natural rhythm.

Meditative Prayer for Patience on the Path

❧

Down-ray the emerald-green ray of balance and
harmony to bring me into divine rhythm so that the
spiritual life may unfold in me in divine time. I trust
in the divine process and know I ascend the spiritual
steps as I have earned the right to do so.

We all make mistakes; it's part of the learning and growth process.
The most important thing is to recognize a mistake for what it is and
correct it. Refuse to condemn yourself as that only serves to keep you in
the energy of the error. At the same time, refuse to whitewash mistakes
as that will keep you repeating them. True redemption can be major
turning points in our lives, opening up new opportunities for spiritual
growth.

Meditative Prayer for Redemption

❧

Down-ray the pure white light into my aura to
release from me any dark corners in my consciousness.
I ask God's forgiveness for anything I have done
that goes against Divine law. May the purity of this
holy Light redeem my soul and bring it back into the
full flow of my spiritual ascent.

You don't walk the path alone, yet at times it can feel that way.
Loved ones may or may not be in harmony with your spiritual aspirations. The key is love. Love those you love regardless of whether they
understand your metaphysical inclinations. At the same time, seek out
those who are walking the path like you. The journey is more exciting
when we can share it with others.

Meditative Prayer for Fellowship with Like-Minded Souls

❧

Down-ray the deep rose-pink of spiritual love to release me of any feelings of loneliness while walking the spiritual path. I know the Divine is with me through every step in the journey. I ask the divine ray of love to flow from my Higher Self Point into the vibrated ethers to attract like-mind souls and fellow spiritual travelers to share the journey with.

Chapter 17

SLEEP AND TRAVELING
TO THE WORLD OF SPIRIT

*Allow not sleep to close your eyes before three times
reflecting on Your actions of the day. What deeds Done well,
what not, what left undone?*
—Pythagoras

*I*N THE LAST two chapters, we looked at tools that help accelerate
your spiritual growth. We explored the essential role of a lifestyle
and conduct of living that is conducive to spiritual evolution and how
daily meditation and prayer are indispensable for growth. Now, we'll
discuss the beautiful yet mysterious relationship of sleep to your spiritual evolution.

Sleep has always had an element of mystery to it. In ancient cultures, sleep was seen as a type of temporary afterlife state—a time to
draw closer to spirit and commune with one's ancestors and the deities
they worshipped. Today, sleep is acknowledged as part of regenerating
the body. We all need a good night's rest. The recuperative power of
sleep is crucial. Science has studied brain/body activity during sleep
and identified some remarkable patterns: light sleep supports relaxation;
deep sleep supports physical rejuvenation; REM sleep serves on the
needs of healthy brain functioning. Yet the benefits of sleep are much

more than biological. Spiritual processes go on during sleep that are of great benefit to the soul.

During sleep, the conscious mind is at rest but the spiritual part of you is active. A spiritual regeneration takes place that helps to refresh our consciousness. Your aura is blessed by the Divine while you sleep. So not only do the Holy Ones work with you during waking consciousness; they work with you in sleeping consciousness as well. This spiritual recuperation is essential for health and well-being—mentally, physically, as well as spiritually. In many ways, you are closer to spirit while you sleep because your mind is not preoccupied with daily affairs. You are more open to the Divine in this deeply relaxed state.

What's more, there is a revelation about sleep and the world of spirit that is well-known to mystics. I have shared with you several of my personal nighttime spiritual travels and the memory I have of these experiences. The skill to bring back conscious awareness of these travels is a talent I was born with and have been developing throughout my years as a clairvoyant and teacher. Yet this talent is not unique to me. Others with similar mystical gifts, such as my spiritual teacher Inez, also have this ability to consciously go to the inner worlds.

What is not generally understood is that, from time to time throughout your life, you are taken out of the physical body to the inner worlds to be refreshed and inspired in the spiritual journey. These occasional inner-world visits happen at night while you sleep. They happen for every soul on Earth regardless of whether they are intentionally pursing a spiritual path. Most often, you don't bring back a conscious memory of the experience, yet you reap the benefits. When these experiences occur, you are not dying, and it's not the same thing as a normal out-of-body experience. This is inner world travel. You are cooperating with the process but not initiating it. This carefully orchestrated crossing is directed by angelic beings to support your spiritual evolution, so it is completely safe and beneficial.

These occasional inner-world visits are done for several reasons. The Divine periodically takes you to the inner realms to keep you connected to the spiritual worlds. Earth is a temporary habitat; the spiritual realms are your real home. Even while in physical life, a part of you remains connected to the spirit world. You are never disconnected from the Divine no matter what is going on in physical life. Going to the inner worlds at night helps to detach from physical cares and refreshes the soul. Another reason for these inner-world travels is to keep you on the spiritual path and support you in completing your purpose.

When you travel to the spiritual worlds, you are aware of what is going on, although (with rare exceptions) you don't remember the experience once you return to the physical body. You don't stay long in these realms because you are still part of earth life. After you return to the physical body, the Divine helps to integrate the spiritual experience into your aura to inspire you in waking life. While conscious memory of inner world travels is rare, it is not uncommon to have vivid dreams that were inspired by them. Once awake, you will unconsciously feel the effects of what was given. Depending on your receptivity, you may find yourself inspired by ideas that were based on inner world guidance.

Where are you taken on the other side? You can end up in a variety of places, but most often you travel to the higher astral worlds and into the temples—the spiritual training centers we have been exploring. How often do these nighttime spiritual travels occur? Depending on what is going in your life, you may go once or twice a month. This can increase as the need arises. You may be taken to the inner worlds when you are in difficult situations and need help. You may be taken if you need healing or are making life-changing decisions. You are taken there for instruction and support in your spiritual growth. Couples getting ready to conceive children will visit the inner worlds to meet the souls who will become their children. If you are doing things that are hurting yourself and others, you may be brought to the inner worlds to see the error of your ways so you can make things right. The angelic beings take leaders to the inner worlds for guidance and direction. Those getting ready to make their transition are often taken to the other side to psychologically prepare.

Why don't we remember these spiritual travels? Of all the aspects of clairvoyant activity, bringing back conscious memory of the inner worlds is perhaps the most difficult. But again, you don't need to see the spirit worlds to connect with them. By keeping an open and receptive mind, you integrate the blessings given. Eventually, your spiritual efforts will lead to direct experiences.

My mother, Zaferia, used to describe some of her inner-world experiences although she was not a trained clairvoyant. She was very religious yet would have metaphysical experiences. One time, she was very sick. At one point, her situation became life-threatening. She told me one morning that she remembered being in a beautiful place on the other side. An angelic being approached her. She was frightened, thinking maybe she was dying, and blurted out, "What am I doing here?!" The angel reassured her it was there to help and that she was in a healing temple. After this experience, my mother did get better. This knowledge of the inner worlds comforted her throughout the rest of her life.

Is inner world travel the same as dreaming? No, the two are different. There is a rich tradition of lucid dreaming and dream interpretation. If you recall, while evolving through the second astral plane, we operated in the dream mind. Even though we have long passed that stage, the dream mind remains part of our mental anatomy. Through dreams, we process experiences without intellectual interpretation. This is why the most irrational combination of activities can seem perfectly reasonable during the dream. Only later when you wake up and reflect on the dream do you start putting together those irrational aspects.

Many feel that the Divine speaks to us through dreams. From the metaphysical perspective, this is both true and not true. The Divine most definitely speaks to us while we sleep, and when this happens, we can recall enough to interpret that Divine experience—not the experience itself but our dream interpretation of that experience. And this can make a powerful impression where you feel very close to the Divine.

FACILITATING NIGHTTIME SPIRITUAL BLESSINGS

To complement your daily meditation practice, we would like to offer a nighttime meditation practice specifically targeted to facilitate the spiritual processes that go on while you sleep. These meditations should be done very close to sleep time. Make this bedtime meditation part of your spiritual practice. The benefits of making a strong rapport with nighttime spiritual work are enormous. This can give you more peace, inspiration, better balance in your consciousness, and more motivation in all you do.

There are five steps in this nighttime meditation practice. While we will go through each step in detail, the actual practice should take no longer than ten minutes.

1. Spiritually prepare your bedroom.
2. Spiritually prepare yourself for sleep.
3. Facilitate sleep-time spiritual regeneration.
4. Facilitate sleep-time blessings from the spiritual worlds.
5. Integrate sleep-time spiritual experience in waking consciousness.

Spiritually Prepare Your Bedroom

Your bedroom is your sanctuary. Spiritually, you want your bedroom and bed to be blessed in the Divine Light. To start your nighttime meditation, it's a good idea to light a candle just before and during the meditation—but don't leave it lit while you sleep! Burning incense is also good. This helps to create the spiritual ambiance that leads to a conducive environment for sleep.

You can do this meditation sitting on the side of the bed or in a nearby chair. Following the Higher Self meditation practice, raise your consciousness and ask the Divine to fill your bedroom with pure white light to release any negativity that might be in the atmosphere. Feel the spiritual power filling the room. Then ask the Divine to surround your bed in a bubble of the golden light of protection.

Meditative Prayer to Bless Your Bedroom

꽃

I ask that you down-ray the pure white light into
my bedroom and area of sleep to release anything
of a discordant nature and uplift the vibration of the
room in Divine Light and Love. Surround
my bed with the golden light of protection to keep
me spiritually protected while I sleep.

If you sleep with a loved one, ask that the golden light surround them as well. If they are distressed, that energy can unintentionally be transferred to you.

Spiritually Prepare Yourself for Sleep

In today's fast-paced world, a good night's sleep seems hard to come by. After a long day of work—often late into the night—or a day full of activities, we often "crash" ourselves to sleep. And with the internet ever present, we live in a 24/7 cycle of activity. The natural cycle of daylight and darkness has also been disrupted as bright lights can stimulate us any time of day or night. In days past, humanity lived at night by candle or firelight. When the sun set, the activities of life naturally slowed down, which moved us into a different rhythm. In many mystical traditions, night was a time to relax, reflect, and be introspective, assimilating the day and preparing for the spiritual process of sleep. Then, when the sun rose the next morning, we were once again engaged and active. Science has taught us that melatonin, the hormone that regulates our waking-sleeping patterns, is greatly influenced by the changing cycles of day and night.

When the activities of the day are complete, it is a good idea to reflect on how well, or not well, you handled things during the day. It's a type of personal inventory to help keep you spiritually on track. Doing at the end of the day is beneficial because everything is fresh in your mind. Then once this reflection period is over and you are actually preparing for sleep, do your best to let the cares of the day go. No matter what happened during the day, clear your mind. If you have insomnia, make sure there are no underlying biological conditions that might be affecting your sleep cycle. If that isn't the issue, insomnia can be caused when there's a lot on your mind. Too many times, we make the mistake of taking our troubles to bed with us. Thinking about our problems while lying in bed stimulates the consciousness, making it more difficult to sleep. We also make the mistake of stimulating consciousness by surfing the internet or watching television just before sleep. When you are ready to slumber, you want your mind quiet and free.

If you haven't done so already, develop a healthy sleep routine. Think of your sleep time in the same way you honor living in harmony with nature. When you stay connected with nature, you stay connected with the rhythms of life. Sleep specialists have outlined good sleeping habits which include a wind-down routine before bedtime and getting seven-to-eight hours of sleep. Avoiding food or caffeine late at night, going to bed at a regular time, and waking up at a regular time are also the components of a healthy sleeping routine.

To help with getting a restful sleep or if you have trouble falling asleep, we suggest working with the white light and the violet ray. The white light uplifts you out of current concerns or worries, while the violet ray is soothing for the nerves.

Meditative Prayer to Facilitate Sleep

Down-ray the violet ray of gentle peace to quiet
my mind and relax my body. Let this gentle energy
flow into my nervous system, releasing any stress,
anxiety, or pressure. (Pause to feel the Light
reaching your spiritual centers and body.)

Then I ask that you down-ray the pure white light to
infuse my body and consciousness with spiritual power
so I receive a good night's rest. May this holy energy
uplift my mind, body, and soul, freeing me of any
concerns and uniting me in the Divine oneness.

Feel the Divine Light quickening all levels of consciousness, the chakras, your aura, and your body.

Facilitate Sleep-Time Spiritual Regeneration

To prepare for the spiritual support you receive during sleep, envision yourself surrounded in white light or a deep rose-pink bubble of light. Ask the Divine to support the spiritual processes you are going through and prepare you for potential nighttime spiritual travel with the following meditative prayer. While you receive divine support nightly, you can't control when you are taken to the spiritual worlds. Whatever happens, this nighttime meditation strengthens your receptivity to spiritual regeneration and supports your connection to the inner worlds. With this meditation, feel the Higher Self point above your head being quickened by the white light.

Prayer to Regenerate Consciousness

᷍

May I be divinely refreshed and recharged with new
life force at all levels of my consciousness while I
sleep. May I fully integrate these powers at all levels
of my consciousness so that upon awakening, I am
regenerated and inspired to meet the new day and the
opportunities that will facilitate my spiritual growth.

Pause in silence for a few moments to feel the Holy Ones making their connections with you.

Facilitate Sleep-Time Blessings from the Spiritual Worlds

In the following meditative prayers, you are requesting the Holy Ones to bless you with Divine Light directly from the temples in the inner worlds. As we have explored, temples are the spiritual training centers on the other side. The word *temple* is defined as a "consecrated space," and truly that is what they are. Receiving spiritual energy from the temples is powerful because, not only do you get the benefit of the Divine Light, you receive from the power of the temple itself. And because this is happening while you sleep, the angels can work with your aura more directly. These nighttime meditations are very supportive for those times when the Divine actually takes you to the inner worlds and are a wonderful complement to a regular meditation.

Pick one or two of these meditations each night when you feel inclined, as part of your nighttime meditation practice.

Temple Meditation for Purification

The orange-red flame of purification is the spiritual power that releases disturbing energies from your aura and consciousness including unhealthy thoughts, anger, resentment, anxiety, jealousy, fear, and so on. In the higher astral worlds, The Temple of Purification is where souls go for deep spiritual release from negativity, either self-created or absorbed from the activities of life. In this temple, the spiritual effects of physical illness and injury are released so the consciousness can better heal itself.

In these meditations, feel your Higher Self point being quickened by the Divine Light you are requesting, and hold to the knowing that during sleep, the Divine will bless you in this power.

Meditative Temple Prayer to Be Blessed by the Orange-Red Flame

※

In Divine Light and Love and if it be Thy will,
I ask to receive the orange-red flame of purification
through the angels from the Temple of Purification
while I sleep. May this vital energy purify me
of all unhealthy and unenlightened energies. Upon
awakening, may I be open and receptive to intuitively
following through on the power and blessings
given. I ask this in Thy Holy name.

Temple Meditation for Healing

The blue-white fire of eternal life is one of the most powerful spiritual energies there is—essential in all types of healing. It brings in the universal life force to recharge and replenish your consciousness. When you expend energy, you need to be refilled again. This holy fire supports that effort. If you are feeling tired, depressed, or low in motivation, the blue-white fire can truly uplift you. The Temple of Healing is one of the largest and most active temples in the spiritual worlds (see Illustration 7.1). Many who are ill are taken there while they sleep for healing and regeneration.

Meditative Temple Prayer to Be Blessed with the Blue-White Fire

※

In Divine Light and love and if it be Thy will, I ask
to receive the blue-white fire of eternal life through
the angels from the Temple of Healing while I sleep.
May this holy power energy charge and recharge

me with new life force and bless me with its healing
powers. Upon awakening, may I be open and receptive
to intuitively following through on the power and
blessings given. I ask this in Thy Holy name.

Temple Meditation for Divine Love

The deep rose-pink ray brings in divine love, compassion, kindness, and
joy. This energy helps to deepen all relationships with others. If you are
in a difficult relationship or feel hurt in matters of love, this energy is
essential to heal the wounds of a broken heart. If you are feeling lonely
or neglected, the deep rose-pink ray connects you with the ever-present,
unconditional divine love. The Temple of Love is one of the most beautiful in the spiritual worlds (see illustration 8.1). If you need to ask forgiveness or need to forgive, blessings offered from this temple can be of
great help. This is a popular temple for enhancing and expanding your
love flow. Not only do we all need love; we need to express love.

Meditative Temple Prayer to Be Blessed with the Deep Rose-Pink Ray

In Divine Light and love and if it be Thy will, I ask
to receive the deep rose-pink ray of spiritual love
through the angels from the Temple of Love while I
sleep. May this sacred power energy uplift me in divine
love and compassion so I feel connected to the divine
source. Upon awakening, may I be open and receptive
to intuitively following through on the power and
blessing given. I ask this in Thy Holy name.

Temple Meditation for Divine Peace

The purple ray of peace, a deeper shade than the violet ray, brings serenity and tranquility to all levels of consciousness. The Temple of Peace is truly a majestic, mystical place. Whenever you feel irritated, anxious, unsettled, restless, hyperactive, or not at peace—for any reason—receiving energy from this temple can greatly help. By calling on this energy, you will re-establish your divine oneness with all life and better embody the glorious spiritual process you are part of.

Meditative Temple Prayer to Be Blessed with the Purple Ray

In Divine Light and love and if it be Thy will, I ask
to receive the purple ray of peace ray through the
angels from the Temple of Peace while I sleep. May
this tranquil power bless me in the "silence of peace
and the peace of silence," stilling my mind, body, and
soul. Upon awakening, may I be open and receptive
to intuitively following through on the power and
blessing given. I ask this in Thy Holy name.

Temple Meditation for Wisdom

The golden ray brings in wisdom and illumination. This is the energy to call on for inner strength, dynamic power, courage, and understanding. We need spiritual strength to get through life's challenges, and the golden ray gives you that power. The Temple of Wisdom is a large, impressive sanctuary with beautiful grounds. This is the temple to ask to visit when you need guidance and direction in your life pursuit or wonder if you have the power you need to accomplish your life's tasks. This temple is the source of illumination for gaining a greater perspective and seeing life from the eyes of the Divine.

Meditative Temple Prayer to Be Blessed with the Golden Ray

In Divine Light and love and if it be Thy will, I ask
to receive the golden ray of spiritual love through
the angels from the Temple of Wisdom while I
sleep. May this divine power strengthen me in my
spiritual journey, illuminating me in understanding
and wisdom. May I feel God walking with me in all
I do. Upon awakening, may I be open and receptive
to intuitively following through on the power and
blessing given. I ask this in Thy Holy name.

Temple Meditation for Prosperity

The turquoise ray brings in the consciousness of abundance and supply. This energy is excellent when dealing with financial worries and distress or if you are looking to build up your prosperity consciousness—not just in finances but also in friendships, health, creativity, and so on. The Temple of Prosperity is where people learn the spiritual foundation of wealth. The Temple of Prosperity is a magnificent place where people are taught by the Holy Ones how to increase this power in their auras and how to navigate the challenges and opportunities that abundance offers.

Meditative Temple Prayer to Be Blessed with the Turquoise Ray

✿

In Divine Light and love and if it be Thy will,
I ask to receive the turquoise ray of prosperity through
the angels from the Temple of Prosperity while I
sleep. May this holy power uplift my mind, body,
and soul so I embody the divine principles of
prosperity and manifest that power in my active
life. Upon awakening, may I be open and receptive
to intuitively following through on the power and
blessing given. I ask this in Thy Holy name.

Integrate Sleep-Time Spiritual Experiences in Waking Consciousness.

Once you finish your nighttime meditations, express your gratitude to the Divine, blow out the candle, relax, and get a good night's sleep. When you wake up in the morning, lie still before engaging in the day and try to recall the first thoughts or impressions that pop in your head. If it helps, write them down. When you first awaken, you are more receptive to whatever spiritually went on the night before. If nothing comes through, don't concern yourself. Hold to the knowing that inspiration will come when you need it.

The process of waking up is as important as the process of falling asleep. So, it's a good idea not to jump out of bed right away or linger too long. If you can awaken without an alarm clock, that is ideal. Another option is to get an alarm clock that wakes you up gently and gradually, as this helps in the spiritual transition from sleeping to waking.

Chapter 18

THE ROAD TO HEAVEN IS
PAVED WITH LOVE

*It's not about how much you do, but how much love
you put into what you do that counts.*
—Mother Teresa

AT YOUR OWN tempo, you will build your talents and skills to reach all of these splendid realms. They are urging you onward and upward. Make every effort to pursue your spiritual path with all you are capable of. If you feel frustrated or disappointed, trust the Divine and hold to the highest ideal for yourself. The spiritually mature life is the greatest life there is. There is no greater source of satisfaction, security, and contentment than to let blossom the immortal attributes of your soul. You are a lamp for the spirit that dwells within you. Let that spirit shine brightly so that all may see and benefit.

In your spiritual journey, love is the key. You cannot climb the spiritual ladder without the constant unfolding of your loving potential. Your spiritual ascent is a path of love. Pain, tragedy, and sorrow are the clouds that pass by; love is eternal. Knowledge of the higher dimensions of life is given to reveal the scope and splendor of the spiritual path and to show you how much there is to look forward to, yet love is always the foundation.

How far can you spiritually climb in a single lifetime? This is determined by your karmic chart. Normally, the progress from one level to the next is steady and slow. As you reach the higher planes, the pace quickens as you are consciously cooperating and supporting your evolutionary process. Today, humanity is truly being given a golden key to accelerate its growth. I urge you with all my heart to take full advantage of the spiritual opportunities being offered. They will carry you far.

How long does it take to reach the spiritual pinnacle? It takes a long time to climb the ladder Home, but it's a graceful and majestic journey and each step is beautiful. In truth, what does it matter how long it takes as long as you get there? The real question is not how long it takes but whether you are doing what you need to do to get there. If you feel stuck in a rut or feel uninspired, there is more you could be doing. If you are over-extended, slow down; spiritual growth is not a race.

Our evolution is a combination of persistence and patience, as well as apparent paradoxes. In one sense, we are as divine and spiritual as we will ever be, yet at the same time we are constantly unfolding greater and more splendid spiritual powers. We are on the road to a glorious destination, yet we live in the eternal now. Our evolution is an unending process, yet there are definite stages and phases that create excitement, mystery, and drama.

Look clearly at the qualities that exist within you. What are your weaknesses and what are your strengths? Make sure you are doing one of the hardest things to do—love yourself. Not a vain love, but one that accepts you wherever you are including your qualities at any given moment. You are part of the Divine as much as everyone else and you have the right to love *you*. Even if you see in yourself things you dislike, start with love. The moment you accept and love yourself, you gain a tremendous power to raise your consciousness. You'll also discover an ability to accept others wherever they are on their journey.

In your spiritual climb, there are many things you will have no physical evidence of, so you will need a strong faith. Not blind faith, when you accept without thought and good judgment, but a dynamic, divine faith that what you have set into motion will come to pass. Your faith has to be constant. You cannot switch it on or off because every time you switch it off, you've switched off something that could have been shown to you.

The other facet you need on the spiritual path of attainment is *hope*. Hope and faith walk hand in hand. Anyone can say, "Heaven is this way." Anyone can give you a picture of something you haven't witnessed or felt yourself. Hope is an essential ingredient to expanding life, learning, and knowledge. The moment you lose hope, haven't you lost life? When everything seems to be crumbling around you and things appear hope*less* is when you need the most hope of all. Many brave souls who have lost many things continue to hope. Best of all, hope, along with faith, eventually lead you into *knowing*—when you discover divine truths through firsthand experience.

Refuse to get discouraged if you are unable to see all that needs to be done. Do what you can and everything else will fall into place. Recognize that every lesson—even the painful ones—helps you to grow. Pay attention to what is being shown to you. That is the only way to recognize when the Divine is speaking to you. Remember: You are *precious* in God's sight. May God bless you in the great journey to your eternal Home.

well as Nigel Yorwerth for his guidance in sales and distribution. And our gratitude goes to Sara Sgarlat for her excellence in public relations, Loma Media for their marketing expertise, and Sarah Kelley for her social media efforts.

ACKNOWLEDGEMENTS

The writing of this book has been a labor of love. As with all our books, it is the inspiration of the Divine that is our guiding light. The Divine Ones brought in many levels of inspiration, and it was amazing to see how much of the inner life they wanted to share in a book designed for the public. This could only mean that many are ready to receive its message. Our hope is that we are worthy amanuenses for their message of encouragement and love to pursue the spiritual life.

We thank all the students, staff, and supporters of Spiritual Arts Institute who gave the space and encouragement for this work to grow. Special thanks to Neil and Anna Mintz for their instrumental support. Our gratitude goes to Barbara's family: Vasilli, Ria, Ken, and Amanda. And to the Moraitis family: Philip, Ann Marie, Ellen, Anne, and Julia; and in memory of Dimitri's father, George, who passed onto the Greater Life.

We are very grateful to Jonathan Wiltshire for his fine art illustrations. It was a joy to work with him. His ability to create on canvas the feeling of the inner worlds is truly remarkable. His oil paintings of these illustrations hang in our training center as an inspiration to all who study at the Institute. A warm thank you to our editor, Matthew Gilbert. He did a wonderful job strengthening the text yet maintaining the spiritual tone and spirit.

We thank Nita Ybarra for her excellent cover and interior design. This is the fifth book cover she has done for us; each one beautifully reflects the mood and feel of the book. Our gratitude goes out to the publishing team at Spiritual Arts Institute—to Melissa Love, Julie Quinn, Janet Cole, and to Simon Warwick-Smith for his years of guidance and support in building the SAI publishing department. We thank

SCB Distributors including Aaron Silverman and Gabriel Wilmoth, as well as Nigel Yorwerth for his guidance in sales and distribution. And our gratitude goes to Sara Sgarlat for her excellence in public relations, Loma Media for their marketing expertise, and Sarah Kelley for her social media efforts.

INDEX

A

Abraham, 65, 73
abundance, 53, 266
acceptance, 54, 174, 190, 205, 270–71
Akashic records, 158
Akkadian eschatology, 58
Alighieri, Dante, 54, 71, 217
ambrosia, 111, 115, 154
angels, 15, 62, 158, 174, 262
  archangels, 105, 121, 178
    Archangel Jibra'il, 73
    Archangel Lucifer, 179
    celestial experiences with, 149–50
    as Holy Ones, 5, 24, 177
    in the spiritual hierarchy, 23, 29, 46, 112,
      182, 187
    support, receiving from, 162, 179, 180
  astral angels, 89, 97, 100, 102, 157, 256
  fallen angels, 219, 220
  as guides, 18, 43, 101, 114, 117, 129, 254
  in Hebrew cosmology, 66, 127
  in *illustrations 6.1, 7.2, 9.1, 9.3,* 104, 124, 140,
    147
  netherworlds, angelic aid to souls in, 215, 218
  sleep, angels working on souls during, 92,
    262
  support, receiving from, 51, 130
  telepathic communication with, 44, 48
  temple angels, 118–19, 132, 263, 264, 265,
    266, 267
animal netherworld kingdoms, 216–17, 218
animals, 46, 50, 146
  animal meat, non-consumption of, 47, 89, 96
  animal souls, 175
  in the spiritual realms, 90, 91, 96, 111, 121
Anubis (Egyptian figure), 63
apple-green, color of, 245, 246
apricot-colored light, 150, 161
Aquinas, Thomas, 71
archangels. *See under* angels
Arjuna (Vedic figure), 62
Arupa-loka (world), 78
Asphodel Meadows, 64
astral planes
  first astral plane, 87, 218
  second astral plane, 88–90, 91–92, 217, 218, 256

third astral plane, 90–93, 97, 216
fourth astral plane, 96, 97, 118, 196, 226
  Earth as closest to vibration of, 95, 110
  interactions with souls on, 111
  physical incarnations as beginning on,
    93, 99
  soul mate relationship changes, 108
  spiritual awakenings, 98, 102–4, 107, 125
  as a staging area for Earth, 159
  visiting the fourth astral plane, 100–102
fifth astral plane, 103, 107, 110
  character-building on, 110–13
  a day in the life of, 115–18
  soul mate relationship experiences, 108
  souls vibrating on the level of, 226
sixth astral plane, 110, 114, 118
  higher self, reaching on, 120–23, 129
  new understandings, unfolding, 107
  soul mate dynamics, 108
seventh astral plane, 129–31, 145
astral sub-planes, 86, 90, 95, 97, 122, 126, 216,
217
astral travel, 20, 21
astro-theology, 45, 57, 61–62, 158, 259
  astral suns, 71, 116, 118, 165
  galaxy, glory of, 34–35
  planets as fields of evolution, 177–78
  solar logi and the solar system, 180
  spiritual cosmology, 37–39
  spiritual planetary travel, 130, 132–33
  spiritual planets, 63
Augustine, Saint, 70
auras, 129, 137, 140, 188, 255
  aura readings, providing, 149
  auric framework, building, 32, 230
  clairvoyant skills, viewing auras via, 4, 205
  colors displayed in, 60, 119, 228, 245–46, 247,
    251
  corruption of the aura through misuse, 176,
    196, 197–98
  disturbing energy, detecting in, 209
  divine light and, 24–25, 226–27, 237, 239, 241,
    242, 261
  full auric power, holding back, 136
  golden light of individuality seen in, 123
  of the Holy Ones, 266

in *illustration 8.1*, 132
Inez Hurd, auric teachings of, 7, 17
Kingdom of God, aura of souls from, 190
little people, auras of, 84
of the planetary spirits, 178
as pure bodies of light, 154
purification of, 102, 114
sleep, work done on the aura during, 254, 262
soul age as reflected in, 165
Aurobindo, Sri, 141
Autobiography of a Yogi (Yogananda), 36

B

Bailey, Alice, 181–82
Beethoven, Ludwig van, 64
Bhagavad Gita text, 174
Bhagavata Purana text, 76
black magic, 200–201, 202
Blavatsky, Helena P., 151, 155
blessings, 16, 147, 238
    from celestial beings, 18, 53, 102, 151
    distress, transforming into blessings, 227, 233
    nighttime spiritual blessings, 257–62
    temple blessings, 5, 160–61
blue, color of, 84, 105, 116, 120, 132
    aqua-blue, 17, 228
    blue-white fire energy, 250, 263–64
    ethereal blue, 157
    powder-blue, 189, 243
    royal-blue, 247
    sapphire blue, 119
Bodhi Tree, 64
Book of Life, 144, 158, 200
Brahma-loka (heaven), 75, 78
Brahman (Ultimate Reality), 28, 74, 75
Buddha Gautama, 76, 78, 79, 146, 226
Buddhism, 74, 76–79, 146

C

candle use, 258, 267
Cathedral of the Soul, 160
causal world, 52, 165, 203
    defining and describing, 141–42
    plummeting from, 202
    reincarnation and, 142–43, 200
cavemen and Neanderthals, 93
chakras, 132, 190, 239, 241, 242–43, 261
character-building, 110–13
children and babies, 47–48, 52, 97, 255
Chinese spiritual tradition, 28, 74, 227
"circus floor" diversion, 208
clairvoyance, 6, 7, 16, 174n3, 200
    auras, clairvoyantly viewing, 149, 189, 197

fruits of cultivating skill in, 128
higher self, clairvoyant sense of, 239
inspiration energy, clairvoyantly
    perceiving, 243
lowly souls, clairvoyantly shining light on, 207
memory of inner worlds, bringing to con-
    sciousness, 256
mystic clairvoyance, 59, 128, 205
outer manifestation of, 131
regaining powers of, 203
vibrations, sensitivity to, 209
compassion, 105, 113, 128, 156, 199
    aura, as reflected in, 24
    of the *devas* and the little people, 84, 174
    in Eastern traditions, 75, 78
    expressions of, 52, 124, 130, 236, 238
    inner worlds, building in, 131
    in the Kingdom of Light, 162
    pink color of, 246, 264
    self-compassion, 122
    in the temple of love, 132, 264
competition, 91
conscious awareness, 4, 31, 90–93, 99, 158, 254
Copernicus, Nicolaus, 59n1, 61
courage, 91, 142, 245, 265
Crown of Life, 163, 167, 175

D

Dante. *See* Alighieri, Dante
death, 7, 50, 100, 178, 219–20
    astral worlds, no death in, 47, 51, 75, 89, 122
    in Egyptian spirituality, 62
    Elysian Fields as after-death world, 64
    etemmu as existence beyond death, 58
    Jonestown as a place of death, 208–10
    nirvana as beyond death, 77
    physical death, souls unaware of, 95
    the portal we call death, 27, 36, 226
demons and demonic realms, 129–30, 219–21
depression, mental, 250, 263
"Desiderata" (poem), 183
desire worlds. *See* astral worlds
Devachan. *See* mental world
devas, 174, 175
devolution, 122
    conditions causing, 197–98
    involution, distinguishing from, 31
    to the netherworlds, 202, 215, 216, 218
devotion, 18, 128, 132
    astral devotion, 142
    in Hindu tradition, 75–76
    meditative prayer to strengthen, 247
    of spirit guides, 231

discernment, 204, 231, 244, 247
The Divine Comedy (Dante), 54, 71, 217
Divine Light, 19, 109, 136, 144, 258
    aura, reflected in, 24–25
    colors of, 46, 150
    earning of, 225–27
    heavens as filled by, 71, 73, 92, 150, 185
    little people, steering back to, 84
    meditating with, 237, 239
    souls in need, practice in sending to, 128
    temples as filled with, 5, 132
    test of evil in turning away from, 129
dreams and the dream state, 12, 85
    divine communication via dreams, 257
    Jacob's ladder, dream of, 66
    second astral plane as a dream state, 88–90,
    91, 256
Duat (underworld), 62

E

Earth, 37–38, 44, 61, 93, 152
    ancient beliefs regarding, 57, 62
    completion of incarnations on, 170
    earthly life, heavenly reflections of, 50, 51, 53, 163
    fourth astral plane and, 95–97, 101, 110,
    120, 158
    in Hebrew cosmology, 65–66
    inspiration, bringing to Earth, 55
    little people as inhabiting, 84
    prayer work for souls on Earth, 127
    as a spiritual schoolhouse, 20, 33, 99
    as a temporary dwelling, 255
ego. *See* Individuality Ego; Personality Ego
Egyptian tradition, 62–63, 200, 203
Ein Soph cosmology, 68–69
Elysium/Elysian Fields, 63–64
emerald-green ray of balance and harmony,
249, 251
emotional chakra, 243
Empyrean (heaven), 62
enlightenment, 155, 186, 204, 231, 237
    as an astral worlds journey, 39, 103, 123
    celestial enlightenment, 159, 163, 166
    in classic thought, 61, 64
    in Eastern spirituality, 74, 76
    *Enlightenment and the Temple of Love illustration
    8.1*, 131–33
    God, rediscovering, 31, 171
    in interplanetary worlds, 135, 145
    mental plane, entering as an enlightened
    soul, 138
    seventh astral plane as realm of, 125–33
Enoch, 66

Etana, King, 60
etheric world, 47–48, 144–47. *See also* spiritual
etheria
evolution. *See* spiritual growth

F

fairies, gnomes, and elves, 83–84
faith, 51, 132, 173
    blind faith, 210, 271
    divine faith, 172, 271
    Hindu faith, 74–75, 227
false prophets, 204–5, 205–8, 208–11
family. *See* marriage and family
Field of Reeds (heaven), 62–63
fifth astral plane. *See under* astral planes
Fire of Spirit, 165–66
first astral plane, 87, 218
float-travel, 87
    as fifth-level astral transport, 111–12, 116, 118
    in *illustrations 7.1, 10.1*, 119, 160
    on the sixth astral plane, 120
forgiveness, 72, 118, 143, 233, 251, 264
Four Noble Truths, 78, 226
fourth astral plane. *See under* astral planes
free will, 30, 85, 93, 99, 129, 154, 179
friendships, 50, 112, 123, 146, 157, 229, 266

G

geocentric model of the Universe, 38, 61
Al-Ghazali, Abu Hamid, 229
God, 15, 18, 24, 237, 247
    in Abrahamic traditions, 65–73
    astral understanding of, 107, 120–21
    co-creating with, 29, 39, 172, 183, 189, 190
    focusing on, 171–74
    God confidence, 236
    God within, 30, 126, 130, 154, 171
    prayer, maintaining connection through, 238
    reverence for, 34, 103
    throne room of God, 187–89
    See also Kingdom of God
gold, color of
    golden bubble of protection, 240, 258
    golden light in the auric field, 123, 258
    golden ray of wisdom light, 245, 265–66
    golden robes, spiritual wearing of, 17, 105, 124
Greek mystery schools, 63–64
green, color of, 120, 187, 245–46, 249, 251
gurus, 231

H

habits, 96, 109, 113, 114, 260
Hades, 64, 66

Hall, Manly P., 61
Halls of Learning, 86, 98, 117
healing, 51, 60, 250
    astral healing, 92, 132, 255
    blue-white fire of healing, 250
    necessity of, 233
    temple of healing, 118–20, 263–64
Heaven and Hell (Swedenborg), 41n, 71
Heaven and the heaven worlds, 31–32, 40, 239
    defining and describing, 15–16, 39, 45–46
    activities and lifestyle in, 49–53
    in Abrahamic traditions, 65–73
    in ancient traditions, 57–58, 60–64
    in Eastern spiritual traditions, 74–79
    glory of, 149–54
    heavenly incarnations, 156–57
    human potential in, 19–20, 151–52
    location of, 35–37
    love, road to Heaven as paved with, 269–71
    preparing for, 135–38
    seven heavenly perfections, 154–56
    as within and without, 41, 152
heavenly hierarchy
    first heaven, 157–59
    second heaven, 159, 161–63
    third heaven, 70, 157, 163, 164–67, 169, 226
    fourth heaven, 174–77
    fifth heaven, 177–79
    sixth heaven, 179–81
    seventh heaven, 181–83
Hekhalot Rabbati text, 67
hell. *See* demons and demonic realms; Hades;
netherworlds
Hermetic Center, 243
Hermetic tradition, 60, 62
Hesiod, 63
hierophants, 231
higher self, 30
    higher self meditation practice, 238–42, 258
    higher self point, receiving energy into,
    239–42, 252, 261, 262
    understanding the higher self, 109–10
Hinduism, 28, 77, 156, 190, 227
    Hindu spiritual tradition, 74–76
    Hindu triune, 171
    mental plane in Hindu metaphysics, 141
Hodsom, Geoffrey, 174n3, 180
Holy Spirit, 127
Homer, 63
hope, 142, 215, 271
humility, 130, 141, 156, 225
    The Perfection of Humility, 155, 182

spiritual success, as fundamental to, 249
    as a virtue, 183
Hurd, Inez, 7–8, 16–19, 22, 150, 254

I

immersed self, 109
incense use, 258
individuality, 27, 30, 128, 190
Individuality Ego, 110, 123
Indra (Vedic figure), 75
infant souls, 29, 130, 164
inner-world travel, 254–55, 256
insomnia, 259. *See also* sleep as spiritual practice
inspiration, 55–56, 96, 237, 239
instinct, 93, 107, 121, 132
    animal instinct, 91, 175–76
    lower instinctual energies, 216, 217, 218
integrity, 196, 205, 227, 232
interplanetary worlds, 39, 155
    causal worlds, 141–44, 165, 200, 202, 203
    etheric worlds, 40, 46, 144–47
    mental worlds, 138–40
intuition, 107, 121, 128, 173, 231, 244
involution of the soul, 31
Irenaeus of Lyons, 70
Islamic Tradition, 65, 72–73, 227
Isles of the Blessed, 63, 64

J

Jacob's ladder, 66
Jannah (heaven), 72–73
Jesus the Christ, 69, 73, 146, 172
jhanas (mental absorption), 78
Jones, Jim and Jonestown, 208–210
Judaism, 65–69, 72, 73

K

Kabbalah, 67, 68–69, 220
Kabir, 173
Kama-loka (world), 77–78
karma, 54, 93, 112–13
    karmic chart, 115, 270
    karmic conditions, devolution due to, 197
    karmic debts, resolving, 136, 145
    karmic history review in Causal World, 142
    Lords of Karma, 51, 143, 144
    reincarnation as affected by, 74, 78, 202
Kingdom of God, 32, 154, 159, 171, 181
    defining and describing, 39, 185
    celestial bodies, maintaining in, 30, 142, 186
    co-creation in the Kingdom, 183
    as the highest spiritual realm, 28–29
    infant souls as descending from, 164

Kingdom of Light body, understanding
via, 163
seven rays of life, needing to enter, 182
soul mate, returning to Kingdom with, 31
Kingdom of Light Teachings, 22, 39, 151, 239
kingdoms of the seven heavens
Kingdom of the Seven Spirits, 40, 155, 181–83
Kingdom of Spirit Light, 40, 155, 179–81
Kingdom of the Inner Light, 40, 155, 177–79
Kingdom of the Gods, 40, 155, 174–77
Kingdom of Creation, 40, 155, 157, 164–67
Kingdom of Light, 40, 161–63, 164
See also spiritual etheria
Krishna, 146, 172
The Kybalion (Hermetic text), 62

L

laws of spirituality, 51, 97, 98, 226, 251
karma as law of cause and effect, 93
law of giving as the perfection of service, 178
natural laws, divine intelligence behind, 171
spiritual laws, breaking, 129, 196
universal laws, 153, 166, 236
left hand path, 201
lemon-yellow ray of concentration, 247
"little people," 83–84, 85, 87
love, 18, 24, 84, 240
astral love, 48, 89, 97, 112, 198
deeper connection to, 108, 112, 128, 142, 163
divine love, 114, 132, 156, 186, 236, 264
Enlightenment and the Temple of Love, 131–33
God, love of, 28, 29, 173, 186
heavenly love, 71, 152, 166, 179
higher understanding of, 107, 152, 191
love as paving the spiritual road, 269–71
loved ones of the other side, 50, 66, 71, 124
loving action, spiritual obligation to take, 238
road to heaven as paved with, 269–71
rose-pink ray of spiritual love, 246, 252, 264
soul mates, love between, 30–31, 108, 160, 186
in the spiritual etheria, 157, 159
spiritual planets dedicated to, 178
temple of love, 114, 119, 131–33, 264
lucid dreams, 256
Lucifer, 179

M

Ma'at (Egyptian figure), 62
Magi, gifts of, 166
Mahabharata text, 75
Maimonides, Moses, 127
Mara (the tempter), 78, 79
marriage and family, 48, 52, 97, 138, 200–203

medieval cosmology, 70–71
meditation, 98, 152, 241, 253
Buddhist meditation, 77, 78
cosmic vision, experience during, 34–35
Divine Light, meditating with, 25, 227, 237, 239
higher self meditation, 238–42, 258
in *illustrations 6.1, 7.2*, 105, 123–24
Inez Hurd, meditative experiences with, 17, 18
meditative color blessings and prayers, 262–67
nighttime meditation practice, 237, 257–62, 267
spiritual growth, meditative prayers for, 243–52
mediums, 205–8
mental chakra, 242
mental world, 138–40, 141
Merkabah tradition, 67–68
Messianic age, 66, 67
metaphysics, 28, 59, 62, 146, 158
heaven, metaphysical perception of, 14
hermetic science as a metaphysical tradition, 60
higher self, metaphysical understanding of, 109–10
holiness, metaphysical perspective on, 176–77
metaphysical education as essential, 230–31, 247
metaphysical journey of the soul, 20, 105
metaphysical principles, 22–25, 161
spiritual cosmology as metaphysical science, 37, 61–62
teaching of, 3, 6, 7, 18, 27, 57–58, 149
moksha (enlightenment), 74
moon. *See* astro-theology
Moses, 68, 73, 146
Muhammed, 73, 146, 185
music of the spheres, 129, 157
mystery schools, 58, 62–64, 121, 200–201, 203
mystic marriage, 136, 146–47, 181
mysticism, 21
Jewish mysticism, 59, 67–69
Kingdom of Light teachings, 22
St. Paul, experiences of heaven, 69–70
Swedenborg, contributions to, 71

N

nature, 119
astral flowers, 17, 115, 121, 153
ethereal gardens, 69, 72, 75, 85, 96, 115
heavenly trees, 17, 46, 115, 121, 132, 150, 153
reified nature, 96, 129, 130, 150
spiritual roses, 132, 160
near-death experiences, 20, 21
netherworlds
defining and describing, 54, 202, 214, 220
animal netherworld kingdoms, 216–17

brute netherworld kingdoms, 218–19
    souls as tested in, 122, 130
New Thought movement, 140
nirvana, 74, 77

O

Ode to Joy (poem and song), 64
Olam Ha-ba (world to come), 65
orange-red, color of, 262–63
Osiris (Egyptian figure), 63
out-of-body experiences, 20–21, 138, 254

P

paradise, 63, 70, 72, 111, 113
patience, 225, 230, 250–51, 270
Paul, Saint, 69–70, 71, 153
peace, 17, 24, 119, 244, 257
    astral peace, 94, 95
    in the *Hekhalot Rabbati,* 67–68
    humility, spiritual peace of, 183
    "the silence of peace," 120–21
    violet ray of peace, 260, 265
Peoples Temple, 208
perfection
    of the creative spirit, 155, 166
    of eternal life, 155, 162
    of the eternal self, 155, 158
    of holiness, 155, 176
    of the infinite spirit, 155, 181
    perfection to perfection, growing from, 151
    of service, 155, 178
    seven heavenly perfections, 154–56
Personality Ego, 109, 110, 122–24, 126, 201, 248
pets, 39, 44, 78. *See also* animals
physical life, 27, 36, 58, 89, 93
    creativity, physical expression of, 166
    out-of-body experiences, 20–21, 36, 136, 254
    physical incarnations, beginning, 99
    physicality as a spiritual necessity, 44
    spiritual body resemblance to physical body, 47
    See also death
pink, color of, 119
    auric field, pink light in, 17
    in *illustrations 6.1, 7.1, 8.1,* 105, 120, 132
    rose-pink light, 246, 252, 261, 264
pinnacle spiritual experiences, 16, 146, 179, 189, 270
    Crown of Life, achieving, 167
    physical Earth, peaking on, 169
    in the seventh levels, 125, 181–83
Pralaya (dissolution), 190
prayer, 69, 150, 173, 199, 253

astral prayer, 92, 97, 98, 187
    auric field, praying to strengthen, 227
    biblical reference regarding, 68
    color energy, prayers to be blessed by, 262–67
    heaven on earth, creating via, 152
    in *illustrations 6.1, 7.2,* 105, 123–24
    Inez Hurd, prayers of, 7, 18
    meditative prayers, 238, 240–42, 243–52
    Muslim prayer practice, 73
    nighttime meditation prayers, 195, 260–61, 262
    prayer work for souls on Earth, 127
Primum Mobile realm, 62
prosperity, 53, 119, 266–67
psychic phenomena, 205–8
psychic warfare, 51
purification, 60, 177
    auric purification, 102, 114
    of the soul, 64, 143
    temple meditation for purification, 262–63
purple, color of
    in *illustrations 6.1, 7.1,* 105, 120
    purple ray of peace, 244, 265
    violet ray, light of, 260, 265

Q

Qliphoth tree of death, 220
Qur'an text, 72–73

R

racial archetypes, 92, 97
rays, 181, 239
    divine source, down-raying from, 240–41
    ray of divine intelligence, 244, 249
    ray of peace, 244, 265
    ray of spiritual love, 246, 264, 266
    ray of wisdom, 245
    seven rays of life, 181–82
    white light, down-raying of, 248, 251, 258, 260
red energy, 197
regeneration of the spirit, 97, 102, 254, 257, 261, 263
reincarnation, 63, 100, 115, 137, 202
    describing and defining, 22–23
    Arupa-loka, rebirth in, 78
    causal world and, 142–43
    in Eastern spiritual traditions, 74, 156
    parents, astrally meeting children before rebirth, 255
    preparation before incarnations, 50, 105, 136
    rebirth, breaking the cycle of, 77–78
    release from the wheel of, 39, 157
    task of reincarnating souls, 166
    temporary nature of, 33, 86

resistance, 54, 98, 110, 217
    divine impulse, rejecting, 104, 174, 189, 195
    in the physical realm, 44–45
    procrastination and, 113
Revelation, Book of, 70, 126
Rose Room, 139
Ruach HaKodesh (Spirit), 127
Rupa-loka (world), 78
Ryan, Leo, 208

S

samādhi (bliss of absorption), 130
Satya-loka (world), 75–76
Schiller, Friedrich, 64
Scholem, Gershom, 59, 67
second astral plane, 88–90, 91–92, 217, 218, 256
self-conscious awareness, 93, 94
Sephiroth tree, 68, 69
seven rays of life, 181–82
seventh astral plane, 129–31, 145
sex and intimacy, 48, 89, 91, 97
Shamayim (the heavens), 65–66, 67
Sheol (underworld), 65–66, 67
Siddhartha. *See* Buddha Gautama
silver ray of divine intelligence, 244, 249
sixth astral plane. *See under* astral planes
sleep as spiritual practice, 73, 118, 139, 194, 257
    angelic cooperation during sleep, 5, 62
    sleep-time insights, integrating into
      consciousness, 267
    spiritual preparation for sleep, 259–61
    spiritual work done while sleeping, 253–55
Solomon, King, 67
Sophocles, 55
souls, 30, 64, 121, 151, 176
    of babies and children, 47–48, 52, 97, 255
    fallen souls, 215, 218, 220
    full soul power, building up, 136–38
    as immortal, 28, 43, 146, 153, 158, 159, 162, 181
    between lives, time spent, 23, 28
    soul evolution as reflected in the aura, 24–25
    soul mates, 146, 157, 175
      on the astral planes, 44, 108
      in *illustrations 7.2, 10.1,* 123, 160
      spiritual journey, sharing with, 30–31,
        186–87
    spiritual maturation of, 95–100, 127
spaceless space, 36
spiritual desire, 234
spiritual education, 59, 90, 156
    inner world travel as part of, 21
    meditative prayer for spiritual knowledge, 247

quality spiritual education, pursuing, 227,
    230–32
Spiritual Etheria, 17–18, 40, 145, 157
    celestial body, inhabiting in, 162–63
    Entering Spiritual Etheria illustration 10.1,
      160–61
    eternal self, as realm for perfection of, 155, 158
    etheric world, not confusing with, 144
    as a prototypal world, 159
spiritual growth, 19–20, 189, 221, 255, 261
    acceleration of, 16, 25, 227, 237, 245–47, 248,
      253, 270
    angels as assisting, 121
    divine light and aura as fuel for, 24–25
    joyous pursuit of, 8, 152
    new opportunities for, 251
    physical life as necessary for, 44
    planets as dedicated to, 177–78
    as a priority, 14, 152, 227, 228–29, 245
    as spiritual ascent, 14, 225–27
    spiritual awakening of the soul, 102–4
    spiritual practice as part of, 61
    ten keys to success in, 234–36
spiritual heritage, 35, 142, 195, 199–203
spiritual hierarchy, 7, 30, 51, 85, 144
    on the astral planes, 46, 50, 89, 112
    becoming a part of, 132
    connecting to, 23–24, 109
    deeper understanding of, 161
    heavens as the headquarters for, 127
    support and guidance from, 31, 179
    as working every day, 127–28
spiritual path, 3, 83, 189, 208, 229
    committed following of, 6, 14, 19, 227
    conscious intent, pursuing with, 86–87,
      196, 233
    falling from the path, 113, 177, 182–83, 196–98
    fellowship with like-minded souls, 252
    fourth astral plane, starting in earnest on, 125
    healing as part of, 233
    importance of, 104, 219, 221, 245, 269
    inner-world visits along the path, 254–55
    pitfalls, handling as spiritual tests, 210, 249
    revelations regarding the spiritual path, 107–8
    soul ages along the path, 29
    spiritual discernment as part of, 204, 244
spiritual surrender, 18, 110, 122, 123
Sumerian spirituality, 60
sun, moon, and planets. *See* astro-theology
Swedenborg, Emanuel, 41, 71

T

Taoism, 28, 74, 227
Tartarus (hell), 64
telepathy, 48, 88, 98, 131, 139
temples, 68, 123, 144, 150, 255
    divine love temple meditation, 264
    divine peace temple meditation, 265
    healing temple meditation, 263–64
    in *illustrations 7.1, 8.1, 10.1,* 119–20, 131–33,
        160–61
    mental plane temples, 140
    prosperity temple meditation, 266
    purification temple meditation, 262
    of the spirit worlds, 5, 17–18, 157
    spiritual energy, receiving from, 262
    wisdom temple meditation, 265–66
Ten Commandments, 226
Theosophy, 1, 7, 21, 138, 141
third astral plane, 90–93, 97, 216
Thompson, Francis, 37
throat chakra, 242
trance mediums, 205–8
Tree of Life, 68–69, 73, 160, 183, 220
Troward, Thomas, 140
truth, 62, 76, 176, 221, 271
    camouflaging of truth, 158
    fallen souls, waking up to, 199
    Four Noble Truths, 78, 226
    integrity, living truth with, 196
    mental plane, living out spiritual truths on, 140
    third heaven, new truths expressed in, 166
    truth-into-wisdom, applying, 155, 227, 229–30
    universal spiritual truth, 58, 68, 151
turquoise ray of abundance, 266, 267

U

Unknown Root of All Existence, 28, 162, 190
Upanishads text, 28
Uranus, 63

V

Vaikuntha (heaven), 75–76
Vishnu (Vedic figure), 75

W

white light, 124, 147, 248, 251, 258, 260–61
willpower, 103, 210, 235
wisdom, 4, 53, 126, 173, 180
    Cathedral of the Soul as representing, 160
    Christos Wisdom, 22
    cultivation of, 14, 24, 84, 86, 136
    golden ray of wisdom light, 245
    in the heaven worlds, 153, 166
    higher self, receiving divine wisdom into, 109
    key of wisdom, turning seven times, 155
    Lord of Wisdom Light, 147
    Moses, wisdom granted to, 68
    mystery schools as providing, 58
    in spiritual cosmology, 38
    temple of wisdom, 114, 265–66
    truth, applying into wisdom, 227, 229–30
    wisdom of God, 127

Y

yellow, color of, 160, 247
Yogananda, Paramahansa, 36

Z

Zohar text, 59
Zoroastrianism, 166

ABOUT THE AUTHORS

BARBARA Y. MARTIN is among the foremost clairvoyants and metaphysical teachers in the world. Affectionately known as the "Mozart of metaphysics," she has been a pioneer in spiritual development for over fifty years. She is co-author of a series of award-winning books that include the international bestseller *Change Your Aura, Change Your Life, Karma and Reincarnation, The Healing Power of Your Aura, Animals of Love,* and *Communing with the Divine.* Barbara is co-founder and co-spiritual director of Spiritual Arts Institute. She has taught thousands of people how to better their lives by working with the aura and spiritual energy.

DIMITRI MORAITIS is co-founder and co-spiritual director of Spiritual Arts Institute. Dimitri has been instrumental in bringing Spiritual Arts Institute to the place it is today as a premier metaphysical school. With Barbara, he is co-author of the international bestseller *Change Your Aura, Change Your Life, Karma and Reincarnation, The Healing Power of Your Aura,* and *Communing with the Divine.* He is an eloquent speaker on a wide variety of spiritual topics, has lectured across the country, appeared on numerous radio shows, and leads the workshops and training classes offered at the Institute with Barbara.

About the Illustrator

JONATHAN WILTSHIRE began drawing at a very young age. His fine art illustrations have been seen in *Angel Times* magazine and *American Artist* magazine and have appeared in numerous books and videos. For twenty years, he was illustrator for the Christian mystic, Flower A. Newhouse. He has been awarded Artist of the Year by the Art Alliance of Idyllwild, California. Jonathan has dedicated his life work to the precept that art is intended to awaken our inner perceptiveness and to encourage and transform the beholder. His images are an exploration of invisible worlds conceived through intuition and imagination.

About Spiritual Arts Institute

Spiritual Arts Institute is the premier metaphysical school for the aura, spiritual healing, and soul growth. The Institute was co-founded by its teachers, Barbara Y. Martin and Dimitri Moraitis, with a mission to help people from all walks of life to accelerate their spiritual understanding and development. As spiritual directors, Barbara and Dimitri lead program training and founder events.

The Institute offers life-changing programs, from single workshops to profound, in-depth training through *The Seven Spiritual Arts Program* and more. All programs are based on a rich, 4,000-year-old mystical tradition and built on Barbara's extensive clairvoyant experiences over five decades. Supported by experienced faculty and staff, the Institute offers certification training in personal spiritual development, Divine Light healing, and metaphysical teaching. Classes are offered online and in person.

The Institute's publishing division produces metaphysical books, videos, and audios based on the work of Martin and Moraitis. Their award-winning books are published worldwide and are designed to share the mystical Divine Light teachings with spiritual truth seekers throughout the world.

Spiritual Arts Institute
527 Encinitas Blvd., Suite 206
Encinitas, CA 92024

Visit the Institute's website:
https://SpiritualArts.org

Phone: (760) 487-1224
Toll Free: (800) 650-AURA (2872)

Facebook: @SpiritualArtsInstitute
Instagram: @spiritual_arts_institute